ISLAMIC
FUNDAMENTALISM

ISLAMIC FUNDAMENTALISM

THE NEW GLOBAL THREAT

by Mohammad Mohaddessin

SEVEN LOCKS PRESS   WASHINGTON, D.C.

Library of Congress Cataloging-in-Publication Data

Mohaddessin, Mohammad.
    Islamic fundamentalism   :   the new global threat / by Mohammad Mohaddessin.
        p.   cm.
        Includes index.
        ISBN 0-929765-32-X — ISBN 0-929765-22-2 (pbk.)
        1. Iran—Politics and government—1979– 2. Islam and politics—Iran. 3. Iran—Foreign relations—1979– I. Title.
DS318.81.M66 1993
955.05'4—dc20

                92–43002
                CIP

A publication of the People's Mojahedin Organization of Iran
Correspondence address:
17, rue des Gords
95430 Auvers-sur-Oise
France
Email: fac@iranncr.org

Manufactured in the United States of America.

SEVEN LOCKS PRESS
(800) 354-5348

PUBLISHER'S NOTE

As a result of the terrorist attacks on September 11, 2001, Seven Locks Press has decided to reissue *Islamic Fundamentalism* with a new introduction and an updated appendix. Radical Islamic fundamentalism is a force the world must reckon with as we enter the twenty-first century. As always, our best weapons in these difficult times are knowledge and education, allowing us to find a solution to this volatile global issue. I hope that this book will shed some light on the chain of events that led to the tragedies in New York and Washington, D.C.

Contents

Foreword   *Georgie Anne Geyer*   **xiii**

Preface   *Dr. Davina Miller*   **xvii**

Introduction: In the Eye of the Storm   **xxi**

I.   **Dogmatism versus Democracy: A Brief History
     of Fundamentalism**   **1**
       The Fundamentalist Appeal
       Fanaticism Versus Liberty
       Kharajites: First Advocates of Dogmatism
       Legitimizing the Status Quo
       Democratic, Antireactionary Islamic Movements
       Shi'ism in Safavid and Post-Safavid Iran
       Iran's Constitutional Revolution of 1906
       Sunnism and the New Era
       Conclusion

II. **The Pillars of the Mullahs' Rule**   **17**
       Two Pillars of Khomeini's Rule
       Velayat-e-faqih in the Constitution

III. **The Post-Khomeini Regime**   **27**
       Constitution Revised
       Moderation an Anathema

IV. **"Mother of All Islamic Lands": The Mullahs'
     Foreign Policy**   **35**

V. Fertile Grounds for Fundamentalism 39
The Power of Islam
A Bastion of Islamic Culture
Decline of Nationalism
Role of Oil
Global Changes
Appeasement: An Ominous Policy
Fundamentalism and Islam's Great Schism

VI. The Iran-Iraq War 59
The War and the Mojahedin
Damages Inflicted by the War
A Dream Unfulfilled

VII. Arms of the Octopus: Exporting Fundamentalism to Central Asia 67
Ties of History and Culture
Iranian-Soviet Relations
After the Soviet Collapse
Azerbaijan: A Special Case
Turkmenistan and Other Republics
Afghanistan
Pan-Islamism Versus Pan-Turkism?

VIII. Fundamentalism in the Arab World 83
The Eastern Mediterranean
North Africa
Saudi Arabia and the Persian Gulf States
The Muslim World at Large

IX. An "International Islamic Army" 97
Ministry of Foreign Affairs
Ministry of Islamic Culture and Guidance
Ministry of Intelligence
The Qods Force
Organizational Structure
Affiliated Units
Training

X. **Terrorism: Iran's Foreign Policy Instrument**   **113**
    Hallmarks of Terrorism
    An International Terrorist Network
    Prospects

XI. **The Mullahs and Middle East Peace**   **125**

XII. **Armed to the Teeth**   **129**
    Conventional Weapons
    Chemical and Biological Weapons
    Nuclear Weapons

XIII. **Crisis from All Sides: Inside the Mullahs' Regime**   **141**
    Political Repression
    Edging Toward Bankruptcy
    Mounting Protests
    The Crisis Continues

XIV. **The Search for a Solution**   **151**
    Nationalism
    Liberalism
    Marxism
    Fundamentalism Misinterpreted

XV. **Modern, Democratic Islam: Antithesis to Fundamentalism**   **157**
    The Antithesis of Fundamentalist Islam
    A Glance at the Mojahedin's Basic Viewpoints

Notes   **173**

Appendix   **191**

Index   **213**

FOREWORD

When the devastating Iran-Iraq War ended in 1988, the virtually unanimous opinion of analysts in the West was that the fanatical and extremist Islamic fundamentalism espoused and pushed by Iran was now dead. The Ayatollah Khomeini, who had fueled the coals of hatred toward the more moderate Muslims of the Middle East, had clearly failed. Finally, it was all over, and the Middle East could go back to seeking more rational and less murderous ways of developing and expressing itself.

The only problem was that it was not all over. The new, supposedly "moderate," regime in Tehran first covertly and then overtly pursued the policies of Khomeini, continuing the efforts to undermine, sabotage, and overthrow the moderate regimes through every kink of extremist terrorism, infiltration, and diplomacy. It was a volte-face because, almost always by the time a fanatical regime has been definitively defeated, the fanaticism has drained out of the people, and their rulers are compelled to turn to more normal ways. That this did not happen in Iran after Khomeini's death was a consequence of his successors' need and desire to hold on to power by reverting to their mentor's tactics and weapons of power.

The new nexus, it soon was learned, began in Tehran with approximately $100 million a year in expenditures; ideas, influence, and money then moved to Sudan, where that country's government transformed it into training camps and influence for fundamentalists from Algeria to Tunisia to Egypt and (again) the Gulf. The situation by 1993 had become so serious that Turkish President Turgut Ozal warned when he came to Washington that the world was now facing basically a "religious war" of extremist and radically politicized Islam against the West.

It had seemed that America's struggles with Iran of a decade ago were fading into history. The American public and news media were focusing on the continuing confrontation between Iraq and the United States and on the peace talks between Israel and her Arab neighbors. Meanwhile, Tehran was again on the move, its continued Islamic fundamentalism as hostile to democracy, human rights, and true social progress as always. Indeed, the mullahs have been presented with opportunities for catastrophic mischief making that Khomeini never dreamed of in his heyday.

Thanks to the disintegration of the Soviet empire, the enfeeblement of Iran's neighbor and rival Iraq, and the West's disregard for the Iranian challenge, the clerical rulers are developing nuclear and chemical weapons, exporting terrorism, torturing the citizenry, and assassinating their opponents abroad.

There was also a new element to the drama. As the Central Asian republics of the former Soviet Union gained independence, Iran began to move into Kazakhstan, Kyrgyzstan, Uzbekistan, Azerbaijan, Turkmenistan, and Tadzhikistan. So far, the Turkish influence has prevailed, but with so many ethnic conflicts already in progress and so many more on the horizon, no one can foresee where the people will turn next.

Meanwhile, the outside world was getting very little in-depth analysis of the developing situation inside Iran. It was, after all, a Byzantine court closed to the world and even to its own people, in whom it inspired hatred. What was going on behind the secreted corridors of power in Tehran?

This book, for the first time, exposes in considerable detail—and in largely rational detail—the inside story of Iran's ongoing Islamic fundamentalism after the Iran-Iraq War, which left probably one million people dead on either side. Mohaddessin takes you inside the pillars of Khomeini's rule, inside the "whys" and "ways" of the export of Islamic fundamentalism, inside the terrorist networks. It is a carefully footnoted book, and a valuable one that can be used well by scholars of the situation and by people who simply want to know more about one of the most important syndromes of our times. I know of no other study like it in terms of depth and interpretation.

The author, of course, is a prominent official of the People's Mojahedin, the major and most active opposition group to the mullahs and the fundamentalists since the beginning of the resistance against the shah. They have fought valiantly for many years, but I personally make no judgments, political or otherwise, on the organization. I speak only for the scholarly aspects of the book, which are considerable.

The reason why Khomeini and his heirs literally "got away with murder" lies deep in the history of Islam. Muslim movements have almost always appealed to popular goals, such as an end to tyranny, by linking them to the original intent of the Quran and the traditions of the Prophet Muhammad. Khomeiniism thus struck—and still strikes—a sympathetic chord in the hearts of Muslims when it promises a return to the values and principles of pristine Islam. This has potent appeal for Muslim nations disappointed with experiments in liberation and renewal that used non-Muslim and ultimately unworkable ideologies. Thus the situation today.

It is a complicated story and an old story, using a beautiful and noble religion for cynical and diabolical goals. It is a story the West ignores at its peril.

Georgie Anne Geyer
March 1993

PREFACE

Islamic fundamentalism, as propagated by the late Ayatollah Ruhollah Khomeini and currently by his heirs, imperils the new world order. The ruling mullahs are using diplomacy, bribery, terrorism, and carefully crafted propaganda to woo Muslim nations, especially the newly independent Central Asian republics of the former Soviet Union. This is especially dangerous because Iran is seeking to acquire nuclear warheads and intercontinental ballistic missiles from these republics.

Policymakers have too often overlooked threats until confronted with a full-fledged crisis. One cannot afford this approach in dealing with Tehran's brand of Islamic fundamentalism. The spread of pro-Iranian regimes, backed by a nuclear-armed government in Tehran, would be a disaster. We have to prevent that threat before it happens.

This book clearly defines the Khomeini form of Islamic fundamentalism and gives a well-documented, authoritative account of its history, reasons for its appeal, and its frightening goals for the future. It also presents a realistic policy to neutralize Tehran's campaign against democracy and peace.

The book's strength is a reflection of the background and position of the author, Mohammad Mohaddessin, who is a ranking member of the People's Mojahedin of Iran. The Mojahedin derive their ideology from Islam, as Khomeini did. But there the similarity ends. Unlike Khomeini and his heirs, the Mojahedin believe in freedom, human rights, and democratic values. The clash between the Mojahedin and the ruling mullahs has been a war between two very different Islams.

In 1965, the Mojahedin formed an underground organization and launched a battle for democracy against the shah's corrupt dictatorship, losing hundreds of men and women in the course of that struggle or to the shah's firing squads.

When the Ayatollah took over in 1979, the Mojahedin immediately denounced the new regime's dictatorial policies and campaigned for democratic rule. The Mojahedin exhausted every opportunity for peaceful political struggle until June 1981, when Khomeini ordered his followers to open fire on a nonviolent demonstration of half a million Tehran residents. This left the Iranians and the Mojahedin with no choice but armed resistance to defend themselves.

The Mojahedin have lost tens of thousands of men and women so far in their crusade for a free and democratic Iran that will follow the laws of the civilized family of nations. They have a full-fledged, highly trained army based along the Iran-Iraq frontier and a huge underground in Iran.

As this book demonstrates, Khomeini-style Islamic fundamentalism leaves no room for "moderates" and "moderation." Any slackening of repression at home will invite a rising by the citizenry that is chafing under a brutal regime. Any real opening to the West will threaten to disclose the ruling clergy's grisly crimes against humanity. Tehran can afford neither. Deception is thus one of the key elements of Khomeiniism that persists to this day. The Ayatollah used it to persuade Iranians that he was fighting for everything they craved: freedom, democracy, human rights, and social justice. Yet after the Pahlavi throne toppled, he ordered the takeover of the U.S. Embassy in Tehran, created an international crisis, and used it to gag his opponents at home, railroad a theocratic constitution, and build institutions of political repression and coercion. In the same way, he used the war with Iraq, which he prolonged for eight years, to equate all popular complaints and criticisms with treason.

The crisis in the Persian Gulf, in this light, was a godsend for Khomeini's heirs. Behind all the blue smoke and mirrors, the ruling mullahs are spreading lies, money, weapons, and agents throughout the region to encourage the creation of one Islamic republic after another, styled after Tehran.

This book is a timely exposé. It offers us a chance to give Khomeini-style Islamic fundamentalism a prominent place on the agenda of public debate here and abroad. We cannot afford to leave unchallenged the claims of Iran's publicists that the regime has become more moderate and "normal."

The Mojahedin's message is that Muslim nations should not look to Khomeini for guidance in their struggles for freedom, democracy, and social justice. The Mojahedin's ideology shows how Islam can support all these ideals. Thus, the Mojahedin illustrate a powerful truth to Iranians and, in my view, to other Muslims: Renouncing Khomeini-style fundamentalism is in no way tantamount to renouncing Islam. On the contrary, renouncing Khomeiniism is the first step for Muslims who want Islam as well as individual liberties and social progress.

The new world order has given the United Nations the moral and physical authority its founders intended. If we use it to unmask Khomeiniism, we need not use force. This is a vitally important mission.

With this book, the Mojahedin have formally launched their battle on a worldwide scale. They deserve support—above all, because of our children. The end of the Cold War means our children can now sleep without fearing death in a nuclear holocaust; by exposing the true nature of the Tehran regime, we can help them continue their untroubled sleep.

Dr. Davina Miller
Lecturer in International Relations
Salford University
Manchester, England
March 1993

Terrorism and Islamic Fundamentalism: Two Sides of One Coin

More than eight years have passed since *Islamic Fundamentalism: The New Global Threat* was first published. During this period, the idea that Islamic fundamentalism led by Tehran—by abusing Islam, the religion of compassion and love—would carry out its ill intentions and would be a threat to peace, security, friendship, and human rights in the world has had many challenges. In academic discussions, some tried to prove that Islamic fundamentalism would moderate over time, while others tried to change the word *fundamentalism* to *extremism*. In politics, many tried—by giving concessions—to open a dialogue and discussion with the leaders of this ominous phenomenon.

The bombing of the Jewish Community Center in Buenos Aires; the unsuccessful attempt to blow up the Israeli Embassy in Bangkok; the assassinations of publishers and translators of Salman Rushdie's books; the terror plot against Maryam Rajavi, the president-elect of the National Council of Resistance of Iran in Germany; the import of huge 320-millimeter "supermortars" rocket launchers to Europe by the Intelligence Ministry; the terror plot against Yasser Arafat; the explosion in Riyadh; the bombing of the Khobar Towers in Dhahran, Saudi Arabia; the bombings of the U.S. embassies in Kenya and Tanzania; 128 terrorist operations against Mojahedin in Iraq, including the bombing of a Mojahedin city bus near a hospital in Baghdad and the firing of 77 surface-to-surface missiles on Mojahedin bases in Iraq—these are but a few of the terrorist and aggressive activities that Tehran rulers and their agents or fundamentalist allies have carried out, killing thousands of innocent people. Yet even when the head of Tehran Radio and Television said, "Missile attacks on the bases of the Iranian [Resistance] in Iraq are a warning to other smaller nations of the region not to play with a lion's tail," many international stakeholders preferred to ignore it.

The September 11 Tragedy: A Strategic Blitz

The tragic events of September 11, 2001—the hijacking of passenger planes in the United States and attacks on the World Trade Center and Pentagon, in which thousands were killed—shocked the world, especially the United States, as the most destructive terrorist incident in contemporary history. One former U.S. government official mentioned in the first few hours after the attack that there was a question of how the terrorists had been able to carry out their plan without U.S. intelligence agencies having any clues or information about it. No one doubts that from a political, economic, and security point of view, the negative impacts of the deadly attacks of September 11 are far greater than those of the Persian Gulf War in the 1990s.

Even if there are doubts about the identities of the perpetrators of this tragedy, there is no doubt that they all belong to one camp: Islamic fundamentalism. They dare to use the name of God and Islam to step on all values and to cross any lines in order to advance their evil intentions. In his address to the U.S. Congress on Thursday, September 20, 2001, President George W. Bush described the perpetrators as radical Muslims and extremists who stand shoulder to shoulder with fascism, nazism, and totalitarianism. If we want to bundle all these descriptions into one name, I believe none can be more expressive than *Islamic fundamentalism*.

It is a deadly mistake if, in a search for a response to the September 11 incident, we lock ourselves in a technical, tactical, and informational labyrinth, attempting to analyze the personalities of the direct perpetrators of this incident. Beyond all the analysis, the past twenty-two years have taught us that in today's world, terrorism is the other side of Islamic fundamentalism and is in fact needed for its existence. When you confront such a dreadful enemy but you try to handle it with friendship and compromise, you certainly will be blitzed.

Islamic Fundamentalism~Based Terrorism

Terrorism is a tactic, a function, and a method whose driving force is an ideological and political goal. Without such a driving force, terrorism would dry up and fail. In the 1960s and 1970s, terrorism was based on nationalist, secular views and in many cases was chauvinistic. For reasons that we will not discuss here, it started to decline in the second half of the 1970s. Despite the fact that reactionary religious movements existed throughout the twentieth century, they were never in a position to engage in terrorist activities until recently.

The roots of Islamic fundamentalism go back to the first centuries of Islam. But Islamic fundamentalism in its current context, theory, and power emerged after Ruhollah Khomeini came to power in Iran in 1979. The Khomeini regime transformed the idea of creating a global Islamic rule from an unachievable ideal to an achievable goal by many fundamentalist groups, and it also gave these groups global backing.

In a historical example, in the second half of the nineteenth century and beginning of the twentieth century, more than a few Marxist parties existed in Europe. But the October revolution victory of Russia's Bolsheviks, who were much younger than many other European parties, made that movement a global one. Until the demise of the Soviet Union, even those Marxist parties that had ideological differences with Moscow used to get their credibility from it.

Export of Revolution: A Specific Goal

Khomeini institutionalized the "export of revolution" and creation of a global Islamic rule, not only as an ideal but as a specific goal and program within various parts of his constitution. The foreword of the regime's constitution reads, in part, "Given the context of Iran's Islamic Revolution, which was a movement for the victory of all the oppressed over the oppressors, it provides the ground for continuation of the revolution inside and outside the country, specifically in spreading international links to other Islamic and people's movements, tries to pave the way for the creation of unique global *ummah* so the continuation of the struggle for the salvation of deprived and suffering nations can be settled." Another part of the foreword, under the headline "Ideological Army," reads, "The Army of the Islamic Republic and the Revolutionary Guards Corps . . . carry not only the duty of protecting the borders but also ideological duty, i.e., Jihad for God and struggle to spread the rule of God's law in the world."

The Eleventh Act of the constitution reads, "The government of the Islamic Republic of Iran is obligated to base its general policy on the coalition and unity of the Islamic nations and to try to fulfill the political, economic, and cultural unity of the Islamic world."

Tehran: The World Capital of Fundamentalism and Terrorism

Iran enjoys a unique position in the world of Islam due to, among other factors, its strategic location, natural resources, and historical and cultural role in the development of the Islamic civilization. Thus, the mullahs' victory quickly turned Tehran into the world capital of fundamentalists— similar to the relationship between Moscow and Marxism. More significant than money or arms, Tehran provided the fundamentalist currents with inspirational, political, regional, and international support.

Fundamentalist movements, which till then were mostly isolated and weak, became the clerical regime's arms for the export of terrorism and fundamentalism, and as such, the menacing phenomenon of terrorism became global. Attempts to separate terrorism from fundamentalism are dangerous or futile at best.

During the 1980s and 1990s, at least 90 percent of the major terrorist attacks were linked either to Tehran as the epicenter of Islamic fundamentalism and terrorism or to its surrogates and agents and movements that managed to thrive only under the light of Tehran's mullahs. Some of the terrorist attacks carried out either by Tehran or fundamentalists under its hegemony and influence are

- The occupation of the U.S. Embassy in Tehran and the taking of American hostages in 1979. This was, in fact, a clear declaration of war by this new phenomenon that effectively demonstrated its anti-West potential and hysteria.
- Taking Westerners, especially Americans, hostage in Lebanon in the 1980s.
- The explosion of the U.S. Marine barracks in Lebanon in 1983.
- The bombing of Pan Am flight 103 over Lockerbie, Scotland, in 1988.
- The explosion of an Air France 747 passenger jet in Tehran's airport in 1983.
- Several bombings in the streets of Paris in 1986, which caused many deaths and injuries among civilians.

- The hanging of U.S. Colonel William Higgins, who worked for the United Nations, in Lebanon.
- The shipment of 51 packages of explosives to Saudi Arabia (which were discovered before detonation) in 1986 in order to kill many pilgrims.
- The massacre of more than 400 pilgrims to Mecca in 1987.
- The bombing of the Israeli Embassy in Buenos Aires.
- The killing of antifundamentalist intellectuals and authors in Turkey.
- The decree to kill Salman Rushdie.
- The killings of many Iranian dissidents, particularly the Mojahedin, in Germany, Switzerland, France, Sweden, Italy, Turkey, Pakistan, and United Arab Emirates.

These terrorist attacks, which have left thousands of casualties behind throughout the world, are just a small fraction of the bloody record of Islamic fundamentalism led by the mullahs ruling Iran.

With such a track record, it came as little surprise that two weeks after the tragic events of September 11, 2001, the clerical regime's supreme leader, Ali Khamenei, said in a speech: "We do not believe that the American administration is sincere in the fight against terrorism. It is not sincere and is not telling the truth. It is pursuing other objectives. We do not regard the United State to be qualified to lead a global movement against terrorism."[1]

Speaking before thousands of his supporters, who were chanting "Down with America," "Down with Israel," "Down with Mojahedin," Khamenei added: "I repeat for the public opinion in our country and throughout the world, we want everyone to know that Islamic Iran will not participate in any movement led by America. . . . The most intransigent and the most evil terrorists are sitting by your side in America."[2]

News agencies reported on September 26 that Mohammad Khatami "strongly lambasted Bush" and said: "The statement by Bush that you are either with us or with the terrorists was the worst kind of dichotomy. . . . A mundane superpower can reach this height of arrogance and illusion because the person concerned thinks he can distinguish what is good and what is bad by himself."[3]

---

1. State Television, 26 September 2001.
2. Ibid.
3. Ibid.

November 4, 1979	American diplomats were taken hostage and held for 444 days in Tehran.
April 1983	A truck loaded with explosives blew up in front of the American embassy in Beirut. Sixty-one were killed and 120 more were injured.
August 1983	An Air France 747 jumbo jet was hijacked after it took off from Vienna Airport en route to Tehran. The plane was blown up by the hijackers on the tarmac of Tehran's Mehrabad Airport.
October 23, 1983	The headquarters of the U.S. Marines in Beirut was destroyed in a suicide attack by Iran's terrorist surrogates, resulting in 241 dead, 80 seriously wounded.
March 1984	William Buckley, an American citizen living in Lebanon, was abducted by Iranian terrorist surrogates. He was secretly taken to Tehran, where he was killed in 1985 by the Revolutionary Guards.
December 3, 1984	Peter Kilburn, a librarian at the American University of Beirut, was abducted by Iran's terrorist surrogates. He was killed in 1986.
May 22, 1985	Michel Seurat, a French writer, was kidnapped by mullahs' agents in Lebanon. He was murdered three years later by the hostage-takers.
June 1985	A TWA Boeing 727 was hijacked en route to Rome and Athens and was diverted to Beirut. One of the passengers on board who was a diver in the U.S. Navy was executed on the plane by the hijackers.
July 1985	Two bombs planted in two restaurants in Kuwait resulted in the death of 10 people and the injury of 80.
November 9, 1985	French police discovered a suitcase containing machine guns, handguns, grenades and bullets in the luggage of the Iran Air crew in Roissy Airport.

February 7, 1986	German police announced that two suspected Iranian terrorists abandoned their car and fled after they were pursued by the police. Their car had been used in previous terrorist attacks in France, and weapons and documents were discovered in the car.
March 18, 1986	Tunisian authorities announced that a terrorist group linked with Iran had been uncovered and 20 of its members had been arrested. The group called itself Hizbollah Al-Mokhtar.
August 28, 1986	A large quantity of explosives, plastic bombs, and weapons was discovered in the luggage of Iranian "pilgrims" arriving in Saudi Arabia for the annual Haj pilgrimage. Saudi police arrested 100 of the undercover agents sent by the mullah regime.
September 1986	A wave of bombings in public places shocked Paris. Fouad Ali Saleh was convicted of killing 12 and injuring hundreds. He was arrested in March 1987 while transferring explosives into a car in Paris.
July 1987	A DC-10 plane belonging to Air Afrique was hijacked by terrorists of the mullah regime. During the hijacking of the plane a French passenger was killed in the Vienna Airport. The president of Switzerland said the Iranian government was responsible.
August 1, 1987	Iranian regime agents staged a riot in Mecca during the Muslim annual Haj pilgrimage as part of a wider plan to destabilize the Saudi regime. The Saudi government said 402 persons were killed and 650 were wounded; 85 Saudi policemen were among the dead.
August 1, 1987	Embassies of Saudi Arabia and Kuwait in Tehran were occupied by government-organized mobs, and a diplomat was killed.
April 5, 1988	A Kuwaiti 747 jumbo jet was hijacked in Bangkok and landed in Mashad, eastern Iran. One of the mullahs' terrorists of Lebanese origin boarded the plane in Iran and led the terrorist operation. During the 15-day ordeal, two passengers were killed by hijackers.

December 22, 1988	Pan Am flight 103 exploded in midair over Lockerbie, Scotland.
February 1989	Khomeini's religious decree to kill Salman Rushdie, an Indian-born British author, for writing *Satanic Verses.*
May 27, 1989	The Turkish daily Hurriyet reported that a 14-man group trying to infiltrate Turkey from Iran to carry out terrorist attacks had been arrested. The group's leader, Esmat Kamal, had been involved in the assassination of a Saudi diplomat in Ankara.
July 31, 1989	Colonel William Higgins, an American officer working for the United Nations in Lebanon, was abducted and executed by the Iranian regime's agents. A video recording of his hanging was given to international news agencies.
1989	During the Muslim annual Haj pilgrimage, three bombs were exploded around the holy site of Mecca. Scores of people were injured.
December 23, 1989	Mehrdad Kowkabi, an Iranian, was charged with the attempted arson of a London bookshop and planning a bomb attack in connection with Salman Rushdie.
January 30, 1990	French Television Channel 1 broadcast an interview with Lotfi Ben-Khala, a terrorist agent who was trained in Iran. He said the mullahs planned a terrorist attack on a French nuclear facility that would have resulted in 10,000 deaths.
July 3, 1991	The Italian translator of *Satanic Verses* was stabbed and injured. The assailant said that he was an Iranian who was seeking Rushdie's whereabouts.
July 21, 1991	Professor Hitoshi Igarashi, the Japanese translator of The Satanic Verses, was stabbed to death.
December 29, 1991	Following the arrest of one of the mullahs' terrorists in Bern, the regime barred the employees of the Swiss embassy from leaving Tehran.

March 1992	Relations between Bern and Tehran were severed after an Iranian terrorist was arrested in Switzerland. A Swiss businessman disappeared in Tehran. Later it was discovered that he had been taken hostage.
March 17, 1992	An attack against the Israeli embassy in Buenos Aires resulted in the death of 20 and the injury of 250 people.
November 21, 1992	French police announced the arrest of two Iranians involved in several assassinations in Europe.
December 29, 1992	Palestinian President Yasser Arafat told Egypt's parliament that the Iranian regime finances Hamas, Islamic Jihad and other radical groups and recently paid them $30 million.
January 27, 1993	The Turkish interior minister said a terrorist network linked with the Iranian regime carried out the assassination of Turkish journalist Ugur Mumcu.
January 27, 1993	Turkish police arrested a group of Turkish Hizbollah members, who were trained in Iran, and charged them with the killing of Hikmet Cettin, a Turkish journalist.
April 25, 1993	The New York Times reported that at least $100,000 had been deposited in the account of the prime suspects of the February 1993 World Trade Center bombing. The money primarily came from Iran.
July 8, 1993	Egyptian security forces arrested 165 Islamic fundamentalists. Two of them had been trained in a terrorist training center in Mashad, eastern Iran.
October 11, 1993	The Norwegian publisher of Salman Rushdie's book, Willian Nigaard, was hit with three bullets from the back in an unsuccessful assassination attempt.
June 2, 1994	AFP reported that U.S. intelligence officials said Iran has secretly planted 400 members of the Revolutionary Guards in Bosnia in order to set up terrorist cells in the former Yugoslavia.

June 3, 1994	Hossein Shahriarifar, an Iranian terrorist, was arrested along with two other Iranians in Thailand on charges of plotting to carry out a suicide attack on the Israeli embassy in Bangkok. His truck was stopped by police as he was driving to the embassy.
July 6, 1994	Reuters reported that the Filipino government had arrested an agent of the Iranian regime named Hosseini on charges of providing financial support for Abu Sayyaf's group.
July 15, 1994	The foreign ministry of Venezuela announced that it had declared four Iranian diplomats persona non grata and asked them to leave the country after they were implicated in the attempted abduction of an exiled Iranian.
July 18, 1994	An attack against the Jewish Community Center in Buenos Aires led to the killing of 26 and the injury of 127 people. Israeli Prime Minister Yitzhak Rabin blamed the bombing on the Iranian regime.
July 31, 1994	Panama announced that two Iranians and a Lebanese had been arrested in connection with the bombing of an airliner on July 19.
May 7, 1995	The Swedish government expelled two suspects from the country for taking part in terrorist conspiracies.
August 1995	Germany expelled two Iranian diplomats. The mullahs' embassy in Bonn intended to dispatch a terrorist team to disrupt the Dortmund meeting in which Maryam Rajavi was due to make a speech.
March 3, 1996	A powerful bomb was exploded in Bethlehem by agents of the mullah regime.
March 13, 1996	The leader of a fundamentalist terrorist group in Turkey was arrested by police. He admitted that he was given weapons by the mullahs' embassy in Ankara to assassinate an antifundamentalist Turkish author.

April 10, 1996	Four diplomats of the mullahs' regime in Turkey were expelled because of their role in the assassination of Zahra Rajabi and a Turkish intellectual.
May 13, 1996	The Iranian Resistance exposed a plan by the mullahs' Intelligence Ministry to attack the residence of Maryam Rajavi, the Resistance's president-elect, in a Paris suburb.
May 23, 1996	Palestinian President Yasser Arafat said: "A clandestine group intended to assassinate me. They acted upon a religious decree from Iran."
June 5, 1996	The interior minister of Bahrain exposed a plan to topple the ruling family by fundamentalist Shiites. The leader of the group, Ali Kazem Almottaqavi, had been living in Iran since 1983. He was led by Brigadier General Ahmad Sharifi of the Revolutionary Guards. (Brigadier General Sharifi, commander of the Qods Force's Sixth Brigade, was one of the eight main operational commanders of the Qods Force).
June 1996	The government of Bahrain announced the discovery of a local Hizbollah terrorist cell, whose members were trained and sponsored by the Iranian regime.
September 24, 1996	An Iranian diplomat was arrested and later expelled by the government of Tajikistan for his role in exporting fundamentalism and terrorism to this country.
February 2, 1997	The Turkish government expelled an Iranian diplomat for active involvement in exporting fundamentalism and terrorism to Turkey.
February 2, 1997	Terrorists were trained in Imam Sadeq's training base near Qom. They were flown to a third country from Tehran in spring 1996. They were transferred to Saudi Arabia and implemented their plans.

October 12, 1998	A government-affiliated institution raised its bounty for Salman Rushdie's head to $2.8 million.
August 23, 1999	The written testimony of Argentina's vice president to the judiciary of this country cited evidence pointing to the Iranian regime's role in the bombing of the Jewish Community Center in Buenos Aires in July 1994.
April 26, 2001	The Conference of Palestinian Intifada in Tehran called for the annihilation of Israel.

The Mullahs Call for Terrorism

The regime's top officials have repeatedly called for criminal acts or have taken responsibility for them. On the seventh anniversary of the U.S. Embassy takeover in Tehran, Hashemi Rafsanjani, the speaker of the Parliament at the time, said: "They hold us accountable for the blow the Americans received and the humiliation they suffered in Lebanon. We are indeed responsible [for it.]"[4]

In a Friday prayer sermon on May 5, 1989, Rafsanjani said: "If for every Palestinian martyred by Israeli mercenaries, five American or French citizens are murdered, they would no longer commit such crimes. . . . The Palestinians might say, in that case, the world will call us terrorists. I say, however, do they not label you already?"[5]

Mohsen Rafiqdoust, the minister of the Revolutionary Guards at the time, said: "In the victory of the revolution in Lebanon and many other places, the United States has felt the impact of our might on its ominous body, and knows that both the TNT and the ideology which in one blast sent to hell 400 officers, NCOs and soldiers at the Marine Headquarters have been provided by Iran. This is well understood by America: that is why they are so helpless in the Persian Gulf."[6]

Mohsen Rezai, then commander in chief of the Revolutionary Guards, said: "The Muslims' fury and hatred will burn the heart of Washington someday and America will be responsible for its repercussions. . . . The day

---

4. Tehran radio, 4 November 1986.
5. *Ettela'at*, Tehran, 6 May 1989.
6. *Ressalat*, Tehran, 20 July 1987.

will come when, like Salman Rushdie, the Jews will not find a place to live anywhere in the world."[7]

Mohammad Khatami, the Iranian regime's president, who is now talking about dialogue among civilizations, once said the following about the British author Salman Rushdie: "Salman Rushdie, the author of the book *Satanic Verses*, must be executed according to the religious fatwa of Imam Khomeini, and there is no way for him to escape the execution of this order. By the publication of blasphemous *Satanic Verses*, the criminal East and West, particularly the British rulers, proved to the world that they are not only an enemy to the Islamic Republic and Imam but are an enemy to the religion of Islam and more than one billion Muslims around the world. The silence on the part of Arab rulers about the publication of *Satanic Verses* proved that they defend Islam and the Quran only rhetorically.[8]

Enmity toward Peace and Freedom

One of the characteristics of Islamic fundamentalism, especially as set forth by the ruling mullahs of Iran, is its enmity toward peace and penchant toward sabotage of the Middle East peace process. The conspiracies of the mullahs and their associates in Palestine and Arab countries against Arafat, the Palestine Liberation Organization (PLO) and the Palestinian Authority continued unabated. In every state-controlled demonstration in Tehran in support of Palestine, "Down with Arafat" and "Down with revisionists" have been routine slogans. So far, several assassination plots against Arafat have been designed by Tehran's regime that were discovered and neutralized. An intifada meeting in Tehran last April basically was aimed at putting pressure on the PLO and boosting opposition and antipeace groups' standings.

As for Israel, the Iranian regime has always wanted its eradication from the face of earth.

Terrorism and Fundamentalism's Financial and Organizational Backing

The regime leaders' remarks on exporting terrorism and fundamentalism enjoy a huge financial and organizational backing from vast networks

---

7. *Kayhan*, Tehran, 21 October 1991.
8. *Kayhan*, Tehran, 8 March 1989.

inside and outside the country. The Intelligence Ministry, the Revolutionary Guards Corps, Khamenei's office, the Foreign Affairs Ministry, the Islamic Culture and Propaganda Organization, the Guidance Ministry, and many other government institutions are involved in exporting terrorism. The regime's organizational structure for exporting terrorism and fundamentalism —compared to eight years ago when this book was first published—has significantly improved.

A large section of the mullah regime's intelligence Ministry is focused on terrorist activities and espionage abroad. Many Western intelligence agencies admit this fact. For example, the Qods Force, as the fifth force of the Revolutionary Guards Corps, was formed specifically for terrorist activities outside Iran. Section IX of this book explains the Qods Force structure and its operations.

The Islamic Propaganda and Communication Organization is a huge system that is present in dozens of countries and has hundreds of millions of dollars in its budget. Besides laying the groundwork for exporting terrorism and fundamentalism, it is engaged in recruiting Muslims and Arabs for the regime's terrorist squads. This organization was formed by merging five large organizations on Khamenei's order, and it operates under his supervision. The regime's embassies and representative offices abroad, as well as other institutions that are apparently involved in cultural and religious services abroad, serve the purpose of exporting terrorism and fundamentalism.

The dimensions of the mullahs regime's atrocities have grown to such an extent that despite economic and political implications, the judiciaries of some countries, especially European countries, have stressed the role of the regime's leaders in those atrocities. Judge Roland Chatelain, the Swiss investigative magistrate, announced in 1990 that the assassination of Dr. Kazem Rajavi was carried out by thirteen Iranian nationals, all of them holding Iranian regime service passports. He stated in June 1998, however, that this assassination was done by the mullahs' Intelligence Ministry.

A German federal court in Berlin, after a four-year-long trial regarding the killings at a Mykonos restaurant, asserted in its verdict that a committee of the highest ranking leaders of the Iranian regime—including the supreme leader, the president, the intelligence minister, and the foreign affairs minister—had ordered assassinations outside the country, including those on Mykonos. Earlier, the Berlin court had issued an arrest warrant for mullah Ali Fallahian, the regime's intelligence minister.

Khatami's Era

Four years ago when Khatami became president of Iran, many believed that everything would change in the regime of the mullahs— the Velayat-e-faqih—and that the theocratic regime would follow the path of moderation. Knowing Khatami and the nature of the Velayat-e-faqih system, the Iranian Resistance made no such misinterpretation.

Nine years ago, when I was compiling this book, while I never thought Khatami would one day become the president of this regime, I mentioned his role as a relatively low-level cleric at the head of the Ministry of Islamic Guidance, a major lever in exporting terrorism and fundamentalism. As one of the chief theoreticians of the regime, he said about the thesis of exporting the revolution: "Where do we look when we are defining our strategy? Do we look at the protection of our territorial integrity or at the expansion? Do we look at expansion or protection? We definitely have to think about expansion.[9]

At another time he stated: "The question is what shall we do to enter the world stage? We need a force that our enemy would not have. This force should be superior to technology and weapons. Our balancing force is the newly born and awakened Islam that is prepared to make sacrifices throughout the world. The Islamic Republic will survive if it is backed by that global force. In Algeria the Islamic movement is serious. We can count on Sudan. New centers of power in the Islamic world are in the making. The rising Islamic force in the world is considerable, and we should seriously include it in our calculations."[10]

He said about the United States: "The U.S. bully is a double disaster. The most cultureless people are Americans—a bunch of bullies, hooligans, adventurers. The worst people from across Europe went there and made money. A baseless culture and with the technology of force. . . . Now Americans, a bunch of the most cultureless people in the world, have the most assets of the world. This is one of humanity's double disasters."[11]

Nevertheless, the presidency of Khatami became an opportunity for some in the West who wanted to do business with the mullah regime. They referred to Khatami as "moderate," a supporter of "civil society" and "removing tensions," and a hope for "democracy." They tried to pave

---

9. *Ressalat,* Tehran, 5 June 1989.
10. *Ressalat,* Tehran, 7 July 1991.
11. *Ettela'at,* Tehran, 7 July 1991.

the way for expanding their relationship by exacerbating the illusion of Khatami's moderation, giving a human face to fundamentalism and identifying Iran under the mullahs' rule as a model for Islamic democracy. But the Iranian People and Resistance knew from the beginning that Khatami neither wanted to reform nor was capable of reforming this regime, nor is this medieval regime reformable.

Khatami's Record

The essence of any real political reform is free elections. This requires abandoning repressive measures; ending suppression, torture, and execution; and allowing freedom of political activities of opponents. In a fair assessment, one has to measure Khatami's four-year record based on these requirements. Khatami has never been faithful to his own early slogans, such as "opponents' freedom," "civil society," and "rule of law" and has used them to give a cosmetic appearance to the religious fascism and absolute rule of the mullahs—that is Velayat-e-faqih—and to gain more shares of power. The Iranian Resistance, which struggles for Iranian people's basic rights, i.e., freedom, democracy, peace, and justice, welcomes any reform and political dialogue and would be the first winner of such a process. But the reality, as Patrick Clawson wrote in the *Wall Street Journal*, July 16, 1999, is different: "Khatami's agenda is not to bring Iran back to the modern world. His goal, instead, is to strengthen the Islamic republic through reforms that would restore its popularity."[12] A glance at Khatami's four-year record provides this image:

- Oppression, torture, inhuman punishments such as public stoning, amputation of hands and gouging eyes, which are aimed at terrorizing the society, are more common than ever. More than 1,100 public executions, 16 announced stonings, and public floggings of thousands of people are part of the disastrous human rights record under Khatami. Khatami played a major role in suppressing the uprising of students and other people of Tehran in July 1999 and personally ordered a crackdown on the demonstrators via television.
- More than 50 publications were closed down during the last four years, and no opposition newspapers were allowed to be published. These publications belonged to the regime's factions.

---

12. Patrick Clawson, *Wall Street Journal*, 16 July 1999.

- No political opposition party, organization, or group was permitted to operate, and even members of the "Freedom Movement," who were tolerated during the past twenty years and acted as a safety valve for the regime, were sent to jail. This group has always maintained its loyalty to the Velayat-e-faqih.
- With the collaboration of Khatami and Khamenei, the perpetrators of political assassinations by the Intelligence Ministry—which claimed more than 120 victims according to the regime's officials—were set free and the related cases were settled behind closed doors.
- Khatami personally ordered the closure of *Arya*, a newspaper of his own faction, because it pointed to Khatami's role in the mass execution of political prisoners in 1988. *Arya* wrote in March 2000: "The main resolution of the suspicious assassinations is to go back to the past and to open the case of mass execution of political prisoners in the summer of 1988. Everybody involved in that must be removed and sent home."[13] *Ressalat*, referring to Khomeini's fatwa for the mass execution of political prisoners, pointed out in April 2000: "This verdict was issued at a time when Mr. Khatami was the cultural deputy of the commander in chief and supported vigorously the Imam's order."[14]
- As explicitly stated by Ali Shamkhani, the minister of defense, the bombing of Iranian Resistance bases within the first few weeks of Khatami's election (September 1997) was with the agreement of all the regime's leaders and specifically Khatami. The decision to launch seventy-seven missiles of mass destruction against the Resistance's bases, according to Mohsen Rezai, the secretary of the Expediency Council, was made in the Supreme National Defense Council, led by Khatami. In its first four years Khatami's regime has launched seventy-seven terrorist operations against the Iranian Resistance abroad. These facts show clearly that Khatami has no hesitation about exporting crisis and terror outside of Iran's borders.

The Growing Trend of Threat

The *International Herald Tribune* on April 3, 2001, reported "the State Department's top Middle East diplomat said that Iran had increased its support for 'terrorism,' one of the key markers by which Washington

---

13. *Arya*, Tehran, March 2000.
14. *Ressalat*, Tehran, 9 April 2000.

assesses the Iranian government. Edward Walker, assistant secretary of state, [stated], 'I would say that in my judgment the problem of Iranian support for terrorism has increased. . . . This is problematic.'"[15]

In May 2001, Secretary of State Colin Powell in a Congressional hearing said that the Iranian regime "continues to hang on to an ideology" that is not relevant to the twenty-first century.[16] The State Department's annual report, *Patterns of Global Terrorism*, published in April 2001, once again named Iran as the world's "most active state-sponsor of terrorism."[17]

The *Los Angeles Times* on May 6, 2001, quoted an American official who said, "Iran has become more active (in terrorism) since last fall. The increase has been pretty steady and pretty intense. . . . In the past, Iran tried to limit direct links to extremist operations. . . . Now the Revolutionary Guards in Lebanon are providing more operational support. According to Arab and US sources 'The Jordanian government is sufficiently concerned about Iran's heightened profile that King Abdullah II raised the issue during his visit to Washington last month. It is a change because in recent years, Jordan had witnessed a drop in Iran's activities, and then they went back up again last fall.'"[18]

Michael Sheehan, then coordinator for counterterrorism of the State Department, in an address at Brookings Institute on February 10, 2000, said: "The primary area of concern for me in counterterrorism today is in Southwest Asia, and specifically in two countries—Afghanistan and Iran. . . . Iran continues to support such terrorist groups as Hezbollah, Hamas, the Palestinian Islamic Jihad, and Ahmad Jabril's PFLPGC, for the purposes of attacking the Middle East peace process. As CIA Director George Tenet recently testified, Iran remains the most active state sponsor of terrorism, and I fully agree with that assessment."[19]

Weapons of Mass Destruction

During Khatami's tenure, not only has the domestic situation deteriorated, including personal and social freedoms, but Iran's policy

---

15. *International Herald Tribune*, 3 April 2001.
16. Colin Powell, testimony before hearing of Senate Appropriations Subcommittee, 3 May 2001.
17. State Department, *Patterns of Global Terrorism* (Washington, D.C.: GPO, 2001).
18. *Los Angeles Times*, 6 May 2001.
19. Michael Sheehan, address at Brookings Institute, 10 February 2000.

regarding terrorism has not changed. George Tenet, CIA director, at a hearing of the Senate Intelligence Committee on February 7, 2001, said, "Islamic militancy is expanding, and the worldwide pool of potential recruits for terrorist networks is growing. In central Asia, the Middle East, and South Asia, Islamic terrorist organizations are trying to attract new recruits, including under the banner of anti-Americanism. . . . Iran's desire to end its isolation has not resulted in a decline in its willingness to use terrorism to pursue strategic foreign policy agendas—Tehran, in fact, has increased its support to terrorist groups opposed to the peace process over the past two years."[20]

The Iranian regime's intense effort to obtain and proliferate weapons of mass destruction continues to be a top priority for Khatami. A report submitted to the U.S. Congress by the National Intelligence Council in September 1999 stresses that "Iran is the next hostile country most capable of testing an ICBM capable of delivering a weapon to the United States during the next 15 years. Iran *could test* an ICBM that could deliver a several-hundred kilogram payload to many parts of the United States in the last half of the next decade using Russian technology and assistance."[21]

In a January 2001 report, the Pentagon stated, "Iran is one of the countries most active in seeking to acquire nuclear, biological, chemical weapons- and missile-related technologies. Iran's NBC and missile programs continued in the last several years notwithstanding President Khatami's moderation of the regime's anti-Western rhetoric."[22]

The Policy of Rapprochement with the Mullahs

Considering the current circumstances, the Western policy of rapprochement with the mullahs has only emboldened them to further pursue their policies and goals. Let us examine a case in point. U.S. officials have long been aware of the mullah regime's role in the explosion of the Khobar Towers in Saudi Arabia (June 1996), which killed nineteen U.S. military personnel. In June 2001, an article published in *New Yorker* magazine as well as an independent UPI report revealed, quoting U.S. officials, that FBI

---

20. George Tenet, testimony at hearing of Senate Intelligence Committee, February 2001.
21. National Intelligence Council, *Foreign Missile Developments and the Ballistic Threat to the United States through 2015* (Washington, D.C.: GPO, 1999).
22. Office of the Secretary of Defense, *Proliferation: Threat and Defense* (Washington, D.C.: GPO, 2001).

director Louis Freeh had prepared a list of individuals responsible for the Khobar Towers explosion. He had submitted the list to the Bush administration for prosecution. This list included the names of some officials within the mullah's regime.

UPI reported on May 6, 2001, that the United States had "airtight evidence" that the mullah regime was the chief culprit behind the June 1996 terrorist bombing. Quoting a U.S. official, UPI wrote: "The FBI reached that conclusion in an early stage but was forced to withdraw it because of political considerations."[23]

The *International Herald Tribune* wrote on April 3, 2001, "Iran-watchers inside the U.S. government say there was pressure from the Clinton White House to play down any criticism of the Khatami administration, which it saw as more conducive to improved ties."[24]

Tehran interpreted Washington's approach as a sign of weakness. This, in turn, made the mullahs more adamant in pursuing their terrorist policies. These policies were considered the government's "Achilles heel." In March 2000, Madeleine Albright, in her speech to the Asia Society, introduced U.S. sanctions on certain Iranian export products and stressed her government's readiness to improve relations with Tehran. The ruling mullahs, who were only too happy to receive such one-sided rewards, seized the opportunity to increase their terrorist activities and the export of fundamentalism. It is ironic that a few months after granting such a concession to the mullah regime, State Department officials complained of witnessing a "noticeable increase" in the mullah regime's terrorist activities within the region. At the same time, the State Department failed to make a connection between that increase and the policy of appeasement and rapprochement with the mullahs.

Crisis in Afghanistan: The End Result of the Mullahs' Rule

Along with a policy of export of revolution and terrorism, the regime has done its utmost to create centers of crisis. Lebanon was the first and perhaps the most costly experience. The mullah regime was able to use the particular circumstances in Lebanon to turn it into a serious center of terrorism and fundamentalism.

---

23. UPI, 6 May 2001.
24. *International Herald Tribune*, 3 April 2001.

The dilemma of Afghanistan was primarily created by the mullah regime and will no doubt continue until the regime is overthrown. In the spring of 1979, after the change of government in Iran, the Soviet Union, relying on the shift in the balance of power in the region, occupied Afghanistan. During the next few years, while maintaining a cordial relationship with Moscow, the Tehran regime tried to exert considerable influence in shaping events in Afghanistan. This task was accomplished through influencing the Islamic movements that were opposed to the Soviet Union. To that end, various branches were created within the Revolutionary Guards Corps and the Intelligence Ministry to further fan the flames of civil war in Afghanistan. Most importantly, due to the presence of the mullah regime in the region and through its continuous efforts to prevent the creation of a democratic and modern alternative, it was able to impede national conciliation in that country.

It would be a superficial assumption if one were to view the developments as the result of a natural course of actions within Afghanistan. The history and background of Afghanistan do not justify the complete lack of any democratic movements. Two preventive factors played a part: one was the active role played by Tehran and the other was the West's, in particular the United States', compromise with various reactionary forces in that country. It thus did not prevent the destructive role of Tehran in the formation of such a climate.

A Historical Error

In order to respond to the question that was raised at the beginning of this writing and to explain the reason for the September 11 surprise attack (outside the tactical and technical realm), we have to emphasize that it is due to not taking Islamic fundamentalism as a major and serious threat. A secondary reason is attempting to appease the mullah government, the center of worldwide fundamentalism. The Mojahedin and the Iranian Resistance have time and time again (including in this book) warned that Islamic fundamentalism and the mullah regime will not cease their terrorism. They should be considered the most important threat to human civilization in this era. Did we have to pay such a heavy price in order to take this threat seriously and to become aware of such an evil force?

A Unilateral Response Does Necessarily Include Tehran

Considering recent events, if we use a military response against terrorism only in Afghanistan (or elsewhere) without concentrating on the totality of fundamentalism, its sociopolitical roots, and its regional center of power, this strategy will act against itself and will further encourage the fundamentalist elements. The response to terrorists should not be selective. This means that while those responsible for the September 11 tragedy should be punished, those responsible for the Khobar bombing, the bombing of the U.S. Marine base in Lebanon, hostage taking in Lebanon and Tehran, and many more terrorist crimes (committed by the agents of the Tehran regime) should not go unpunished. Allowing this would strongly undermine the seriousness of the fight against terrorism.

Fundamentalism, as well as its twin, terrorism, will remain a threat to peace, stability, and tranquility as long as its worldwide capital is in operation. Only by overthrowing the mullah regime and its capital will the threat be removed. At that time, even if the fundamentalist elements continue to exist, similar to the fate of Communist parties following the collapse of the Soviet Union, they will either have no role or at the very least will not constitute a threat.

If, along with military measures, we do not focus on political, regional, and international efforts, the Tehran regime will remain the heart of fundamentalism. Without a political force of action against the Iranian regime, all military, political, or ideological measures against Afghanistan or any other interested party will not render the desired end result. As William Safire, in his September 17 *New York Times* column, concluded: "If . . . the great majority of peaceful Muslims can be helped to win their internal theological war, today's military solutions need not beget tomorrow's tragedies."[25]

I believe that in dealing with Islamic fundamentalism, in addition to security and military solutions, there is a need for political and cultural solutions as well. This is the best and only practical way to demonstrate that the goal is to fight against terrorism and fundamentalism, not animosity against Islam.

---

25. William Safire, *New York Times*, 17 September 2001.

The Symbol of a Tolerant and Democratic Islam

The symbol of a tolerant, antifundamentalist and democratic Islam is Maryam Rajavi. She has played a key role not only in exposing the true nature of the misogynist regime ruling Iran but in preventing the fundamentalists from taking advantage of the religious sentiment of the People for their objectives.

In a speech before some 15,000 Iranians and foreign dignitaries in Germany in June 1995, referring to the fundamentalists ruling Iran, she declared: "These demagogues commit their crimes in the name of Islam, a despicable and horrendous act, and itself one of their most heinous crimes. As a Muslim woman let me proclaim that the peddlers of religion who rule Iran in the name of Islam, but shed blood, suppress the people, and advocate export of fundamentalism and terrorism, are themselves the worst enemy of Islam and Muslims. The day will come when they will be forced to let go of the name of Islam."[26]

A year later on the anniversary of the beginning of the Resistance, in a huge gathering of some 25,000 people in London, she called for the formation of an international front against fundamentalism. She said in part of her speech:

> From Tehran, the beating heart of theocracy, the octopus of fundamentalism has extended its blood-drenched tentacles into Islamic states and Muslim societies around the world. It is the main threat to global and regional peace. Exploiting the religious beliefs of more than one billion Muslims, the mullahs ruling Iran promote expansionism, while exporting crisis and discord. Their foreign policy consists of meddling in the affairs of Islamic countries, issuing fatwas to murder foreign nationals, and launching terrorist operations abroad. Other aspects of this policy include spending huge sums on armaments of all kinds, especially weapons of mass destruction such as biological, chemical, and nuclear.

> Such a foreign policy is inherent to the fundamentalists' nature. The theocracy ruling Iran thrives on crises. It is hostile to the most important global peace initiative in the Middle East, and its policies and actions only nourish warmongering extremists and fundamentalists. These realities demonstrate how the ominous specter of religious fascism haunts global peace. The world community, for its turn, has a moral duty to confront and overcome this phenomenon.

> I again emphasize here that these reactionaries who suppress the Iranian people, and particularly Iranian women, and export terrorism and fundamentalism

---

26. Maryam Rajavi, "Freedom," speech given at Westfallenhallen, Dortmund, Germany, 16 June 1995.

under the cloak of religion, have nothing to do with Islam. They are the peddlers of religion and exploit the name of Islam to advance their sinister,
inhuman objectives. Islam is the religion of peace, freedom, liberty, equality,
love, mercy, and liberation. The mullahs' fundamentalist mindset, however,
rests upon vengeance, enmity, and ignorance and is at war with human values
and world peace.

As we approach the end of the twentieth century, fundamentalism's brazen
enmity toward human values and world peace has spilled onto issues of international concern. . . . The international community has failed to demonstrate
enough sensitivity to the dangers of appeasing the religious, terrorist dictatorship ruling Iran. Hence, the mullahs still find opportunities to take advantage
of such conciliation. Through terrorist blackmail, they take the policies and
even the moral principles of governments hostage.[27]

Finally she declared: "A common front against fundamentalism serves
the interests of global peace and will preclude a repeat of the bitter experience of appeasing fascism on the eve of the Second World War."[28]

—Mohammad Mohaddessin

---

27. Maryam Rajavi, "Women: Voice of the Oppressed," speech given at Earls Court
Exhibition Center, London, 21 June 1996.
28. Ibid.

I

Dogmatism Versus Democracy: A Brief History of Fundamentalism

Let there be no compulsion in religion.

—Holy Quran, Sura II, Baqara, Verse 256[1]

In critically analyzing the history of Islam, experts and orientalists have generally seen the Shi'ah-Sunni conflict as the main source of strife within the Muslim communities. This conflict has certainly continued at various times and to various degrees, whether in the form of scholarly debates and canonical discussions or bloody confrontations. Often overlooked, however, is the profound antagonism between the opposing interpretations of Islamic ideology and the message of revelation, a conflict which has persisted for fourteen centuries, since the founding of the Islamic community in the seventh century by Prophet Muhammad.

On one side is the dogmatic outlook, which is unable to comprehend the true essence of the teachings of the Quran and the Prophet of Islam, i.e. mercy, liberty, and guidance of the individual and society toward moral and material evolution. To the dogmatist, compassion, love, freedom, and progress are not absolute values; the tendency is toward brutality, vengeance, intolerance, ignorance, and superstition. These qualities contradict the approach and practices of Islam's great Prophet. Fourteen centuries after the birth of Islam, Muhammad continues to symbolize to his followers all the sublime qualities of a human being. The hopes for the one who has been sent as "mercy for the worlds" and will intercede for his followers on Doomsday are extremely high, especially among the masses.[2]

Throughout the history of Islam, there have also been Muslims who followed Muhammad's genuine message of mercy and liberty from the Quran, rejecting dogmatism and fanaticism despite threats of excommunication or charges of heresy. This ideological clash has never been limited to Shi'ites versus Sunnis. It has persisted to varying degrees within all Islamic communities. Conflicting ideological interpretations are common to all religions. With Islam, however, the issues have immediate political overtones more volatile than theoretical discussions or academic disputes. The conflicts may last for centuries, because Islam's distinctive characteristic is a model of life, not just of worship. Hence, differing interpretations of the teachings of Islam directly and immediately translate into political conflicts.

A closer look at this linkage of politics and religious sentiments of the Muslim masses is essential to understanding how religious demagogues and fundamentalists—chief among them Khomeini—have exploited this bond to usurp power, and why Marxism, nationalism, and liberalism (especially in their antireligious form) have failed to serve as an alternative to the religious forces in the Islamic world. The only alternative capable of countering fundamentalism is modern, democratic Islam, which opposes the union of church and state, for both political and religious reasons.

The Fundamentalist Appeal

Throughout the tortuous history of the Islamic world, religious attitudes have been interwoven with politics. Researchers rarely find a political philosophy that has not been influenced by the indigenous religious culture. All intellectual trends in the past century that aimed to eliminate Islam from the political life of Muslim society were unable to extend their reach beyond small intellectual or academic circles. This singular characteristic of Islamic societies colors the specific demands of the masses and their image of the ideal society. Iran and Algeria provide clear examples.

In the course of Iran's antimonarchic revolution in 1978–79, foreign journalists interviewed a large number of "revolutionaries," including youths, white-collar workers, housewives, and bazaar merchants, all of whom aspired for the revival of Islamic values in society. When asked their specific demands, they usually gave similar answers: liberty, freedom of the press, a multiparty system, justice, full realization of social and political rights, and an end to censorship, repression, unemployment, economic privation, corruption and bribery. All insisted that Islam would meet these demands.

Fourteen years later, antigovernment protesters in Algeria cite similar reasons for their chants of "Islam is the only solution."[3]

The difference, however, is that for more than a decade the people of Iran have gone through a painful process of disillusionment with Khomeiniism and its demagogic promises, medieval philosophy, administrative incompetence, and reign of terror. Ironically, while Khomeini, his heirs, and his reactionary ideology are held in deep contempt by the majority of Iranians, his brand of Islamic fundamentalism still finds some appeal in Muslim societies far away from Iran's borders. But the youth of Algeria, Morocco, Tunisia, and many other Muslim countries know little if anything about Khomeini's decrees against the Muslim Mojahedin, such as permitting the Guards to drain the blood of the Mojahedin before execution, or sanctioning the rape of Mojahedin women on the eve of their execution.[4] Iranian propaganda depicts Khomeini as a paragon of Islamic virtue.

Khomeini was, of course, not the first ruler in the history of Islam to take advantage of the canon to justify his authoritarian dictatorship. Many tyrants and oppressive sultans used the clergy to legitimize their despotic rule and justify their suppressive policies. In post-Islamic Iran, however, Khomeini was one of the very few *faqihs*, or "scholars of Islam," to propose that Muslim clergymen take the reins of political power in their own hands, and certainly the first one who actually seized power.

Fanaticism Versus Liberty

The first thing Prophet Muhammad did when his army of Muslims conquered the city of Mecca in January A.D. 630 was to declare a general amnesty. The people of Mecca were free to choose or reject Islam. Among the pardoned were the powerful leaders of the Quraysh tribe who were guilty of unspeakable atrocities against Muslims. For years they had harassed and hounded the Prophet and organized more than one attempt on his life. This first act as ruler attests to the spirit of the man entitled the Messenger of Compassion and Emancipation. The life of the Prophet of Islam glows with examples of forgiveness and mercy and with a love for the lofty ideals of the human race. His eminent traits reflect the teachings of Islam and the Quran, the holy book whose every chapter begins "In the Name of God, the Compassionate, the Merciful."

There were instances, even during the Prophet's lifetime, when some

3

of his followers—and occasionally even his close companions—were at a loss to understand the noble spirit of Muhammad's actions and decisions, and protested to him. Such encounters have been recorded, for example, when the Prophet signed the *Al-Hudaybiyah* peace pact with the Meccan leaders one year before the conquest of Mecca, and when he pardoned a Muslim who had fled Medina to join Muhammad's enemies, but was captured en route to Mecca. That some early Muslims argued against such decisions by Muhammad emanated from their inability to grasp the profoundly humanitarian essence of the message of Islam and its rejection of the notion that human character is immutable.

Kharajites: First Advocates of Dogmatism

The Kharajites (seceders) were among the first historical examples of dogmatism and fanaticism in the name of Islam.[5] During the caliphate of Ali ibn Abi Taleb (the Prophet's son-in-law and cousin, and the first Shi'ite Imam), a group of Muslims rebelled, with the motto "*la hokmo illa lellah*" (there are no verdicts but God's), forming the anarchist sect of the Kharajites. One of them assassinated Ali in 661.

The Kharajites continued to exist as a rebel group for two centuries, then disintegrated and virtually disappeared as a sect. They are noteworthy, however, because they were the first to advocate a fundamentalist outlook of Islam and the Quran as their official ideology, opposing any dynamic interpretation of the Quran which Ali pioneered and symbolized. The Kharajites also espoused a formalistic interpretation of the Quranic command to "enjoin good and forbid evil" as vindicating truth with the sword. Their anarchist ideology made the Kharajites highly inflamatory terrorists intolerant of established political authority or almost any opposition to their views.

The Kharajites rebelled against a unique man. Ali was foremost among Muslims for his profound understanding of the Quran and the Prophet's tradition and his tolerance for opposition and of those who criticized him personally. The confrontation between the Kharajite zealots and Ali was the first ideological battle between two diametrically opposed interpretations of Islam.

Ali spent many long days arguing with the Kharajites, convincing several thousand of them to leave the rebels' ranks. Pointing, for example, to the Kharajites' formalistic manipulation of the verses of the Quran to justify their dogmatic viewpoints, Ali said: "They are the ones who use (some) words of the truth to allow falsehood to prevail."[6] The

Kharajites left a legacy of zealotry and dogmatism which continues to influence a wide range of Islamic political thought. Some contemporary fundamentalists continue to admire the Kharajites for their "strong will and righteous deeds."[7]

Legitimizing the Status Quo

Within the spectrum of Islamic fanaticism, the Kharajites represented the anarchist tendency. Most of history's Islamic fundamentalists, however, have rationalized and legitimized the despotic, authoritarian governments in power. For the most part, they were members of the clergy and religious jurists, although at times even the theories of the most renowned Islamic philosophers were used in practice to serve the very same purpose.

Islam's history shows a clear demarcation between that group of jurists and thinkers who—contrary to the teachings of the Quran and the Prophet—provided religious justification for oppression by despotic rulers, and the philosophers, scientists, and movements which resisted this distortion of Islam. Between the eleventh and fourteenth centuries, for instance, the Sunni clergy demonstrated more flexibility than their Shi'ite counterparts in adapting their views to those of ruling regimes. But once Shi'ism was established as the official religion in Iran by the Safavid dynasty (sixteenth century), many Shi'ite clerics also legitimized the despot in power. There was a readiness, even among distinguished Muslim scholars, to accept the most tyrannical rule, as long as it could to some degree guarantee the community's security and peace. In the eleventh century, Abu Hamid Muhammad al-Ghazzali, one of the most revered philosophers in the history of Islam, wrote: "These days, the government is completely dependent on military power. The (rightful) caliph is whomever the holders of military power vow allegiance to."[8]

The tolerance of despotism finally reached a point where security alone took precedence, not freedom and justice. Many jurists paid more heed to a ruler's ability to keep law and order than to his honesty or piety. Ibn Taymiyah, another famous Islamic scholar (thirteenth century), wrote: "It is far better even that an oppressive sultan seize power than that no man take charge. As is said, sixty years under an oppressive ruler is better than one night without a ruler."[9] To that effect, "tyranny is better than anarchy became a favorite theme of the Jurists."[10]

According to the orientalist A. Von Kremer, "In the final run, therefore, the Muhammadan jurisprudence transformed into a theory of

5

unlimited acceptance and recognition of the rights of the most powerful. ... No longer were there talks of a bilateral contract between the ruler and his subjects or of their right to oust an oppressive caliph."[11] In general this notion advocated that for the Muslims "the civil duty of the subject was obedience; ... only when the faith itself was in danger had he the right, under proper leadership, to resort to force."[12]

Judge Abu Bakr Al-Baghlani, a tenth-century statesman and the Abbasid caliph's ambassador to Constantinople, wrote in his book *Al-Tamheed*: "The Caliph cannot be deposed and it is not permissible to revolt against him even if he were corrupt and oppressive, or plundered the *ummah's* [nation's] wealth, or crushed the people under the blows of his whip, or violated all divine laws. He should only be given counsel."[13]

Ten centuries later, in presenting the theory of the "absolute sovereignty of the jurist," Khomeini virtually repeated the words of Judge Abu Bakr Al-Baghlani. The only, yet very important, difference was that Judge Abu Bakr and others endorsed the rule of someone else, while Khomeini was himself in power.

Numerous cases exist of arbitrary distortions of the teachings of Islam throughout its history. Hafiz Yahya Al-Nawawi, a jurist and chief of the Syrian *Dar Al-Hadith* (center for the collection of narrated traditions of the Prophet), for example, wrote in the thirteenth century: "Muslims concur that despite the corruption and oppression of a caliph or a ruler, rebellion and waging war on him are forbidden."

The Prophet's traditions have disappeared altogether from the words of such jurists. The Prophet is quoted as saying: "The most precious martyr in my *ummah* is he who rebels against a tyrannical leader, enjoins him to good, forbids him from evil and is killed by him." The Prophet's own grandson, Hussein bin Ali, rebelled along with his family and disciples against the corrupt ruler of his time, Yazid, and was slain in battle in the seventh century. The democratic and freedom-loving tradition of Prophet Muhammad was gradually distorted over time as despotic fundamentalists (or "traditionalists") veiled their backward views in the guise of Islam. The Umayyad (661 to 750) and Abbasid (750 to 1258) dynasties issued orders for the torture, pursuit and inquisition of their opponents, primarily the Prophet's descendents and their supporters. A few centuries later, Shah Isma'il, founder of Iran's Safavid dynasty, ordered the harshest punishment inflicted on anyone who refused to insult Abu Bakr and Umar (the two caliphs who succeeded the Prophet), resulting in the massacre of numerous Sunni sheikhs.

Democratic, Antireactionary Islamic Movements

The history of Islam and specifically Iran also contains a considerable number of movements and thinkers who steadfastly resisted despotic rulers and who offered dynamic and democratic interpretations of Islam. The *Ikhwan as-Safa* (Brethren of Purity) movement, around the tenth century, demonstrated one such open-minded approach to religious and political affairs in Islam's early centuries. The *Rasa'il* (*Letters*) of the Brethren is the first known Islamic encyclopedia, containing a significant collection of the sciences and traditions of that era. Its authors tried diligently to remain anonymous, doubtless to protect themselves from dictatorial rulers. Lengthy chapters in the *Rasa'il* demonstrate that its authors paid particular attention to Muslims' social plight, trying to identify reasons for the moral bankruptcy and submission to despotic systems. The *Ikhwan as-Safa* lashed out at "worldly tyrants," urging respect for the liberty and free will of the faithful. Throughout the work, the emphasis was on knowledge and awareness as the requirements for salvation in the material world and hereafter. The essays of the *Ikhwan as-Safa* reflected a commitment to the spread of scientific knowledge among the ordinary people. At the time, science commonly meant knowledge of the religion, but the *Ikhwan as-Safa* also promulgated worldly sciences and education because the authors believed that science was worthwhile only if it served practical purposes. They perceived a bright future for humanity and reiterated the return of tranquility to the world: "Although destructive elements such as wars, calamities and havoc occur, causing the ruin of some cities and retardation of development and prosperity among some nations, they ultimately lead towards a more desirable situation and well-being."[14]

In the fifteenth and sixteenth centuries, a series of antidespotic Shi'ah movements emerged in various parts of Iran. The most prominent among them was the Sarbedaran movement, active during the fourteenth and fifteenth centuries in north and northeastern Iran. Founded by Sheikh Khalifa Mazandarani, the *Sarbedaran* (meaning in Farsi "those hanged" or "the self-sacrificers") rebelled against the ruling system and fanatic jurists who legitimized the oppressive rule of the local sultans. The clergy soon took advantage of its privileges, issuing a decree sentencing Sheikh Khalifa to death for apostasy, a common fate for advocates of new ideas or liberty. He was subsequently hanged in the courtyard of a mosque in Sabzevar, Khorassan Province.

After Sheikh Khalifa's death, one of his disciples, Hassan Jowri,

7

continued to disseminate his ideas, secretly organizing traders and peasants for a revolt against the ruling system. The Sarbedaran's influence gradually spread. They defeated the sultan's forces, conquering large parts of Iran and ruling for many years. Compared to contemporary regimes, the people enjoyed more peace and freedom under the Sarbedaran, whose sovereigns had seized power out of antagonism towards fundamentalist Islam and after defeating despots and the clergy supporting them. Hafiz Abru, a famous fifteenth-century Iranian historian, writes in his works about the prosperity of Khorassan's Beihaq region under the Sarbedaran, noting that the town of Sabzevar, the Sarbedaran's capital, had become one of Iran's largest and most prosperous cities.

Shi'ism in Safavid and Post-Safavid Iran

The spread of popular Shi'ite movements opposing fanaticism and fundamentalism continued elsewhere in Iran after the Sarbedaran. Upon assuming power, the Safavid dynasty (1502–1736) adopted a new approach, intended both to impede these movements' growth and consolidate the ruling regime. Shi'ism was declared Iran's official religion, thereby allowing the Safavid rulers to legitimize their dictatorial rule and interests under a religious cloak. Shi'ism also provided a powerful element of national identity at a time when the Safavids were facing an eastward drive by the Ottoman rulers to expand their empire. The reactionary Shi'ite clergy allied itself with the shahs, and for the first time Shi'ite jurists who espoused fanatic positions became the apparatus of the official church. Not only did they legitimize attacks on the Sunnis, but also sanctioned the brutal suppression of antifundamentalist Shi'ites and advocates of freedom. In this context, this era of Iran's history can be compared with Khomeini's rule. Tens of thousands were killed for their religious beliefs or political tendencies.

According to historians, philosophers and libertarians were not the only ones despised and oppressed under the Safavid reign; the Sufis, who for the most part were open-minded and enlightened, were also targets of the kings' wrath. Meanwhile, the number and influence of the dogmatic clerics increased. During Shah Abbas's reign, the campaign to eradicate the Sufis' influence was so harsh that in just thirty years, three centuries of general affection toward the Sufis gave way to prejudice and violence. Mullah Muhammad Baqir Majlisi, a notorious cleric at Shah Abbas's Court (1588–1629), issued *fatwas* (decrees) for the Sufis' murder. The reign of terror denied that era's greatest philosophers, such as

Mir Damad and Molla Sadra, the opportunity to express their social and philosophical views openly.

The Safavid sultans benefited greatly from the dogmatic clerics in maintaining their grip on power. For their part, the mullahs were granted special privileges which kept them quite satisfied with the status quo. The demise of Iranian literature, arts, and the sciences accelerated as the theocracy imposed its dark rule on society.

During the reign of the Qajar monarchs (1786–1925), the reactionary clerics continued in the footsteps of their predecessors in the Safavid era. Haji Molla Ali Kani, a senior cleric and a big landowner during the reign of Naser od-Din Shah (ruled 1847–96), opposed any intellectual or social progress under the banner of defending Islam. In one of his personal letters to Naser od-Din Shah, he expressed his abhorrence at the "despicable word 'freedom.'" Naser od-Din Shah and Molla Kani feared that with the penetration of such ideas as democracy and the advancement of public awareness, the people would no longer submit to absolute dictatorship. Their concern was well founded.

During the Qajar period, the influence of reactionary mullahs steadily increased within the ruling apparatus. The situation became so extreme that mullahs began to preach that God created the Westerners to work and provide what is needed so that Muslims can pray with peace of mind. He had given the material world to Westerners and set aside the Hereafter for the Muslims.

Haj Mirza Nasrollah Malik ol-Motekallemin was among those clerics who rebelled against the ruling despotic regime and the reactionary clergy supporting it. The king ordered him arrested and put to death in Tehran in 1905. In his book *Royaye Sadeqeh* (*Truthful Dreams*) in 1897, Malik ol-Motekallemin used the device of a dream to illustrate the unbridled corruption plaguing the clerical establishment in Iran. Addressing Aqa Najafi, his contemporary and one of the most influential reactionary clerics, he wrote:

> On what equitable terms did you marry hundreds of 10- to 12-year-old virgins to satisfy your lust, and then let these poor souls go after a short while of pleasure, forcing them into prostitution and begging? For what reason did you prohibit the study of divine philosophy and brand theologians infidels? According to which religion or Shari'ah did you label modern schools the houses of Satan and their founders apostates and non-believers, declaring the adherents of these sacred principles faithless blasphemers and the shedding of their blood legitimate?[15]

9

Iran's Constitutional Revolution of 1906

The 1906 Constitutional Revolution stands out in Iran's modern history as an illustration of intense confrontations between the two conflicting interpretations of Islam—one democratic and the other dogmatic. By the end of the nineteenth century, a combination of factors—an influx of Western culture, establishment of publishing houses, increase in trade with the outside world, merchants' travels, dispatch of students to Europe, and publication of books describing the tremendous scientific and industrial advances in Europe—gradually set Iranian society in motion. Popular protests against the absolute monarchy gained momentum in the form of demonstrations and sit-ins in various cities. Eventually, Muzaffar od-Din Shah signed the Constitutional Decree in 1906, transforming the ruling system, at least on the surface, into a constitutional monarchy.

The constitutional movement found Muslim jurists and clerics in opposing camps. The majority advocated the status quo, opposed any reform, and backed the shah. A powerful minority of liberal-minded and democratic clerics, however, favored the establishment of a parliamentary government and the realization of democratic rights.

The fanatic mullahs were led by Sheikh Fadhlullah Nuri, whom Khomeini revered as a role model. Faced with a nationwide constitutional movement, Nuri insisted that all laws take effect only after they were reviewed and confirmed by a group of clergymen. Seventy years later, Khomeini incorporated exactly the same principle in the constitution of his own regime, appointing a Council of Guardians to confirm or reject legislation.

Sheikh Fadhlullah Nuri was profoundly reactionary. Admonishing Iranians in the early years of the century for beginning to pick up the "evil" habit of reading newspapers, he declared:

> Today, your senses and perceptions have changed, so much so that you read newspapers. Now you relish socializing with Westerners and atheists. Shame on you, Muslims, for thinking that reading these newspapers has been a source of your progress and perception, for spending your wife and children's money on newspapers, and for dissociating yourselves from Islam and the *ulema* (religious scholars) to the point that it seems as if you have never shared the same faith as theirs.

Of course, Sheikh Fadhlullah Nuri and the like had concrete reasons to fear a constitutional government and to defend the status quo; each of these mullahs was among the wealthiest and biggest landowners in Iran. Conversely, clergymen such as Seyyed Muhammad Tabataba'i, Seyyed Abdullah Behbahani, and Seyyed Jamal od-Din Va'iz, basing their views on the teachings of the Quran and Islam, defended the right to popular suffrage and considered a constitutional government indispensable. A number of progressive clerics, including Seyyed Jamal od-Din Va'iz and Aqa Mirza Ali Seqat ol-Islam e-Tabrizi, were assassinated by the ruling regime in the course of the Constitutional Revolution.

Other clerical authors of this era, citing the genuine teachings of Islam, refuted the reactionary mullahs' rationale for their opposition to freedom and constitutional system. One of the most invaluable works in this field is *Tanbihol Umma va Tanzihol Millah* (*Raising the People's Awareness and Purifying the Ideology*), a treatise by Ayatollah Mirza Hussein Na'ini, a senior Shi'ite cleric of the late nineteenth and early twentieth centuries. In this treatise, Na'ini elaborates the argument that from a Shi'ite perspective, a constitutional regime is essential.

The confrontation between the democratic constitutionalists and the reactionary dogmatists of the early years continued throughout the first half of the twentieth century. A turning point came in the early 1950s. Dr. Muhammad Mossadeq, leader of the Iranian nationalist movement who had nationalized the oil industry, became prime minister in 1951. During his tenure, however, his conflict with the dictatorship of Shah Muhammad-Reza Pahlavi reached a climax. Twenty-seven months later, on August 19, 1953, a coup ousted Mossadeq and restored the shah's rule.

The most significant domestic factor in the failure of Iran's nationalist movement was the antagonism of an unholy alliance of anti-Mossadeq forces, ranging from the pro-Moscow Communists to the fundamentalist mullahs, led by Ayatollah Abolqassem Kashani. An associate of Kashani, Khomeini was heavily involved in the fanatic mullahs' conspiracies against Mossadeq's government. After seizing power in 1979, Khomeini recalled: "In those same years in the 1950s, I told the Aqa [Kashani] that Mossadeq would be slapped in the face. And it did not take long before he was slapped. Had he survived, he would have slapped Islam."[16]

After the 1979 revolution, Hassan Ayat, one of Khomeini's close confidants and a founder of the now defunct Islamic Republic Party, wrote a book, entitled *The True Visage of Mossadeq ol-Saltaneh*, in which he said: "History attests that in contemporary Iranian history, the clergy and Islam were never so insulted as during Mossadeq's rule. One is ashamed to repeat such insults."[17] The vengeful attitude of Kashani, Khomeini, and their clique toward Mossadeq contrasts sharply with the view of figures like the late Ayatollah Seyyed Mahmoud Taleqani, loyal supporter of Mossadeq who criticized the policies adopted by the reactionary mullahs against the nationalist leader. Twenty-five years later, Taleqani was one of the key figures in the antimonarchic revolution that toppled the shah. He warned against the monopoly of power by the fanatic mullahs, led by Khomeini, and reiterated that "dictatorship under the cloak of religion" is the worst form of tyranny. Taleqani passed away a few months after the revolution, never living to see his prediction realized, the return of dictatorship in the guise of religion.[18]

The Feda'ian-e-Islam was among the most fanatic religious sects of the Mossadeq era and was rewarded with a significant share in the ruling hierarchy after Khomeini's rise to power. Founded by Mojtaba Navvab Safavi, the Feda'ian-e-Islam became active after World War II. From 1945 to 1963, its members carried out a series of political assassinations, whose targets included not only government officials but also many whom the group considered apostates or renegades. Ahmad Kasravi, the prolific Iranian historian and author, and Dr. Hussein Fatemi, Mossadeq's deputy and foreign minister, were among the victims. The Feda'ian-e-Islam's dogmatic and superficial interpretation of the Quran and Islamic teachings—similar in many respects to that of the early Kharajites—transformed the group into an armed gang of fanatics advocating blind terror. Their ideology lacked a cohesive or well-defined interpretation of Islam and disdained rational criteria. On Khomeini's orders, Sadeq Khalkhali, an activist of the Feda'ian-e-Islam, was appointed "religious judge of the Islamic Revolutionary Courts" after the shah's downfall. His extensive use of the death penalty earned him the nickname "the Hanging Judge." Khalkhali later acknowledged he was acting under Khomeini's personal decree. Like all of Khomeini's religious judges, Khalkhali used the terms "waging war on God and His Messenger" and "corruption on Earth," in passing sentences on the accused, whether political dissidents or people charged with armed robbery or drug trafficking. Khomeini and Khalkhali's use of such religious justifications for their crimes distorted the religion of compassion and liberty, violating the spirit of the Prophet when he declared a general amnesty upon conquering Mecca. The religious and legal interpretations of the judicial concepts of "corruption on Earth" and "waging war on God and

His Messenger," developed by Islamic schools of thought and scientists, were disregarded. Instead, the regime's religious judges adopted a wholly formalistic application of the terms to justify the execution and physical elimination of their opponents, the Muslim Mojahedin and other political opponents. This dogmatic approach by Khomeini and the Feda'ian-e-Islam was essentially the same. After Khomeini seized power, it was applied to the whole of society, with calamitous consequences.

Sunnism and the New Era

Throughout Islamic history confrontation has not been limited to the differences between the Shi'ah and Sunni; the pivotal conflict has been between dogmatic (fundamentalist) Islam and dynamic (modernist) Islam. Whether in the cloak of a ruler or a clergyman, there have always been individuals or groups who have misused and manipulated Islam to protect their own material interests or to legitimize their rule. Opposing them, however, have been persons and movements who earnestly strove to realize the genuine essence of Islam—emancipation from the chains of servitude and material well-being.

Among the Sunni philosophers of the past century who fought against fanaticism and dogmatism, Abdur-Rahman Al-Kawakibi (1849–1902) was particularly prominent. Al-Kawakibi was born in the Syrian city of Aleppo (Halab). At the age of 20, he published the city's first Arabic magazine, which featured articles critical of the autocracy of Ottoman Sultan Abdulhamid, and he defended the political rights of the people of Syria. The Turkish governor of Aleppo soon shut down the publication, but Al-Kawakibi produced two masterpieces, *Tabaye' ol-Istibdad* (*Nature of Despotism*) and *Umm ol-Qura* (*The Mother of All Lands*). *Tabaye' ol-Istibdad* rapidly became famous among both Arab and non-Arab Muslim readers. During Iran's 1906 Constitutional Revolution, the book was translated into Farsi and distributed in the country, where it had considerable influence on Iranian intellectuals.

Tabaye' ol-Istibdad is a treatise on Ottoman despotism, upon which the caliphate was based and which Khomeini called his model. Al-Kawakibi defined despotism as "an unbridled rule which arbitrarily confiscates any aspect of the life of the serf without fear of being questioned." He rebuked the Sunni jurists who believed despotism could coexist with the Shari'ah, their maxim being, "sixty years under a despot is better than one night without a ruler." Al-Kawakibi argued, "A despot rules over the lives of the people, not according to their will or religious beliefs, but according to his own. He knows that he is a usurper and an invader. He therefore tramples upon the mouths of millions of people to silence them and deny them the chance to speak or demand the truth."[19] According to Al-Kawakibi, despots have always taken advantage of religion to consolidate their rule. He concluded that "no despot has ever adopted a holy image except for himself and in order to share in God's authority."[20] The Quran, he wrote, exhorts us to safeguard equality and freedom. Referring to verses from the Quran, he emphasized counsel and councils even at the highest levels of government, and the need for parliamentary, representative rule.

In the *Tabaye' ol-Istibdad*, Al-Kawakibi revealed another aspect of progressive Islamic thought in his approach to religious minorities. Addressing the non-Muslim Arabs, he wrote:

> Dear fellow Arabs—and I am hereby referring to those whose language is Arabic but who are not Muslims—I invite you to forget the wrongdoings and your rancor and forgive whatever our fathers and ancestors have done.... Let us have mercy on each other, help each other in hardships, and in accordance with "indeed, the believers are brothers," be equal in times of happiness.[21]

Al-Kawakibi's invitation to forget "wrongdoings and rancors" is in reference to the nineteenth-century wars between the Christians and Muslims in Lebanon. He underlined the spirit of religious tolerance so conspicuous in the words, deeds, and teachings of the Prophet of Islam and so hysterically opposed by the dogmatists.

Although a prominent example, Al-Kawakibi is by no means alone among antifundamentalist scholars. Seyyed Jamal od-Din Assad Abadi (1838–1897), one of the nineteenth century's most renowned Muslim leaders, and the famous Egyptian scholar and reformist Muhammad Abdoh (1849–1905) also played significant roles in exposing the dogmatists and reactionaries. Seyyed Jamal od-Din was at the forefront of the struggle against the absolute dictatorship of the Qajar king, Naser od-Din Shah, in Iran. He relentlessly strove to enlighten the public and expose the corrupt, reactionary mullahs, whose efforts were wholly focused on providing religious justification for the corruption and atrocities of the shah and his court. Refuting the distortions which tainted Islam with ignorance, Seyyed Jamal od-Din called for a return to the authentic sources of Islamic thought and urged the Islamic world to learn the new sciences.

He was imprisoned in Istanbul on the orders of the Ottoman caliph, Abdulhamid, and died in prison.

Conclusion

In sum, the historical confrontation we are addressing is not between the Shi'ah and Sunni, but between the advocates of reaction and the advocates of freedom and democracy in both branches of Islam. From this perspective, Khomeini's predecessors are found not only among the dogmatic Shi'ite mullahs of the Middle Ages in Iran, but also under the cloaks of the Ottoman caliphs and the backward jurists of the Dark Ages of Islam.

Khomeini was the first ruler of a Muslim state since 1258—the year of the conquest of Baghdad by the Mongol ruler Hulagu Khan—to wield both political and religious power. A master of demagogy, he committed atrocities in the name of Islam. Not even the Umayyad and Abbasid caliphs had ever simultaneously held both political and religious powers. In the case of the Ottoman sultans, non-Turkish jurists and clerics never recognized their claims as legitimate. Before Khomeini and his entourage seized power in Iran, the clerical apparatus was always secondary and subordinate to the royal court and ruling regime, basically acting to legitimize the tyranny in power. Under Khomeini, however, the reactionary clerical apparatus actually rose to power. For this reason, the magnitude of the tyranny taking place over the past fourteen years in Iran is unparalleled in the nation's history. No other so-called Muslim tyrant had ever shed the blood of so many Muslims, especially the Mojahedin.

In studying the history of Islam, it is clear that the fundamentalists were always defeated by the school of religious thought that advocated democracy, opposed dogmatism and zealotry, and relied on its faith in the exalted values upon which Islam is based. Religious reactionaries have always managed to use demagogy to parry attacks by nationalists and other secular philosophers, thereby preserving their sway. They have no weapon but brute force and repression to confront the genuine Islamic ideologies, which expose their distortion and abuse of the religion. ▣

The Pillars of the Mullahs' Rule

The vali-e-faqih *is empowered to abrogate the religious commitments he has undertaken with the people should he find them contrary to the interests of the nation and Islam. Governing is one dimension of the absolute authority of the* velayat-e-faqih *and takes precedence over all secondary commandments, even prayer, fasting, and the hajj.*

—Khomeini's open letter to Ali Khamenei, January 7, 1988[1]

The government of Khomeini and his successors is based on a theory of government called *velayat-e-faqih*, literally meaning the guardianship of the religious jurist. The essence of the theory, developed and applied by Khomeini, is that one man with a thorough knowledge of Islamic law is designated as *vali-e-faqih*, heir to the Prophet Muhammad and the *Imams* (Leaders). He also acts as vice regent to the Mahdi, the messianic Twelfth Imam of Shi'ite Islam. The vali wields absolute authority and sovereignty over the affairs of the entire Muslim nation. No public or private matter concerning a Muslim or anyone living in the Islamic world is beyond the vali's jurisdiction.

Velayat-e-faqih is in fact the essence of the Iranian mullahs' Islamic Republic. Incorporated into the constitution after the shah's overthrow, the immense powers bestowed on the vali-e-faqih have been expanded since Khomeini's death. An understanding of exactly what the doctrine of velayat-e-faqih is and how it functions is essential to understanding the theocracy in Iran and its drive to export fundamentalism.

◈ ◈ ◈

The abolition in 1924 of the Ottoman Caliphate by Turkey's Great National Assembly was a turning point in contemporary Islamic history. For centuries, the Ottoman sultans had proclaimed themselves to be caliphs, the absolute civil and religious leaders of Muslims. Although the Ottomans governed only part of the Islamic world and their authority was challenged even within their empire, the abolition of the caliphate generated profound debate among a wide spectrum of Islamic political thinkers. Various theories and hypotheses emerged on the role of religion in the Islamic community. In Egypt, for example, a group of Sunni fundamentalists put forth the thesis of the "Islamic state."

Nearly half a century later, Khomeini published his absolutist views on the Islamic state in Najaf, site of one of Shi'ite Islam's two major theological schools. He had taken up residence there after being exiled to Iraq by the shah. At the time, Khomeini could not have foreseen that he would one day be able to put his theory into practice. His book, entitled *Velayat-e-faqih*, is essentially limited to a general discourse on the necessity of the Muslim *ummah*'s (nation's) being ruled by "just theologians."

Without elaborating on the economic, political, or social outline of his proposed system of government, Khomeini stressed that "there are no real boundaries between Islamic countries." He wrote: "If a competent person possessing these characteristics [those of a faqih] arises and forms a government, his authority to administer the society's affairs is the same as that Prophet Muhammad enjoyed. Everyone must obey him. The idea that the Prophet had more authority as a ruler than His Holiness Imam Ali [the first Shi'ite Imam], or that the latter's authority exceeded that of the vali is incorrect."[2]

Most of the Shi'ite clergy strongly opposed Khomeini's doctrine, saying it contradicted the principles of Islam. As a gesture of protest against his views, many of the students and instructors boycotted Khomeini's classes in Najaf seminary, a rare act in Muslim theological schools. Other religious authorities viewed Khomeini's ideas as the scholastic dissertations of a mullah in a seminary. Once in power, however, Khomeini demonstrated that the book was the blueprint of his rule, a blueprint on which he later elaborated, granting himself far greater authority than that which even the Prophet had assumed. When, in

January 1988, the incumbent president and future vali-e-faqih, Ali Khamenei, said in a Friday prayer sermon that "governmental authority is contained within the bounds of divine edicts,"[3] Khomeini lambasted his protege in an open letter:

> The statements of your Friday prayer sermon indicate that you disagree with the premise that governance, in the sense of the absolute guardianship bestowed upon the Prophet of God, which constitutes the most imperative divine decree, should take precedence over all secondary commandments. Such an interpretation of my words—that the government's authority is limited by divine edicts—totally contradicts my statements. If the government's authority were bound by secondary commandments, I would have to say that the divine rule and absolute authority conferred upon the Prophet would be devoid of meaning and content. ... I should point out that governing is one dimension of the absolute authority of the Prophet's velayat-e-faqih. It is one of Islam's primary decrees, and takes precedence over all secondary commandments, even prayer, fasting, and the hajj. ... The vali-e-faqih is empowered to unilaterally abrogate the religious commitments he has undertaken with the people should he find them contrary to the interests of the nation and Islam. He can ban any religious or non-religious matter contrary to the interests of Islam. ... The statements made, or being made, derive from a lack of knowledge of divinely ordained absolute rule.[4]

Khomeini likened the vali's authority over the people to that of a guardian over a minor or mentally incompetent adult. "The velayat-e-faqih is like appointing a guardian for a minor. In terms of his responsibility and status, the guardian of a nation is no different from the guardian of a minor."[5] This dismissal of the notion of popular will characterized Khomeini's rule, during which he repeatedly declared that if the entire population advocated something to which he was opposed, he would nevertheless do as he saw fit.

Interestingly, as he rose to power prior to the shah's fall, Khomeini made no mention of the velayat-e-faqih theory in his many interviews in France. Asserting that he intended to withdraw from politics, Khomeini claimed that neither his desires and inclinations, nor his age and position would permit him to personally play a role in the post-shah government.[6] When asked if he sought to serve as the head of an Islamic state and if he intended to involve himself in the daily affairs of government, Khomeini reiterated his previous answer, adding that the people's elected representatives would choose the government.[7]

Khomeini's dissembling helped him ride on the wave of popular religious sentiments and hijack the leadership of the 1979 revolution. He exploited the Iranian people's abhorrence of the shah's open antagonism toward Islam and Islamic traditions. Moreover, two generations of the Pahlavi dictatorship had kept the general public largely unaware of political realities and complexities. The shah's secret police, SAVAK, had brutally suppressed in the 1960s and '70s all active opposition groups, notably the People's Mojahedin. When the shah reluctantly eased the repression and restricted the powers of SAVAK in the mid-1970s, the Khomeini-led clerical network was the only entity outside the government capable of acting as a cohesive political alternative.

Two Pillars of Khomeini's Rule

Although Khomeini usurped the leadership of the 1979 revolution, he was incapable of directing a nation of sixty million toward freedom, economic prosperity, and social progress in the final decades of the twentieth century. As his velayat-e-faqih doctrine dictates, he chose a two-pronged policy to stay in power: repression at home and export of revolution abroad. As the first ruler in Iranian as well as Shi'ite history with supreme religious and political authority, he was able to advance both policies, particularly the brutal enforcement of oppression.

Terror

In the first weeks after the shah's ouster, the mullahs laid the foundations for suppression, mobilizing terror squads to intimidate all opposition to their rule. Within two and a half years, they had formed such repressive organizations as the Islamic Revolutionary Guards Corps (the *Pasdaran*), Islamic Revolutionary Courts, Islamic Revolutionary Committees (the *Komitehs*), Guards Corps Mobilization (the *Bassij*), and others in government offices, schools, universities, the armed forces, and the bazaar. This sprawling apparatus made possible a reign of terror to support the velayat-e-faqih.

The early years of the clerical rule also saw a return to censorship, closure of nongovernment newspapers, and more extensive attacks on political rallies and gatherings than during the shah's time. Election rigging and fraud prevented the election to parliament or high office of any opposition candidate. When Massoud Rajavi, the popular leader of the People's Mojahedin and candidate of the democratic opposition, ran for president in 1980, Khomeini issued a decree formally declaring him ineligible to run for the office, because the Mojahedin had boycotted the referendum on the new constitution.[8]

By June 1981, several thousand political prisoners had been tortured and nearly 100 supporters of the People's Mojahedin Organization murdered. Finally, on June 20, 1981, Khomeini ordered the Guards to open fire on 500,000 Tehran residents who participated in a peaceful demonstration held by the Mojahedin to protest the return to despotism. That date marked the beginning of mass executions, sweeping arrests, and general suppression.[9] The mullahs' most outrageous crimes, such as sending pregnant women before firing squads, were all sanctioned by religious *fatwas* (decrees) issued by Khomeini or by religious judges.

But as Khomeini had repeatedly emphasized, the duties of the vali-e-faqih were not limited to political or governmental issues. The vali supervised and ruled over all of the relations and affairs of every individual member of the society, whether ideological, intellectual, private, or public. The mullahs' network acted as "absolute guardian" over the people, in much the same manner as the Catholic Church had ruled during the medieval Inquisition. Khomeini even declared it a religious duty for family members to spy on one another.

Export of Islamic Revolution

But suppression was not, by itself, a sufficient safeguard for the new regime. The antimonarchic revolution had released the energy of Iran's youth, which, as in most developing countries, represented a sizeable force. The enormous changes within the society raised the younger generations' expectations that the new regime would resolve the country's economic and social problems. Prior to the outbreak of the Iran-Iraq War in September 1980, an increasing number of young people, disillusioned by the mullahs' betrayal of their prerevolutionary promises, joined the growing ranks of the opposition. Within two years, the Mojahedin had emerged, according to independent polls, as the largest political party and best organized force in the country, outranking the ruling Islamic Republic Party.[10]

The Saudi weekly, *Al Majalla* (4 December 1991), quoted a member of the post-shah editorial board of a major Iranian newspaper, *Kayhan*, as saying:

> In the early months of the Islamic Republic in Iran in 1979, one of the more popular dailies conducted a poll on the popularity of parties, political organizations and personalities directly involved in the victory of Iran's revolution. Under the circumstances at the time, the daily's editors were obviously fright-

ened, and thus declared Khomeini as the most popular personality, although he had come in fourth. Next was Massoud Rajavi, the leader of the Mojahedin Organization, who was favored by 90% of the readers. Rajavi was first among 80 political parties and organizations.

To consolidate his rule and contain the desertion of his followers to the ranks of the opposition, Khomeini stepped up the suppression of dissidents. But he also began to rely on the second pillar of the velayat-e-faqih, the export of revolution and fundamentalism. Only nine months after the shah's downfall, the Khomeini regime occupied the American Embassy in Tehran, the first essential step in focusing public attention on foreign targets. Using "anti-imperialist" slogans, Khomeini first purged internal rivals. Within days, he disposed of Mehdi Bazargan's cabinet, which he had the previous year proclaimed the "government of the Mahdi (Messiah)," and granted greater authority to the clergy to run the country's affairs.[11]

Next, he tried to use what he claimed were threats from abroad to combat the Mojahedin's demand for political freedoms. On the pretext of an anti-imperialist struggle, he accused the democratic opposition forces, and particularly the Mojahedin, of "liberalism" and of close ties with the United States. Khomeini thus set the stage for a final crackdown.

As the newspapers' headlines of that period show, Rajavi had in an earlier meeting with Khomeini reminded him that freedom and democracy were the spirit of the revolution and essence of true Islam. By his "anti-imperialist" motto, Khomeini was trying to make it appear that any demands for democracy and freedom were petty and diversionary. In his efforts, Khomeini enjoyed the support of a dozen Marxist-Leninist parties, especially the Tudeh Party, which cooperated with Khomeini in the Mojahedin's suppression.

Concurrent with the hostage crisis, the clerics pursued a policy of aggression, encroaching on neighboring Muslim countries, especially Iraq. Khomeini referred to the devastating eight-year war that followed as a "divine blessing," exploiting it to divert millions of Iranians awakened by the 1979 revolution. Under such pretexts as "defending the Islamic nation" or "liberating Qods [Jerusalem] through Karbala," the mullahs issued "keys to heaven" to children sent over the mine fields, and made maximum use of the conflict to justify the domestic repression. The twin pillars of the velayat-e-faqih—repression at home and export of revolution—kept the Khomeini regime in power despite all odds.

Velayat-e-faqih in the Constitution

Before the shah's overthrow, Khomeini had promised in Paris that the constitution of the future regime would be determined by a popularly elected constituent assembly. Well aware, however, that such an assembly would never support his absolutist doctrine, Khomeini, once in Tehran, replaced the promised constituent assembly with a smaller body called the Assembly of Experts, chiefly composed of mullahs close to his line of thinking. That assembly drafted a constitution that incorporated the principle of velayat-e-faqih.

The preamble to the constitution ratified by the Assembly of Experts notes: "Based on the principle of the Guardianship of the Islamic State and the Leadership of the Muslim Nation, the Constitution provides a basis for the leadership of a fully qualified faqih whom the people consider as Leader, to ensure that no institution deviates from its Islamic mandate."[12] Principle 4 elaborates on the mechanism by which the vali-e-faqih has universal jurisdiction, providing quasi-legal justification to the supremacy of the vali's will over the law. "All civil, penal, monetary, cultural, military, and political laws must be based on the Islamic principles."[13] Naturally, the interpretation of what is or is not an "Islamic principle" falls within the authority of the vali-e-faqih and the Council of Guardians, another body of mullahs appointed by the vali. Despite the superficial separation of the three branches of government, the constitution delegates their control entirely to the vali-e-faqih. Principle 57 says: "The legislative, executive, and judicial branches in the Islamic Republic of Iran are under the supervision of the vali-e-faqih and the Imam of the Islamic ummah." Since supreme religious and political authority rests in the hands of one person, the Imam's power far exceeds that of any contemporary head of state. Principle 110 of the constitution lists the vali-e-faqih's powers as follows:

A. Appointing members of the Council of Guardians;
B. Appointing Head of the Judiciary;
C. Supreme Command of the Armed Forces as the following:
   1. Appointing and dismissing the Chief of Staff of the Armed Forces
   2. Appointing and dismissing Commander in Chief of the Islamic Revolutionary Guards Corps
   3. Forming the Supreme National Defense Council of the following seven members:
      - President
      - Prime Minister

- Minister of Defense
- Chief of Staff of the Armed Forces
- Commander in Chief of the Islamic Revolutionary Guards Corps
- Two advisors designated by the Leader

4. Appointing the supreme commanders of the three forces upon the suggestions made by the Supreme Defense Council;

5. Declaring war, peace, and troop mobilizations upon the suggestion of the Supreme Defense Council;

D. Signing the decree naming the President after popular elections. The competence of presidential candidates, as per the conditions stipulated by the Constitution, must be approved prior to the elections by the Council of Guardians and confirmed by the Imam during the first electoral round;

E. Impeaching the President for reasons of national interest pursuant to a verdict by the Supreme Court confirming his violation of his legal duties or a vote of no confidence by the Islamic Consultative Assembly, as per Principle 89;

F. Pardoning convicts or commuting their sentences.

Accordingly, no civil or military affair falls beyond the vali-e-faqih's jurisdiction. Khomeini and his aides added two other prerogatives to further consolidate the vali's position:

1. The formation of numerous institutions comprised of mullahs personally appointed by the vali-e-faqih to control other governmental organs. These institutions include the Council for the Determination of Exigencies of the State, the Council for Constitutional Revision, and the Council of Guardians.

2. The establishment of representative offices of the vali-e-faqih in all ministries, administrative offices, military and security organizations, universities, judicial organs, and so on. These representatives, all of them mullahs, act as ideological commissars. The bitter rivalries between the bureaucratic and clerical hierarchies breed tension and crisis in the governmental apparatus.

The various powers invested by the constitution in the vali-e-faqih, however, were still fewer than those envisioned by Khomeini, who in the previously cited open letter to Khamenei, introduced the notion of *velayat-e-motlaqeh-faqih* (absolute rule of the jurist). On Khomeini's instructions, Ahmad Azari-Qomi, a senior conservative cleric, defined the theoretical basis of such absolute rule in a series of newspaper editorials:

The velayat-e-faqih means absolute religious and legal guardianship of the people by the faqih. This guardianship applies to the entire world and all that exists in it, whether earthbound or flying creatures, inanimate objects, plants, animals, and anything in any way related to collective or individual human life, all human affairs, belongings, or assets. It also applies to God's religion, whether the primary and secondary commandments, worship, politics, social or family affairs and obligations, or what Islam recommends, tolerates or prohibits. [14]

Discussing the "meaning of *velayat*," Azari-Qomi wrote: "During his rule, God's representative [the vali-e-faqih] may temporarily ban prayer, fasting, the hajj, and the promotion of virtue and prohibition of vice as he sees fit. In these circumstances, he may order the home of a Muslim demolished, or order him to divorce his wife."[15] In another editorial, Azari-Qomi wrote: "Islam prohibits the marriage of a virgin girl without the permission of her father and her own consent. Both of them must agree. But the vali-e-faqih is authorized to overrule the father or the girl and to order them to act contrary to their shared view."[16]

Azari-Qomi further noted: "All members of the Iranian nation, including all Muslims, religious minorities, and opponents of the revolution, must legally recognize, accept, and obey the rule of velayat-e-faqih as stipulated in the Constitution of the Islamic Republic and obey its eminent leader. The verdict of the Islamic ruler is incumbent upon, and mandatory for, all individuals, even for an Islamic jurisprudent or expert who does not accept the principle of the velayat-e-faqih, or those who accept the principle but do not accept its absoluteness."[17]

The Post-Khomeini Regime

In all affairs, the pivotal role of the velayat-e-faqih must be accepted as fundamental.

—Hashemi-Rafsanjani, October 10, 1991[1]

Khomeini's death on June 3, 1989, deprived the Tehran regime of the sole person capable of uniting its disparate political and ideological factions. A few months before his death, Khomeini had dismissed Hussein-Ali Montazeri, his officially designated successor, for Montazeri's "weak and flexible approach" to the Mojahedin.[2] Montazeri had, in a series of letters to Khomeini, objected to the massacre on Khomeini's order of thousands of Mojahedin political prisoners immediately after the 1988 cease-fire in the Iran-Iraq War. "This kind of massacre without trials of prisoners and captives will definitely benefit [the Mojahedin] in the long run," Montazeri wrote. "The world will condemn us and they will be further encouraged to wage armed struggle. It is wrong to kill to contain thoughts and ideas. . . . The People's Mojahedin are not individuals; they are an ideology and a worldview. They have a logic. It takes right logic to answer wrong logic. You cannot solve the problem with killings; it will only spread."[3]

With Montazeri gone, Khomeini's death confronted his regime with a succession crisis. Fearing that the absence of a leader could mean imminent collapse or overthrow, the ruling mullahs of the Assembly of Experts were compelled to act quickly. They appointed Ali Khamenei as vali-e-faqih even though his credentials were clearly deficient. Khamenei's rank of *hojjatolislam* (a relatively junior position in the Shi'ite clerical hierarchy) did not meet the constitutional requirement that the faqih have the rank of *marja'iat*, or superior standing within the Shi'ite clerical hierarchy with some following among the faithful. He was promoted to *ayatollah* overnight. But he still fell far short of being qualified for the velayat-e-faqih, prompting Khomeini's heirs to attempt to make the constitution subordinate to velayat-e-faqih.

The day after Khamenei's appointment, Ahmad Azari-Qomi, an influential member of the Assembly of Experts, argued: "Let's suppose that Ayatollah Khamenei's election apparently violates the letter of the Constitution. But does the spirit of the Constitution permit the Islamic Republic to remain without a leader? I believe that anyone appointed to this post by the Assembly of Experts is the *Vali-e-amr* [Guardian of All Affairs] of Muslims, and obedience to him is obligatory, although he might not be a faqih."[4]

Abolqassem Khaz'ali, another member of the Assembly of Experts, also reasoned: "*Marja'iat* is not the problem at hand. For the time being, due to the need of the society, the experts deemed it appropriate to choose . . . someone with insight and management skills."[5]

A propaganda campaign was also launched to solicit the *bei'at* (oath of allegiance) to Khamenei from the regime's foreign proxies in a bid to reinforce his position at home. Among those who swore loyalty to Khamenei, according to Tehran radio, were the leader of the Lebanese Hizbullah; Ahmed Jibril, leader of the Popular Front for the Liberation of Palestine—General Command (PFLP-GC); Muhammad-Hussein Fadhlullah, a senior Lebanese Shi'ite cleric; and the head of the Shi'ite Clerical Center in Pakistan.

As "Vali-e-faqih of the World's Muslims" and "Leader of the Global Islamic Revolution," Khamenei from the outset of his rise to power stressed the need to continue Khomeini's policies. "Iran's Islamic revolution cannot be confined within borders, nations, or ethnic groups," Khamenei told a visiting delegation of the Lebanese Hizbullah group. "It is in our revolution's interest, and an essential principle, that when we speak of Islamic objectives, we address all the Muslims of the world, and when we speak of the Arrogant West, we address all the oppressors of the world."[6]

He and other clerical leaders have also repeatedly stressed the importance of velayat-e-faqih and the need to obey it since Khomeini's death. "Ayatollah Khamenei said opposition to velayat-e-faqih is tantamount to opposing the most essential principles and fundamental bases of the Islamic Republic," Tehran radio reported. "Ayatollah Khamenei said, 'According to the Constitution, the positions declared by the leadership apparatus are the principal policies of the State. Those who oppose these positions at critical junctures are doubtless opposed to velayat-e-faqih.'"[7]

Such assertions were subsequently echoed by other Iranian officials. "The gravest danger threatening our revolution is disobedience to velayat-e-faqih," emphasized Mullah Mohsen Shabestari, a member of the Assembly of Experts. "We do not have any disputes over the principles of the revolution and loyalty to the State. We are all followers of the Imam's Line and the Leader."[8] Muhammad-Sa'id Raja'i-Khorassani, former ambassador to the United Nations and later a majlis deputy, remarked, "Velayat-e-faqih is the principle to be preserved and safeguarded in all the organizations and classes of our society."[9]

Constitution Revised

With Khomeini's death, the entire velayat-e-faqih regime was endangered because the religious charisma and marja'iat which safeguarded the system were gone. Khomeini's heirs therefore defied the expectations of foreign observers who believed that Khomeini's death would mean the end of the velayat-e-faqih and the beginning of moderation. They soon formally recognized the principle of absolute rule. In an attempt to keep the Islamic Republic on its feet, they revised the constitution to enhance the status of the vali-e-faqih and gave him more authority. For example, the post of the prime minister was eliminated and, more importantly, the president became even more dependent on the vali-e-faqih.

Other parts of the constitution were also changed to strengthen the vali-e-faqih:

Principle 5: Among the criteria originally set for the selection of the vali-e-faqih was his acceptance by the majority of the populace. This stipulation was deleted from the new constitution; henceforth, the vali would be chosen, not nominated or approved, by the Assembly of Experts. In addition, Principle 107 in the original constitution stated that a council whose members qualified f or the post could serve jointly as velayat-e-faqih. This possibility was also omitted and the velayat-e-faqih restricted to an individual.

Principle 57: The original constitution designated the president as the supreme coordinator of the three branches of government. The new constitution entrusted this prerogative to the vali-e-faqih. With the post of prime minister eliminated, the president was put in charge of running the executive branch and forming the cabinet.

Principle 109: The key qualification originally specified in this principle for the vali-e-faqih was that the candidate be a *marja-e-taqlid* (preeminent jurist with followers.) The new constitution contains no such stipulation.

Principle 110: The powers of the vali-e-faqih were dramatically increased, giving him control over almost everything. His powers are enumerated as follows:

A. Determining the general policies of the Islamic Republic in consultation with the Council for the Determination of Exigencies of the State;
B. Supervising the proper implementation of the general policies;
C. Ordering referendums;
D. Supreme command of the Armed Forces;
E. Declaring war, peace, and troop mobilization;
F. Appointing, dismissing, and accepting the resignations of the:
    1. Members of the Council of Guardians
    2. Head of the Judiciary
    3. Director of the Voice and Vision of the Islamic Republic of Iran (Radio and Television Organization)
    4. Chief of Staff of the Armed Forces
    5. Commander in Chief of the Islamic Revolutionary Guards Corps
    6. Commanders in Chief of the military and security forces;
G. Resolving differences and regulating relations among the three branches of government;
H. Resolving, by means of the Council for the Determination of Exigencies of the State, problems which cannot be resolved by ordinary means;
I. Signing the decree naming the President after popular elections. The competence of presidential candidates, as per the conditions stipulated by the Constitution, must be approved prior to the elections by the Council of Guardians and confirmed by the Imam during the first electoral round;
J. Impeaching the president for reasons of national interest pursuant to a verdict by the Supreme Court confirming his violation of his legal duties or a vote of no confidence by the Islamic Consultative Assembly, as per Principle 89;
K. Pardoning convicts or commuting their sentences in accordance with Islamic criteria and subsequent to a request from the Head of the Judiciary.

The vali may on occasions delegate his duties and powers to other persons.

Principle 113: The right to regulate the relations of the three branches is withdrawn from the president and transferred to the vali-e-faqih. The president heads the executive branch, but his powers are limited by the clause that says "except those affairs directly relevant to the vali-e-faqih."

Principle 122: The original constitution specified that the president was accountable only to the populace. This article adds that he is also accountable to the vali-e-faqih.

Principle 130: The revised constitution includes an article stipulating that the president submit his resignation to the vali-e-faqih.

Principle 131: In the case of the death, dismissal, resignation, or illness of the president, the original constitution provided for the formation of a council of certain people who would carry out his duties. The new constitution stipulates that, with the vali-e-faqih's approval, the first deputy president would carry on. In the absence of a first deputy, the vali-e-faqih is to appoint the new president.

Principles 157 and 158: According to these two articles in the new constitution, a single individual appointed by the vali-e-faqih heads the judicial branch. The original version provided for the formation of a Supreme Judicial Council consisting of five members, two of whom were appointed by the vali-e-faqih in consultation with the Supreme Court judges and three of whom were chosen by their peers.[10]

Moderation an Anathema

In the years after Khomeini's death, his regime's fundamental policies have undergone no significant changes. Mass executions and torture have persisted. The United Nations Human Rights Sub-Commission noted in a resolution that the number of executions had tripled between 1990 and 1991. In March 1992, the UN Human Rights Commission expressed grave concern about the persistence of human rights violations in Iran, including the increase in the number of executions. Human rights were systematically violated, and women continue to be denied their fundamental rights. The foreign policy of Khomeini's heirs is more sophisticated in strategy and tactics, and encompasses a broader scale, but the objective remains the same: export of the Islamic revolution. As Hashemi-Rafsanjani, who became president in July 1989, spelled out, "Conditions might have changed, but our policy has not."[11]

There have been no basic changes, despite the much noted gestures of moderation by Rafsanjani, for the simple reason that the medieval doctrine of velayat-e-faqih, the theocracy's body and soul, renders the system intrinsically incapable of moderation. The system is in a delicate balance; a crack in its pillars would rapidly become a rift, bringing down the entire system.

To be sure, there are factions within the political system. They do occasionally come into serious conflict, especially over the distribution of power. But such differences are clearly of secondary importance, because the interests of all of the regime's leaders and major factions dictate allegiance to the doctrine of velayat-e-faqih, upon which all of their fortunes ride. The search for a moderate trend within the clerical oligarchy is, therefore, an exercise in futility. A "moderate velayat-e-faqih" is a contradiction in terms. For each of the regime's factions, breaking out of the theocratic mold altogether is tantamount to rejecting their own political and ideological justification. The velayat-e-faqih legitimizes the system as a whole and the role within it of each individual cleric, including Rafsanjani.

Rafsanjani, often described as a "moderate" in the West, has acknowledged being one of the five top aides, perhaps foremost among them, who made all key decisions during the eleven years of Khomeini's rule. He admits, "Despite poisonous imperialist propaganda—which tries to project the idea that the Iranian nation is hopeful of entering a new era and choosing a new path—I am confident that we and our people will choose nothing else. I myself have been one of this regime's decision makers. Should anyone seek to question the country's five top officials regarding the national affairs, certainly I have been one of them."[12] Rafsanjani had established himself as Khomeini's most trusted lieutenant by the time Khomeini died, closer to him even than Muhammad-Hussein Beheshti had been.[13] In 1979, it was Rafsanjani who, on Khomeini's behalf, handed the prime ministerial decree to the first postrevolutionary prime minister, Mehdi Bazargan, although the ceremonies were attended by mullahs of more senior rank, including Beheshti and Abdulkarim Moussavi-Ardebili, who was appointed chief justice afterwards. In 1988, when Mir-Hussein Moussavi submitted his resignation after eight years as prime minister, Khomeini rebuked him for not seeking out officials of superior standing, pointing specifically to Rafsanjani, then Speaker of the Majlis.

If we, nevertheless, assume that Rafsanjani is now earnestly seeking to make an about-face and move toward moderation, can he do it? He is confronted with a dilemma: If he leaves the velayat-e-faqih intact, moderation becomes impossible. But if he begins to dismantle the velayat-e-faqih, he is dismantling the foundations upon which he stands. To allow political freedoms, loosen the restrictions on parties and the press, and remove the obstacles to public gatherings would set in motion a process which would fatally weaken Rafsanjani's grip on power. Had such a potential for change existed within the regime, there would have been no need for 100,000 political executions. Even in the simplest terms, allowing public gatherings would provide the means for the friends and relatives of these victims, as well as those of the 150,000 victims of torture, to unite. Rafsanjani cannot be assumed to have forgotten the final months of the shah's rule.[14]

Political freedoms, therefore, are too much to expect. Rafsanjani, however, might at least take more modest steps: observing social freedoms, respecting women's rights, stopping interference in people's private lives, ending political and religious persecution, complying with the accepted norms of international conduct. In other words, he could choose to be content with the role of a twentieth-century dictator, like the shah, and relinquish the religious character of the regime, which lends it a distinctively medieval flavor. But if such a change were made, Rafsanjani would be among the first to go, because he is himself a cleric. A secular dictatorship has no need of clerical tyrants; in every third world country are generals and technocrats ready and willing to do the job.

Even analysts who regard Rafsanjani as a "realist" admit that a metamorphosis of the "Islamic Republic" from within is an impossible task. One analyst, calling Rafsanjani's rule the "Second Republic," wrote: "What the realists [Rafsanjani's faction], perhaps to their peril, do not realize is that it may yet require a complete metamorphosis before the ghost of the First Republic can be laid to rest; and this is a feat which looks as if it might be beyond the natural capacities of the children of that First Republic. One thing they realize, though, is that if such a metamorphosis were to take place, the end-product would more than likely bear no resemblance to an Islamic Republic at all."[15]

Any moderation or reform in the mullahs' regime, therefore, presupposes a weakening or elimination of the velayat-e-faqih, which implies an end to the regime itself. Rafsanjani, like his regime, is neither inclined to, nor capable of, moderation. In founding his theocracy on the doctrine of velayat-e-faqih, Khomeini implanted within it the seed of its own destruction, the inability to change. ◈

"Mother of All Islamic Lands": The Mullahs' Foreign Policy

We have a huge position in the Islamic world. No country other than Iran can lead the Islamic world; this is a historical position.

—Muhammad-Javad Larijani, August 7, 1989, principal foreign policy advisor to Rafsanjani[1]

The Rafsanjani administration's approach to foreign policy may differ from Khomeini's, but the ultimate goal remains the same: expansion of the rule of the Islamic Republic and establishment of a caliphate similar to the Ottoman Empire but controlled from Tehran. The present state of the world—especially the collapse of the Soviet Union and the Eastern Bloc—has encouraged the mullahs to believe that they can realize this goal. Tehran's rulers reason, however, that a comprehensive, step-by-step strategy is required to export the Islamic revolution. As Khomeini's right-hand man for a decade and acting commander of the armed forces, including the Revolutionary Guards, Rafsanjani oversaw a series of extraterritorial terrorist operations, such as kidnappings, hostage takings, assassinations, and ill-fated coups. But the overextended, random, and incoherent mix has outlived its usefulness. Describing Tehran's new methods of exporting its revolution, Muhammad-Javad Larijani has said:

The first [source of our national strategy] is our position within the Islamic world. This means Iran must not be limited by its geographic boundaries. . . . Iran is not just one among many Islamic countries. Today we face a division of the world into geographic states that has no justice and that has a very bitter past. Now, should we accept these frontiers or not? . . . We do [in fact] accept the world's geographic boundaries—in order to avoid trouble. [But] our Islamic responsibility does not [just] go away. This responsibility crosses borders. . . . We have to plan our policies and our diplomacy in such a way that they match our position in the Islamic world. No country other than Iran can lead the Islamic world; this is a historical position.[2]

Elsewhere, Larijani, who is sometimes described in the West as a moderate, asserted: "The true velayat-e-faqih is in Iran. This velayat is responsible for all of the Islamic world." He enumerated the "three vital objectives of the Islamic Republic: The first is maintaining the Islamic nature of our regime and our status in the Islamic world. The second is defending the republic's security, and the third is expansion."[3]

After Khomeini's death, his successors recognized that his absence would make the domestic situation far more precarious. Lengthy, detailed discussions among members of the Supreme National Security Council, chaired by Rafsanjani, led to a consensus that the "Islamic Republic" could not survive without the spread of the Islamic revolution beyond Iran's borders. Advocates of this theory referred to the split between Trotsky and Stalin after the Russian revolution. They argued that the Soviet Union's disintegration confirmed the validity of Trotsky's theory of a "permanent world revolution," which asserts that the proletarian revolution confined within the borders of a single country will suffocate. The clerics, borrowing Trotsky's thesis, claimed that the only way to preserve their Islamic revolution was to foment Islamic revolutions in other countries.

Muhammad Khatami, minister of Islamic culture and guidance and a chief policy maker in Rafsanjani's cabinet until spring 1992, explained the doctrine of export of revolution in a roundtable discussion on the "National Security Strategy of the Islamic Republic of Iran."[4] Khatami argued: "Where do we look when drawing up our strategy? Do we look to preserve the integrity of our land, or do we look to expansion? Do we look to *bast* (expansion) or to *hefz* (preservation)? We must definitely focus on expansion."[5] (Ironically, Khatami was ousted by the conservative faction in April 1992 for being too liberal. In July, Rafsanjani appointed Ali Larijani, a Revolutionary Guards commander, to succeed Khatami.)

Rafsanjani echoed the same theme: "Islamic Iran is the base for all Muslims the world over. There is not the slightest doubt in my mind, and I am certain that His Holiness the Imam would have said that we do not want this revolution only for ourselves, that we care about others. He truly and deeply hated the idea that we be limited by nationalism, by race, or by our own land."[6]

Muhammad-Sa'id Raja'i-Khorassani, chairman of the Majlis Foreign Relations Committee and former ambassador to the United Nations in New York, also dubbed a "moderate" by some Western observers, commented on the golden opportunity presented for the export of the Islamic revolution by the fall of communism: "Disappointed by materialist and worldly governments, the world has turned its attention today to the Islamic nation and sovereignty of God. People have concluded that a government not ruled by Islam is doomed to destruction and annihilation. Today, the victory of Islamic Iran in the international arena is the victory of the Islamic world. And the Islamic world sees its salvation as dependent on the Islamic government of Iran."[7]

The regime's policy planners, such as Larijani, refer to Iran as *Umm ol-Qura*, or the "Mother of All Islamic Lands." From this perspective, Iran is the center of gravity for the world's fundamentalist Islamic movements and the source of their momentum. The mullahs believe that without the Islamic Republic's active moral and material support, the fundamentalist movements in other countries would be incapable, as in previous decades, of expanding beyond an isolated religious sect or of seizing power in any country.

The events of the 1970s support this assertion. Serious political, social, and economic grievances—from unfair distribution of wealth to sprawling and corrupt bureaucracies—existed to varying degrees throughout the region. But until the fundamentalist clerics seized power in Iran in 1979 and began to actively export their revolution by providing organization, finances, and training to fundamentalists in other countries, these forces never posed a serious threat to their governments.

The mullahs therefore believe that their regime must act as the model and the nurturer, providing moral and material sustenance (arms, training, money, and propaganda) to religious fundamentalists in Islamic countries. Explaining the Umm ol-Qura theory, Larijani maintained:

Why do I believe our duty is not limited by land or geographic boundaries? Because in the Islamic Republic, we do not have merely an Islamic government;

we have and have had the velayat, both during the Imam's [Khomeini's] time and during Ayatollah Khamenei's. This velayat is a righteous jurist ruling the entire Islamic nation. Muslims may not even realize that we have such a jurist ruling here, but this does not undermine the reality of this guardianship. Of course, it affects the ruling jurist's effectiveness, but not the principle. As long as this guardianship exists, the velayat is responsible for the Islamic world, and it is the duty of the Islamic world to protect the ruling jurist. . . . As long as our country is the seat of the true ruling jurist, we are responsible for the whole Islamic nation, and the Islamic nation is duty-bound to safeguard the Umm ol-Qura.[8]

Similarly, in a recent speech Rafsanjani said, "Iran is the base of the new movement of the world of Islam. . . . The eyes of Muslims worldwide are focused here."[9] The minister of Islamic culture and guidance commented on foreign policy:

As far as resources and equipment are concerned, I think we have a long way to go to catch up with our enemies. No matter how much we acquire, the enemy still has the upper hand. We should forget this wishful thinking that someday we might be able to challenge our main rivals in technology and arms. Hence, the question is, What can we do to enter the international arena? We need a power that the enemy does not have, a power superior to technology and arms. Our power lies in the nascent Islamic force awakening the world over, in those prepared to sacrifice themselves. The Islamic Republic's survival depends on the support of such a global force. The Islamic movement in Algeria is serious, and we can count on Sudan. New centers of power are taking shape in the world of Islam. Growing Islamic forces abound in the world, and we must truly depend on them.[10]

The export of revolution and fundamentalism is thus indispensable to the Iranian clerics and is the basis of their national security strategy. The Muslim world's receptivity to fundamentalism, as well as the collapse of the Soviet Union, have convinced the clerical rulers that the policy of *bast*, or expansion, is the only guarantee for their survival.

The velayat-e-faqih government's guiding foreign policy principle dictates "the establishment of the worldwide sovereignty of Islam." "From an Islamic standpoint, the world is generally divided into two camps: *dar ol-Islam* (the home of Islam), where the divine laws of Islam are implemented and Islamic rule prevails, and *dar ol-kofr* or *dar ol-Harb* (the home of blasphemy), where the ruling regimes do not act in accordance with Islamic laws. On this basis, Islam recognizes only one boundary, purely ideological in nature. Other boundaries, including geographic borders, are rejected and condemned."[11]

V

Fertile Grounds for Fundamentalism

Iran's Islamic revolution has awakened all the Islamic countries. . . . Islam recognizes no borders. We cannot put off establishing Islamic governments and administering the divine laws. The objective of the Islamic Republic and its officials is none other than to establish a global Islamic rule. . . . Political means and methods may differ, but no revolutionary Muslim ever forgets the objective.

—Ahmad Khomeini, January 11, 1992[1]

In the course of his much publicized visit to Khartoum in December 1991, Iran's President Rafsanjani gave glad tidings to his Sudanese hosts: "The Islamic revolution of Sudan, alongside Iran's pioneer revolution, can doubtless be the source of movement and revolution throughout the Islamic world."[2]

Although Khomeini's heirs differ, as his son Ahmad puts it, in their "political means and methods," they have never abandoned "the objective": to impose their hegemony over the entire region and ultimately monopolize the leadership of one billion Muslims worldwide. Pursuing a carefully planned strategy, the Iranian regime seeks to combine an assortment of diplomatic, cultural, propaganda, subversive, and military activities into a powerful network of proxy groups and followers in all Islamic countries. Such a "Fundamentalist International," with Iran at its center, is expected to realize the regime's objectives and interests.

This strategy was laid out in a top secret analysis, drafted by experts of the Supreme National Security Council as part of a policy paper in January 1992, following Rafsanjani's trip to Sudan:

> Climaxing the political and propaganda pressures brought to bear on Sudan by the West and Egypt, a U.S. State Department official warned the government of Sudan: The United States will spare no effort to prevent Sudan from becoming a center for terrorist activities. The U.S. has already begun contacting those countries neighboring Sudan and in the region about adopting appropriate decisions.

The analysis goes on to argue that this pressure is motivated by geopolitics:

> The Arab Republic of Sudan in Africa is one of the largest African states and is second only to Egypt in Arab population. Its Red Sea coastline and proximity to the Suez Canal lend it enormous geopolitical importance. Thus, the presence of any regional power, such as the Islamic Republic [of Iran], in Sudan would be of great significance, especially in view of the regional rivalry between the Islamic Republic, Egypt and [Saudi] Arabia, and the rapid growth of Islamic movements in the area. In light of recent political developments in the Horn of Africa and the decline of Ethiopia, Somalia, and Kenya as regional powers, leaving Sudan as the dominant player, the added influence of the Islamic Republic of Iran in Sudan and the expansion of bilateral security and military ties will certainly affect the other countries in the region, specifically [Saudi] Arabia, and Egypt. Overall, the consolidation of relations between Tehran and Khartoum will contribute greatly to revolutionizing the Islamic tendencies in North Africa and enhancing Iran's political stature in regional contests.[3]

What are the bases for this "rapid growth of Islamic movements in the region," that is, expansion of fundamentalism? Several important regional and international factors provide a fertile ground for the spread of fundamentalism.

The Power of Islam

The Islamic world includes very different societies and tribes, stretching from Southeast Asia to North Africa. Muslims comprise over 85 percent of the populations of Afghanistan, Algeria, Bangladesh, Egypt, Indonesia, Iran, Iraq, Jordan, Pakistan, Saudi Arabia, Senegal, Tunisia, Turkey, and most of the newly independent republics of Central Asia and the Caucasus. In Albania, Chad, Ethiopia, and Nigeria, Muslims make up 25 to 85 percent of the population; and India, Myanmar (formerly Burma), Cambodia, China, Greece, Yugoslavia, Thailand, and the Philippines have significant Muslim minorities.

Despite their ethnic, cultural, and social variety, these societies share striking similarities. Ernest Gellner, a specialist on Islam, has written:

> For all their indisputable diversity, the remarkable thing is the extent to which Muslim societies resemble each other. Their traditional political systems, for instance, are much more of one kind than were those of pre-modern Christendom. At least in the bulk of Muslim societies, in the main Islamic block between Central Asia and the Atlantic shores of Africa, one has the feeling that the same and limited pack of cards has been dealt. The hands vary, but the pack is the same.[4]

The political and economic objectives of most Muslim societies today are to achieve democracy and freedom, economic growth, and improved living standards. Relatively high birth rates and shorter life expectancy have meant a persistent decline in the average age of the citizenry in most of these countries. The impact of such global developments as the collapse of communism and the growing influence of the international mass media on the younger generation, better informed and less apathetic than their forefathers, will have far-reaching repercussions, and the demands for freedom will become more vociferous.

Given the profound religious roots prevalent in Muslim societies and the absence of any other viable alternative, the quest for democracy and struggle against dictatorship often assumes a religious, and specifically Islamic, character. Hence religious reactionaries and fundamentalists endeavor to exploit Islam in directing political and social development toward their own ends. They cite "alienation from Islam" as the cause of every problem in Islamic societies, and a "return to pure Islam" as the undefined cure-all. This lack of specifics allows the fundamentalists to impose their own views and policies under the banner of "Islam" while benefiting from the legitimacy religion grants them in the hearts and minds of the Muslim masses. The most obvious example of such manipulation is Khomeini's usurpation of the leadership of Iran's antimonarchic revolution in 1978–79.

For the millions of Iranians who took to the streets in 1978 to vent their anger and frustration against the shah's dictatorship, the word *azadi* (freedom) had a magic ring. Freedom had been denied them for more than half a century by the shah and his father before him. The demand for freedom unified a wide spectrum of the populace and soon acquired a religious connotation. In the eyes of the average Iranian, the brutal repression and endemic corruption of the royal family and court reflected the ruling regime's antipathy toward Islam and basic Iranian values. Despite the iron-fisted controls imposed on the society through the dreaded secret police, SAVAK, virtually everyone had heard rumors of the fabulous wealth of the shah and his entourage in Iran. Even Iranians only nominally Muslim were offended by the ruling elite's moral corruption. It was, therefore, natural for the antishah movement to take on a religious tone when it ultimately surfaced in the streets.

In the minds of Iranians, Islam has traditionally been synonymous with struggle against dictatorship, despite the Shi'ite clergy's record of having served the interests of the court. For the general public, Islam was symbolized by such figures as Imam Hussein, the Prophet's grandson. Vastly outnumbered, Hussein was slain in 680 with seventy-one of his companions at Karbala in a revolt against a corrupt ruler. This epic struggle has profoundly influenced the Iranian social psyche. For centuries, people in every town and city gathered on the anniversary of Hussein's martyrdom to follow a white horse out of the city as part of the symbolic ceremonies honoring his memory. These rites often had a political theme directed against the contemporary rulers. During the antimonarchic revolution, Imam Hussein's defiant revolt against injustice was a prominent symbol for millions of Iranians, both devout Muslims and secular intellectuals, who praised his struggle for freedom from dictatorship in their writings.

The compatibility of Islamic beliefs and democratic struggle in Iran is considered by many to be symbolized by the political and social movement of the People's Mojahedin Organization. Particularly after 1971, some of the most prominent and popular opponents to the shah's regime belonged to this movement. Muhammad Hanifnejad, the organization's founder, was among the leading Mojahedin members sentenced to death and later executed by a military tribunal.[5] Massoud Rajavi, the Mojahedin's leader, was among the leaders of resistance under SAVAK's torture. That the Mojahedin, an antishah, Muslim, independent movement, rapidly gained widespread support among the people shows the degree to which the antidictatorial struggle in Iran derives from the democratic precepts and traditions of Islam.

In 1978, the Iranian masses thus sought in Islam democracy and an end to dictatorship. They demanded freedom of political parties, political prisoners, and the press. It was only in the second stage of the revolution that Khomeini and the mullahs succeeded in taking advantage of the popular religious sentiments to usurp leadership and move Iran toward an "Islamic Republic."

The Iranian experience is not unique, however. The socio-political awakening of Muslim societies began with colonialism's decline in the 1950s and early 1960s. The end to the Western empires' domination of the Islamic world set the various countries on different paths, which nevertheless converged in the political revival of Islam.

From an economic perspective, for example, so long as they were dominated by the European colonists, these lands were used as sources of raw materials for European industries. After their independence, the new governments moved towards industrialization, building factories and workshops. For various reasons, including mismanagement, inadequate planning, weaknesses in the infrastructure, and political instability, the process of industrialization was generally a failure, with disastrous repercussions: unchecked urban migration resulting in the destruction of agriculture and the helter-skelter expansion of urban centers. Cairo, Istanbul, Tehran, Jakarta, and Lahore became magnets for millions of peasants deserting their ancestral homes in search of a better life. The cities of dreams, however, held nothing for the vast majority but shantytowns and poverty. Isolated from their traditional culture and shunned by the new, alien civilization of well-to-do city dwellers, many urban immigrants sought both solace and a means of freeing themselves from their misery and destruction in Islam.

The trend toward independence also brought fundamental changes in the educational system. The colonial administrators had often excluded courses from the curricula that would have acquainted the younger generation with their precolonial national, cultural, and religious identity in a bid to prevent the growth of proindependence sentiments. In Algeria, for instance, school children learned French rather than their own language until 1962. But this attempt to blot out the Islamic heritage failed. In fact, it made the people in many countries want to learn more about Islam once independence came.

Different third world countries chose different paths to resolve their mounting problems. Successive failures in the Arab world caused their governments to veer between ethnic nationalism (Pan-Arabism) and state nationalism. Many Muslim countries, such as Egypt, Turkey, and Indonesia, experimented with various types of capitalism and socialism; yet neither brought them out of crisis and socioeconomic misery.

The failure of imported forms of government convinced Muslim laymen, especially the intelligentsia, that these systems could not respond to the complex problems of the Islamic world. Starting in the 1960s, this growing awareness led many to turn their attention to Islam. According to American scholar and researcher Daniel Pipes, "After a generation of experimentation, the time had come to try something different."[6] A consensus was reached by Muslims that no imported political philosophy, however credible or crucial to the freedom and well-being of Muslims, could successfully mobilize the masses in harmony with their spiritual consciousness.

This search for a compatible system that was "something different" was not in essence fundamentalist or reactionary. Muslim communities' rejection of emulating the West and Western forms of government— liberalism, socialism, and so forth—was never meant to imply that they shunned such universal values as democracy and freedom. The message, rather, was that a new formula must be used to fulfill their yearning for democracy and economic growth while conforming to their cultural, traditional, and religious—in other words, Islamic—beliefs and values. Such a formula would achieve the kind of political stability, economic prosperity, and social freedoms and equity for which the Muslim masses yearned.

This has been the basis of the philosophy advocated by the People's Mojahedin in Iran since the movement's inception in the 1960s. The Mojahedin believed that no imported ideology could alleviate the problems plaguing Iranian society, pointing to the failures in twentieth-century Iran of nationalism, Marxism, and liberalism. Similarly, the Mojahedin denounced fundamentalism and reactionary interpretations of Islam, rejecting the calls for a revival of the Ottoman Empire. The organization emphasized that a governing regime in Iran must be suited to the particular culture and religion of the Iranian masses while remaining committed to the cause of democracy. Theocracy must be avoided at all costs.

A Bastion of Islamic Culture

Throughout the history of Islam, from the early decades to recent times, the Iranian intelligentsia has played a active role in shaping the policies and cultural identity of Islamic societies. The current rulers of Iran have used this historical legacy to their own advantage, but to the disadvantage of other Islamic nations.

In the mid-seventh century, the Arabian Peninsula had converted to Islam. Only a decade after Prophet Muhammad's death, the army of Umar, the second caliph (the second successor to Muhammad), conquered Iran following the battles of al-Qadisiyah (Iraq) in 636–637 and Nahavand (western Iran) in 642. When a Muslim delegation sent by Umar was given an audience before the battles began by the last of the Sasanid kings, Yadegerd III, the Muslims described their mission as breaking the shackles of bondage and setting free the masses from oppression.[7] Though rejected by the king, this message had enormous appeal to ordinary Iranians. Although Iranian society was significantly more advanced than that of her Arab neighbors, Iranians quickly accepted Islam's message of peace and equality as a welcome alternative to the despotic rule of the Sasanid dynasty. Islam's appeal explains in part the embarrassing defeats of the Sasanid's much larger and better-equipped armies at the hands of a small, poorly trained, but motivated Arab contingent. In the al-Qadisiyah battle, for example, the 30,000-man Muslim army succeeded in crushing the Iranian force, which was four times larger.[8]

Despite their defeat, the Iranians displayed a remarkable resilience. They used the newly found religion to shape and formulate Islamic culture and civilization and to advance the ideals of the Prophet Muhammad and the Quran. Iranians wrote the four major Shi'ite books on Hadith, considered the primary source on the traditions of the Prophet after the Quran and *Nahj-ol Balagah*. The six source books on Hadith in the Sunni sect were also written by Iranians.[9]

In philosophy, logic, mathematics, medicine, astronomy, chemistry and other sciences of the era, the Islamic world led the way. And within the Islamic world, Iran was often at the forefront. Iranian contributors to the quest for knowledge included such scientists as Avecinna (Ibn Sina, 980–1037) a renowned physician and philosopher whose books were translated into English and French and were taught in Western universities; Fakhr-e Razi, a twelfth-century philosopher from Ray (a southern district of present-day Tehran); and Zakariya-ye Razi, the famous fifteenth-century chemist and mathematician from Ray.

Many of the leading interpreters of the Quran and Islamic history were Iranians as well, including Qazi Bayzawi, from Shiraz, who wrote *Anwar ot-Tanzil va Asrar ot-T'avil* (*The Rays of the Quran and Secrets of Interpretation*). Iranians soon mastered the art of Islamic teaching and jurisprudence. The first Arabic grammar was written by Sibevayh, the author of *al-Ketab,* who lived in the seventh century in Shiraz in Fars Province. Many of Arabic literature's greatest works were written by Iranians; and many of the great Shi'ite jurists were Iranians, as were many early Sunni jurists. Bu'l-Fazl-i Bayhaqi (995–1077), one of the most renowned Muslim historians, wrote the first major prose work in New Persian, *Jame' ot-Tawarikh* (*A Comprehensive History*). Muhammad Jarir-e Tabari (died 953), the author of *Jame' ol-Bayan* (*A Comprehensive Statement*) and *Tarikh ol-Omam-e val Molouk* (*The History of Nations and Kings*), was another famous Iranian historian from northern Tabarestan (now Mazandaran) Province. Zamakhshari, who lived in the eleventh century in Khorassan Province (northeast Iran), wrote *Tafsir-e Kashaaf* (*A Comprehensive Interpretation*) and *Assass ol-Balaghah* (*The Fundamentals of Eloquence*).

The rise of the Ummayads led to the massacre of the Shi'ites, who had branched off from the majority after the death of the Prophet. (See Chapter I.) Muhammad's followers and descendants sought refuge in Iran, where they were warmly welcomed. They led many Shi'ite rebellions against the ruling caliphs. Iran thus became a center of rebellious popular movements against oppressive regimes and the status quo. Thousands of relatives of the Prophet and Ali, the first Shi'ite Imam, were buried in Iran, and Iranians still worship at their shrines. Shahrbanoo, the wife of Hussein (the third Shi'ite Imam), was the daughter of the last Persian king, Yazdegerd III.

The reign of the Abbasid caliphs, who ruled the Islamic world from Baghdad for five centuries, was strongly influenced by Iranians from the mid-seventh to the thirteenth centuries. The Abbasids' interest in fostering Islam in the East prompted the new caliphs to employ the methods and procedures of governance used by their Iranian predecessors. Many top officials brought into the caliph's court came from the ranks of influential and well-known Iranian families. For instance, the Abbasid caliph Harun ar-Rashid (ruled 786–807) drew into his service prominent members of the Iranian Barmakid family. For all practical purposes, the Abbasid caliphs functioned in a largely ceremonial role, while the day-to-day governing was conducted by Iranian rulers, such as the Ghaznavid (tenth century) and the Khwarezm-Shah (1077–1231) dynasties.

The enormous impact of Iranians on science and other areas of knowledge, particularly during the first seven centuries, and their attempts to restore the spirit of equity and tolerance, two original teachings of Islam, gave Iran long-lasting prestige in the eyes of all Muslims. Iran, in fact, is unique in this sense; no other Arab or Muslim country could exert the same influence. As a result, when the mullahs try to spread their dogmatic philosophy beyond Iran, they carry with them the credibility earned by the remarkable contributions Iran has made to Islamic civilization. This credibility enhances the mullahs' appeal among the Muslim and Arab masses.

The mullahs, exploiting the Iranian legacy, are attempting to turn Iran into an Umm ol-Qura of fundamentalism (see Chapter IV). Thus, in spreading fundamentalism, Tehran has come to play the same role Moscow played in spreading communism.

Decline of Nationalism

The decline of Arab nationalism, or Pan-Arabism—which was for several decades a source of tremendous strength for Arab countries and their governments—has also contributed to the growth of Islamic fundamentalism. The absence of an attractive democratic alternative caused many political groups throughout the Arab world to turn away from Arab nationalism and toward Islamic fundamentalism. (See Chapter XIV.)

In non-Arab Muslim countries, nationalism is also succumbing to the mounting wave of religious fundamentalism. Even in Turkey, where a fiercely secular government has ruled since the 1920s, religious fundamentalism poses a serious challenge. While a wave of ethnic nationalism and regionalism has engulfed the European countries of the former Eastern Bloc, deep-seated Islamic tendencies in the Muslim republics of the former Soviet Union have raised concern about the expansion of fundamentalism even after seventy years of religious repression.

Role of Oil

The Persian Gulf region has 65 percent of the world's total oil reserves. Of the 3.1 billion tons of oil on the market in 1990, some 843 million tons were produced in the Middle East. To appreciate the importance of oil in preparing the ground for the Khomeini regime's export of fundamentalism one need only imagine how much less attention Islamic fundamentalism would have received had Khomeini seized power not in Iran, but in another third world country located far from the Middle East.

Under the shah, Iran was the second largest exporter of oil in the world. It also had great geopolitical importance, because it was seen in the West as a buffer between the Red Army and the world's largest oil reserves. These factors made events in Iran front-page news in the West. Through Western news agencies and media, therefore, Muslims around the world learned in minute detail of the shah's overthrow and Khomeini's rise to power.

Oil also provided the funds with which Khomeini and his heirs exported their revolution and fundamentalism. The huge oil revenues paid for the extensive political and propaganda campaigns abroad, funded the worldwide networks created to recruit and train fundamentalists, provided the financial and logistical support for Khomeini's allies and surrogates throughout the Islamic world, and enabled the clerics to bestow gifts of free oil to certain countries to increase influence. Between September 1991 and February 1992, for example, Rafsanjani's government "spent more than $500 million and sent out 1,300 Islamic fundamentalist preachers to influence the newly independent Muslim republics of Central Asia."[10] On the average, the mullahs have spent $100 million annually in recent years to reinforce and maintain their operatives in Lebanon.

Looking at the region as a whole, oil has also indirectly paved the way for fundamentalism's growth in the Middle East. Since 1975, of the thirteen members of the Organization of Petroleum Exporting Countries (OPEC) all except two (Ecuador and Venezuela) have been Muslim countries. Six (Iran, Iraq, Saudi Arabia, Kuwait, Qatar, and the United Arab Emirates) are located in the Persian Gulf region and two (Algeria and Libya) in Muslim North Africa. Indonesia's population is over 90 percent Muslim. Half of Nigeria's population is Muslim, and most of the time a Muslim has ruled the country. Although Muslims are a minority in Gabon, President Omar Bongo converted to Islam in 1973. Hence any major change in oil prices has extensive economic repercussions that may act as political catalysts in these Muslim countries.

In 1955, Arabian light crude was posted as high as $2.08 a barrel. In 1961, the price dropped to $1.80, where it stayed for most of the 1960s, prompting Western industries to switch from coal to oil as their main energy source. At the same time, OPEC members signed new contracts with smaller oil companies, strengthening their position vis-a-vis the major oil consortiums. In 1970, declining oil production in the United States and Venezuela, the explosion of the Saudi pipeline to the

Mediterranean, and rising demands caused by the severe oil shortage led to a new surge in oil prices. After several increases, the price of oil rose to $2.01 per barrel in September 1973. Then the Arab-Israeli War inspired two price hikes, in October 1973 and January 1974, and oil-producing countries were suddenly earning $9.27 per barrel, 4.5 times the previous rate. This new rate remained stable for several years, until the fall of the shah, when prices again shot up, to $34 per barrel.

Meanwhile, many countries had also been boosting their production. Saudi oil production jumped from 3.5 million barrels a day in 1970, to 7.3 million in 1973, to 10 million barrels per day in 1980. Saudi revenues rose accordingly, from $1.2 billion in 1970, to $29 billion in 1974, to $101 billion in 1981.[11] This enormous wealth, of course, brought political power incomparable with the past, and raised these countries' international prestige and presence overnight.

The flow of petro-dollars, however, was a two-edged sword. The rapid oil price increases meant equally rapid energy price increases in oil-importing countries, such as Turkey, Pakistan, and Egypt. The consequent economic problems fomented social turmoil, and the resultant rising tensions provided fertile ground for the growth of fundamentalism.

For the oil-producing countries, the situation was worse. The flood of petro-dollars and consequent economic upheavals quickly led to the unraveling of these countries' social fabric. The newly acquired wealth created havoc with people's daily lives. Corruption, bribery, extravagance, greed, and—most importantly—the widening rift between the very rich elite and the poor majority in countries such as Iran brought fundamental changes to societies whose social structure had remained essentially unchanged for decades. A Nigerian political analyst's description of the situation applied to all the oil-producing countries: "There is unprecedented indiscipline in Nigeria these days. . . . There is smuggling, there is corruption, money permeates society."

The corruption accompanying the enormous wealth worked to the advantage of the fundamentalists, who declared that the only solution was to seek refuge in the "Islam" they represented. Such simplistic answers attracted the deprived masses to the fundamentalists' fold. Iran provides a classic example.

Iran's oil revenues rose from $4.4 billion in 1972–73 to $9.6 billion in 1973–74, and then to $20.6 billion the following year, where they leveled off until the shah's ouster.[12] The new income meant tremendous wealth for a very few, while the many were left out. The flood of money in 1973–75 also raised the general public's expectations; but when the prices stabilized in the following years, the shah's regime suddenly found itself short of funds to continue its ambitious plans. Inflation soared, and villagers' migration to the shantytowns skirting the major cities changed the urban environment. Economic discontent rose sharply among the populace, already chafing under the political repression. Meanwhile, the Pahlavi family and those entrepreneurs with connections to the court deposited billions of dollars of oil revenues in their foreign accounts and spent lavishly in Iran.

After 1976, the shah was forced by international pressure to loosen the grips of repression. Khomeini jumped at the opportunity to exploit the widespread social discontent and political vacuum created by the brutal clampdown on organized opposition. Relying on religious demagoguery and a nationwide network of like-minded mullahs, Khomeini hijacked the leadership of the antimonarchic revolution.

It should be emphasized, however, that although economic and social factors play an important role in the growth of fundamentalism, it is a misperception to view the phenomenon as merely a product of social destitution or the unfair distribution of wealth. True, Khomeini and his followers took maximum advantage of the poverty and deprivation in Iran to advance their own political interests. But fundamentalism also has historical, cultural, and social roots which do not necessarily grow out of economic factors. All of the material components of the present crisis—poverty, bureaucratic corruption, and so on—existed in the region in the 1960s and '70s, but fundamentalism's appeal remained limited to small religious sects until the mullahs took over in Iran. After 1979, Khomeiniism was exported; fundamentalists were organized and nourished morally and financially by the Iranian mullahs. Had Khomeini not assumed power in Iran, "Islamic fundamentalism" would not have been the issue of global concern it is today.

Global Changes

The restructuring of the world in recent years has also meant great turmoil and change for the Middle East. Topping the list is undoubtedly the collapse of the Soviet Union and its aftermath. The sudden end to the Soviet presence in the Middle East, where it had been a key player for several decades, created a vacuum felt throughout the region, upsetting the balance of power. The Soviet and Eastern European trends toward democracy could have contributed to a similar process in the

Middle East. Instead, conditions have benefited the fundamentalists. Again, the primary cause has been the absence of a credible democratic alternative.

The interest of the former Soviet Union (and its predecessor, the Russian Empire) in its neighbors to the south has a long history. In the years following World War II, Soviet foreign policy in the Middle East focused on the Arab-Israeli conflict. Moscow initially went along with the idea of a State of Israel, and from 1949 to 1954 the Soviet delegation to the United Nations abstained in all key votes on the Arab-Israeli dispute. Before long, however, the Soviets came out in favor of the Arabs. The shift was motivated in part by Moscow's concern at the emergence of nationalism in Egypt and Gamal Abdel Nasser's rise to power, as well as military pacts like the Baghdad Pact (later called CENTO) signed between the United States, Britain, and their regional allies.

The Soviets soon became the main suppliers and source of political support for a number of Arab countries. Although relations with some of these countries, such as Egypt, were occasionally stormy, Moscow succeeded in establishing itself in the Middle East in the 1960s and '70s. Under Leonid Brezhnev, important political, military, and economic pacts were signed with South Yemen, Libya, Algeria, and Morocco, among others. At this time, the Soviet Black Sea fleet was transformed from a coast guard force into an awesome naval power in the Mediterranean and Arabian seas. Friendship accords were signed with Egypt, Syria, Iraq, South Yemen, and Afghanistan. To advance its political goals in the region, the Soviet government gave priority to economic assistance to Middle Eastern countries over other regions of the third world. Between 1954 and 1979, eight of the ten major recipients of Soviet aid were Middle Eastern counties: Turkey, Morocco, Egypt, Afghanistan, Iran, Syria, Algeria, and Iraq.

Throughout the Arab-Israeli War in 1956, the Six-Day War in 1967, the October War in 1973, and the Israeli occupation of Lebanon in 1982, the Soviet Union was perceived by the Arab masses as being on their side. Despite some major Soviet setbacks in the region, the Soviet Union enjoyed considerable influence among the Arab nations. Even on oil-related issues, the Soviet Union's policy was diametrically opposed to that of the Western governments. As the world's largest oil producer and a major exporter since 1974, the Soviets gave their full support to OPEC's measures to increase oil prices.

Moscow's influence in the Middle East began to wane in the early

1980s. By the middle of the decade, the effects of the Soviet decline had surfaced in virtually every country. This process coincided with the 1979 military invasion of Afghanistan, a Muslim and nonaligned country, as well as the establishment of a fundamentalist government in Tehran. The most important catalyst, however, was the Soviet Union's own internal collapse. Just as the reactionary mullahs of Iran were preparing to export their fundamentalism to the farthest corners of the globe, the Soviets began their rapid exit from the Middle East (and indeed the world arena), leaving the field to Khomeini and his supporters, who were claiming "Islam is the only solution."

Khomeini's famous letter to Soviet President Mikhail Gorbachev in January 1989 (see Appendix), although preposterous on the surface, had a message for the targets of the Khomeini regime's fundamentalist propaganda in Islamic countries. Khomeini sought to implant the idea that with the Soviet departure from the international scene, only his ideology and form of government could stand up against the remaining superpower and offer a solution for the harrowing problems of the Islamic world. Khomeini wrote:

> If you intend to untie socialism and communism's difficult economic knots by seeking refuge in the arms of Western capitalism, you will not only fail to cure the ills of your own society, but will oblige others to come and compensate for your mistakes. Today Marxism has reached a practical impasse, economically and socially. The Western world is also entangled in a different way in similar problems.... In conclusion, I declare with frankness that the Islamic Republic of Iran, as the largest and most powerful base of the Islamic world, can easily fill the ideological void of your system.

While Soviet influence in the Middle East was, for a time, considerable, the indigenous communist parties never attracted significant support among the Middle Eastern peoples, despite profound political and social discontent and other factors that could have contributed to the spread of communism much as in postwar Europe. In addition to the majority of these parties' total dependence on Moscow, the most important cause of their failure to attract followers was the unshakable faith of the Muslim masses in Islam.

With the exception of South Yemen, which ultimately decided to dismantle its Marxist government and merge with its non-Marxist northern neighbor, no Middle Eastern country took the "noncapitalist path of growth" advocated by the Kremlin for the third world. The

Soviets had hoped that the ruling regimes of Egypt and Sudan would adopt such a strategy and gradually move toward socialism by means of state control over production. It never happened. The rise of state capitalism in these countries did not impede their change of foreign policy toward the West. Anwar Sadat's sudden expulsion of the Soviet advisors in Egypt in June 1972 was a bitter pill. Shortly afterwards, Egypt opened its doors to foreign investors.

◈ ◈ ◈

Appeasement: An Ominous Policy

When Neville Chamberlain gave in to Hitler's demands in Munich in September 1938, the word "appeasement" took on new meaning. The attempt to conciliate Hitler instead of confronting him only emboldened the German dictator to go further.

The policy of appeasement which the West, notably Western Europe, has adopted toward the Iranian government is not unlike the Munich approach. It has similar effects. Whenever the mullahs see that their support for fundamentalism beyond Iran's borders does not meet with an adverse reaction, they are encouraged to do more. Western leniency towards Tehran, especially after the Persian Gulf War, so emboldened the mullahs that in private meetings with European officials, they even requested help in promoting Islamic fundamentalism abroad. French Foreign Minister Roland Dumas was asked in a February 1991 meeting by his Iranian counterpart, Ali-Akbar Velayati, for France's support for the fundamentalists in Jordan, Algeria, and Tunisia. Such a policy of placation has been opposed by a wide range of Western politicians, who have repeatedly warned of grave consequences.

A firm approach, on the other hand, means decisively and unambiguously confronting the main exporter of religious fundamentalism, the Iranian regime. This approach calls for close cooperation among all the antifundamentalist forces throughout the Islamic world. If those countries which supported peace, human rights, and democracy do not target the heart of fundamentalism, world peace and the modern era will be in danger. Left unchecked, fundamentalism misuses democratic processes to democracy's detriment. In Algeria, for instance, the Iranian regime exploited domestic problems to advance its policy of export of fundamentalism. Ironically, the Algerian government had opened its doors to the onslaught from Tehran by establishing close ties with the mullahs' regime over the past ten years. In other words, Algeria played right into Khomeini's hand, preparing the ground for the crisis that has befallen the country. Its experience should be a warning to others.

Fundamentalism and Islam's Great Schism

Some analysts have expressed doubts as to whether Shi'ite Iran could act as a center for export of fundamentalism to a Muslim world dominated by Sunnis.[13] Although the spread of Khomeiniism in the Sunni countries of North Africa and Central Asia has resolved such doubts, a few points still need to be made.

Most of the key Shi'ah-Sunni disputes have changed little over the centuries. According to the late Iranian scholar Hamid Enayat, the debate is essentially over the issues argued between Hilli and Ibn Taymiyah, renowned jurists of Shi'ism and Sunnism respectively, in the fourteenth century.[14] The issues can be divided into two broad categories: those that deal with the prominent personalities of early Islam, and those regarding religious rites and decrees.

The differences are basically rooted in the issue of the Prophet's succession. Shi'ites believe that before he passed away, Prophet Muhammad publicly designated his son-in-law and cousin, Ali ibn Abi Talib, as his successor. Ali had been one of the Prophet's closest disciples and confidants from the onset of his mission. During a stopover on his return to Medina from what came to be known as the Prophet's "Last Hajj," Muhammad turned to the thousands of Muslims accompanying him and declared that whoever followed him should also follow Ali. The Shi'ah view this incident as a formal proclamation of Ali as successor to the Prophet. After the Prophet's death, however, the Muslim dignitaries who gathered to resolve the succession issue ultimately chose Abu Bakr, one of Muhammad's close companions and his father-in-law, as their leader. The decision split the community. Those later to be known as Shi'ites established an independent identity as defenders of "the violated right to leadership" of Ali and his progeny. They gradually grew in numbers to become Islam's largest minority sect.

Over the years, the Shi'ite-Sunni dispute over the succession evolved to include religious ceremonies, laws, and theology. In the mid-nineteenth century, however, a new wave emerged in Islamic religious circles, and the Shi'ah-Sunni barriers began breaking down. Jamal ad-Din Assad Abadi and Muhammad Abdoh, distinguished scholars from

Iran and Egypt, contributed greatly to religious tolerance and did much to remove the deeply rooted prejudices and mistrust among Muslims. Shi'ite authors of the past few decades have noticeably toned down their criticism of the first three caliphs (Abu Bakr, Umar, and Uthman) in a bid to bring the Shi'ites and Sunnis closer. Prominent Shi'ite scholars noted for their efforts in this regard include Abdul-Hussein Sharafoddin Al-Moussavi (died 1958), leader of the Lebanese Shi'ites, and Muhammad-Hussein Kashef Al-Qeta' (died 1954), famous for his conciliatory approach in discussion with Sunnis.

In February 1959, Sheikh Mahmoud Shaltout, dean of Al-Azhar University of Cairo, issued a decree sanctioning the teaching of Shi'ite *fiqh* (jurisprudence) in the university, and formally declaring Shi'ism equal in status to the four recognized schools of law in Sunni Islam. Sheikh Shaltout's decree, printed in the official publication of the university's mosque, ended a 900-year ban on the teaching of Shi'ite jurisprudence at Al-Azhar University. The decree's impact extended far beyond a simple reform in the university's curriculum. It represented an important psychological change in the Sunni perception of Shi'ism. It is said that friendly correspondence between Shaltout and some senior Shi'ite scholars in Iran and Iraq prompted the sheikh's decree.

Strained relations between the government of Gamal Abdel Nasser in Egypt and the shah's regime in Iran inadvertently also led to greater intimacy between the Shi'ites and Sunnis in later years. In July 1960, Egypt broke off diplomatic ties with Iran in protest to the shah's de facto recognition of Israel. The common denominator between the shah's opponents in Iran (the great majority of them faithful Shi'ites) and Arab nationalists supporting Nasser laid the grounds for closer ties between the two sects. In August 1960, some 150 Sunni scholars issued a statement in Cairo calling on the world's Muslims to wage *jihad* (holy war) against the shah and his pro-Israeli policies.

By the time Khomeini seized power in 1979, the old hostilities between Shi'ites and Sunnis had to a great extent subsided. With the exception of extremists on both sides, who slandered each other as apostates or heretics, the majority of Muslims lived in a new atmosphere of mutual understanding and reconciliation. Khomeini exploited this new harmony to try to extend his religious leadership beyond Shi'ism, portraying himself the qualified leader of the entire Muslim world. Early on, the regime's official propaganda referred to Khomeini as the Leader of the World's Muslims. Keenly aware that the Shi'ite-Sunni rift would be the first ideological obstacle to his dream of reviving the Ottoman Empire, Khomeini always tried to stand above factional infighting and adopt a "patriarchal" posture. His early speeches were filled with generalized, vague emphases on unity between Shi'ites and Sunnis, calling upon both sects to seek "unity of word" (i.e. one voice). Khomeini preached that "there are no privileged peoples in Islam, be they Shi'ite or Sunni, Arab or Persian, Turk or non-Turk. . . . We are brothers with the followers of Sunnism."[15]

At the same time, Khomeini attempted to provoke the Muslims of various countries to revolt against their "oppressive rulers" and establish an "Islamic government" modeled after his own and subject to Iranian hegemony. To this end, his regime embarked on a campaign to create, organize, and strengthen various groups of religious fundamentalists, both Shi'ite and Sunni, in different countries.[16]

Within Iran, however, Khomeini's treatment of Sunnis was both discriminatory and brutal. In Kurdistan, the northeastern regions inhabited by the Turkoman tribe, and Baluchistan, Iranian Sunnis opposed to Khomeini's rule were harshly repressed. In practice, the mullahs revealed that the calls for Shi'ite-Sunni unity were rhetorical, intended to enhance their influence and prepare the ground for the export of fundamentalism.

When Khomeini's book *Islamic Government* was published in 1970, many Shi'ite scholars dismissed the concept of velayat-e-faqih as contrary to the principles and traditions of Shi'ism. After the Iranian revolution in 1979, Khomeini again tried to inject the velayat-e-faqih idea into the debates surrounding the drafting of the new constitution, outraging secular intellectuals and democratic Muslim forces. A broad spectrum of clerics and theology students at Iran's seminaries also protested.

This Shi'ite opposition to Khomeini's version of the Ottoman Caliphate came from two very different groups. The first were Shi'ite traditionalists, who controlled the majority of the religious schools and seminaries. Despite their acquiescence to the status quo, they dispute Khomeini's interpretation of Islam. These traditionalists rejected the velayat-e-faqih as a fabrication inspired by some Egyptian Sunni fundamentalists and alien to Shi'ism. Even the Quranic verse used by Khomeini to legitimize his theory, "O ye who believe! Obey God, and obey the Apostle, and those charged with authority among you," has been often used throughout Islamic history by Sunni jurists to legitimize contemporary regimes.[17] Shi'ite traditionalists contended that the *velayat* (guardianship) is confined to the twelve Shi'ite Imams, and in the absence of the "hidden" Twelfth Imam, or Mahdi, neither Khomeini nor anyone else had the right to declare himself Imam and claim absolute guardianship. They also accused Khomeini and his followers of neglecting the essence of the Shi'ite concept of velayat, meaning the protectors of the Prophet's family and the children of Ali ibn Abi Talib.

Initially, Khomeini opted to appease the Shi'ite traditionalists, who wielded great influence in the clerical hierarchy, and gave them a share of power to enlist their support. As the conflict intensified, Khomeini began to lash out, calling the traditionalists "dogmatists." One such group, the Hojjatieh, was subsequently dissolved, despite its previous alliance with the Khomeiniists. But the debate continued. In the final year of Khomeini's rule, the traditionalists made headway in attacking his decrees and theory of government, especially after Khomeini was forced to drink the "chalice of poison of a cease-fire" at the end of the Iran-Iraq War, and his authority decreased dramatically. After Khomeini's death, the traditional clerics never submitted to Khamenei's leadership. As a result, Khamenei has never been able to establish his credibility as the country's spiritual leader in the seminaries and theology schools.

It was, however, the second group, namely the Shi'ite modernists, who waged the most effective opposition to Khomeini's theory of velayat-e-faqih. They argued that Khomeini's theory was basically a mantle which fit only him and had nothing to do with Islam or Shi'ism, being merely a philosophical justification for religious despotism. Citing the traditions and sayings of the Prophet of Islam and the Shi'ite Imams, the modernists reasoned that the "absolute guardianship of the jurist" and Khomeini's other theories of government blatantly contradicted the magnanimous methods, collective decision making, forbearance, and religious tolerance of the historical Shi'ite leaders. These views were compiled and advocated most extensively in contemporary Iran by the People's Mojahedin Organization.

VI

The Iran-Iraq War

*War is a divine blessing, a gift bestowed upon us by God.
The cannon's thunder rejuvenates the soul.*

—Khomeini, September 1980[1]

The eight-year Iran-Iraq War was Iran's first major external conflict since the Russo-Iranian wars of the first decades of the nineteenth century. The Iranian mullahs' policy of exporting fundamentalism ("spreading the Islamic Revolution") to Iraq played a key role in the outbreak of hostilities. Indeed, the Khomeini regime's determination to export revolution to Iraq was a major cause of the eight-year war.

Ten years ago, the Mojahedin obtained and published a top-secret analysis of the Iran-Iraq conflict formulated by the leaders of the now defunct Islamic Republic Party after extensive discussions among Khomeini, Rafsanjani, and Khamenei. The analysis reads in part:

> There is no need to mention the dangers of an imposed peace in the current circumstances. Everyone has a general idea of the unwelcome repercussions of such a peace. If we win the war, however, the situation will change completely. The euphoria of victory will strengthen the revolution's pillars as never before, and the invincibility of Islam will inject fresh blood into the veins of our tired society. This in and of itself will enable the ruling system to handle any military or political confrontation. Victory in battle will enhance Iran's political stature. Iran's triumph will prove that "Muhammad's ideology cannot be defeated," thus raising the morale of Muslims throughout the region. This will mean more domestic difficulties for America's lackeys.
>
> It must be recalled that in discussing the war, the morale of the Muslim peoples of other countries is an important issue. Our present propaganda

capabilities are not equal to the magnificence of the Islamic Revolution. Peace with Iraq would mean confronting the seven-headed dragon of Imperialist propaganda. Any peace with Saddam will be characterized as a defeat for Iran by the international media, even if we succeed in gaining many concessions from Iraq. For us, there is no such thing as a victorious peace. Only a military victory over Iraq can establish in the minds of the Muslims of other countries that Iran has achieved its goal. One should not underestimate the impact of making peace with Saddam on weakening the hope for exporting the Islamic Revolution.

The final significant point to be made in this analysis is that accepting peace will have ramifications far beyond the Muslims' loss of faith in Islam's power to confront blasphemy. One of the principal conditions of any peace agreement between the two countries is noninterference in each other's internal affairs. On the surface, this principle may not seem so important. But [Swedish Prime Minister] Olaf Palme [peace mediator at the time] describes the practical implications of such a peace as follows: Eliminating from Iran's mass media broadcasts and speeches by the Islamic Republic's leaders anything which might instigate the people of Iraq against the Ba'athists, or which urge them to turn to genuine Islam; probably an end to most of Iran's Arabic radio broadcasts; expelling or restricting the activities of the opponents of the Iraqi regime residing in Iran . . .

In this light, the dimensions of this principle [of non-interference] can be better understood. If the Islamic Republic were to be insensitive to the realities beyond its borders or did not want to acquaint other nations with the truth of Islam, the Iran-Iraq War would not have essentially started.[2]

It is clear from the above analysis, particularly the concluding sentence, that the Iran-Iraq War, or at least its final phase, could have been avoided were it not for the mullahs' obsession with exporting revolution. Other factors contributed to the outbreak of hostilities, among them border claims, the dispute over the Shatt al-Arab waterway, and various historical and national enmities. But in the final analysis, these only became important because of the Iranian regime's policy of export of revolution.

As the postrevolutionary provisional government's foreign minister for some time before the war, Ibrahim Yazdi was involved in Tehran's conspiracies to install a vassal government in Baghdad. He has described the Iranian regime's objectives in Iraq as follows:

First, the dispatch of an ambassador knowledgeable about Iraqi affairs and capable of establishing sufficient and secret contacts with anti-Saddam Muslim groups in Iraq. This was an essential step. Another part of our policy against Iraq and other Arabs, especially the Iraqi people, was to broadcast propaganda in Arabic. At that time, numerous meetings were held at the Foreign Ministry to coordinate these aspects of the Islamic Republic's foreign policy. In these meetings, particularly those dealing with Iraq, Iran's ambassador to Iraq was present and the main outlines and principal guidelines were considered and formulated. This undertaking indeed played an effective role.[3]

About five months before the war, in a meeting on April 13, 1980, Hussein-Ali Montazeri, at that time Khomeini's designated successor, asked him to assume the leadership of the "Islamic Revolution" in Iraq: "These days, Iraqi brothers repeatedly approach us saying, we expect His Eminence Imam Khomeini to lead the Iraqi Revolution as he did the Iranian Revolution."[4] The ruling Islamic Republic Party's newspaper constantly wrote about Iraq's "Islamic Revolution" and the conquest of Iraq: "Upon the call by the Imam, Commander in Chief of the Armed Forces, the Forces of the Revolution declared their readiness to conquer Iraq with the support of Muslims."[5]

But why did the Khomeini regime choose Iraq as the first target for exporting its revolution and installing a client Islamic Republic? The most important reasons are the large number of Shi'ites, who make up nearly the entire population of southern Iraq, and the presence in Iraq of the most sacred Shi'ite shrines—the tomb of Imam Ali, the first Shi'ah Imam, and that of his son, Hussein, known to Shi'ites as "the Lord of Martyrs." For many centuries, Iraq has been the most important center of Shi'ism in the Arab world, and the city of Najaf the main seat of Shi'ah learning and theological seminaries.

Moreover, Khomeini had lived in Iraq for fifteen years and knew that from a geopolitical standpoint, Iraq would be the best springboard for export of the "Islamic Revolution" to the Arabian Peninsula, Turkey, the eastern shores of the Mediterranean, Jordan, and Egypt. Iraq's 1,200-kilometer border with Iran and its vast oil reserves (second only to Saudi Arabia's), also made Iraq the most tempting target.

Establishing an Islamic Republic in Iraq became top priority. Such slogans as "liberating Qods (Jerusalem) through Karbala" reflected Khomeini's extraterritorial designs. Iran's clerical leaders even went so far as to produce a map showing the eastward expansion of the Islamic Republic, again depicting Iraq as the staging ground for the subsequent phases of the plan.[6]

The war also enabled the mullahs to fortify the pillars of their velayat-e-faqih rule and justify domestic repression, thereby providing a ready-made scapegoat for every crisis and shortcoming—including the catastrophic economic situation—deriving from the clerical regime's theocratic rule. Khomeini described the war as a "divine blessing," and for many years, his regime insisted on prolonging hostilities when Iraq was willing to negotiate.

Iran's conduct of the war also reflected Khomeini's fanaticism. Following the capture of Iraq's southernmost town, Faw, in 1986, the mullahs saw themselves on the verge of victory. Khomeini formally replaced the slogan "war, war, until victory" with "war, war, until the obliteration of *fitna* throughout the world." The term *fitna*, meaning sedition or disorder in Arabic, had been carefully chosen for its vagueness and could be conveniently interpreted by the clerics to include a range of "targets," from Iraq to other Arab or Muslim countries. With the war with Iraq "nearly won," the mullahs now prepared themselves to take on Jordan, Kuwait, Saudi Arabia, and other Arab countries as Iraq's partners and backers in the war.

To legitimize his belligerent policies and lend an Islamic appearance to his decisions about the war, Khomeini issued a voluminous supply of fatwas, or religious decrees. *Decrees on Defense and the Front*, a book published by the Islamic Revolutionary Guards Corps, contains the full texts of Khomeini's decrees on war-related issues. In accordance with the traditional format of fatwas, Khomeini pronounced his decrees in the form of answers to questions from unidentified adherents. One question asks: "Under the present circumstances, is parental consent necessary before [children] can be sent to the war fronts?" Khomeini replied: "So long as forces are needed at the war fronts, serving there is a religious duty and there is no need for parental consent." The objective of this particular decree was to pave the way for the forcible dispatch of hundreds of thousands of children—even 9- and 10-year-olds—to the fronts despite the opposition of their families. The overwhelming majority of these children never returned; they were used as cannon-fodder or mine-sweepers and made up the bulk of Iranian casualties in each offensive.

Khomeini was also asked whether the killing of elderly men and of women and children who cooperate with the forces of evil is permissible. His reply: "In the name of God, they must be treated as aggressors." (See Appendix.) Khomeini thus gave his Guards free rein to perpetrate any crime against the civilian population. In another religious decree, he sanctioned the execution of prisoners of war. Documents confirm the execution of thousands of Iraqi POWs by the Guards Corps.

The War and the Mojahedin

To counter Khomeini's fanatical commitment to the war—which was to the detriment of the Iranian people—after Iraq withdrew its forces from Iranian territory in May 1982, the Mojahedin leader Massoud Rajavi declared that the war was no longer legitimate. He added that its continuation only served the Khomeini regime's interests, harming the peoples of both countries. The Mojahedin subsequently began a national and international campaign to expose the belligerent policies of the mullahs and counter the hysteria the mullahs tried to whip up in Iran.[7] Thus the Mojahedin deprived Khomeini of his most important excuse for brutally cracking down on all dissent: the claim that there was no alternative to war.

The formulation of a comprehensive peace plan by the National Council of Resistance (NCR) of Iran in March 1983 was the high point of this strategy.[8] The many attacks on the Mojahedin for the peace policy were essentially a smear campaign provoked by the ruling mullahs and did little to lessen the Mojahedin's resolve to pursue peace.

Damages Inflicted by the War

The mullahs' insistence on continuing the war at all costs resulted in tremendous material destruction. Rafsanjani put the colossal war damages at one trillion dollars, equivalent to Iran's oil revenues for the century. He concluded: "Every Iranian became 50 percent poorer during the war."[9]

Of greater significance, however, was the human toll. Hundreds of thousands of children died on the battlefields. On the Iranian side alone, one million people were killed and an equal number gravely wounded or maimed. Three to four million other Iranians lost their homes and property and became refugees. The scars of the war years still torment the Iranian people, who blame the ruling clerics for continuing and losing a futile war. A sharp reminder of the widespread feeling of frustration on this issue have been demonstrations and protests by handicapped veterans. These victims, daily reminders of the war's human toll, have always been the subject of much propaganda by the government, which called them *janbazan* (those ready to sacrifice their lives.) Gradually realizing that it was only hollow rhetoric that once incited them to go to the front, the janbazan have begun to voice their protests.[10] The authorities have been deeply embarrassed by such strong criticism of the government coming from those who have been much praised by the clergy as "living martyrs." Antigovernment feelings on the question of the war have been fueled by the fact that four years after the cease-fire, the government has not taken any serious steps to reconstruct the war-stricken regions. Officials acknowledge that the budget for construction is one-fifteenth of the military expenditures.

A Dream Unfulfilled

The objectives for which Khomeini fanned the flames of war were finally left unrealized. The regime was defeated, and Khomeini, in his own words, "drank the chalice of the poison of the cease-fire" in July 1988.[11] The defeat, however, did not destroy the mullahs' dream of dominating Iraq and installing a client fundamentalist regime. After the cease-fire, the mullahs strengthened their clandestine network in Iraq and waited for an opportune moment to revive their efforts toward realizing the old objectives. That opportunity came at the end of the Persian Gulf War.

When Iraq occupied Kuwait on August 2, 1990, the clerical regime played both sides to advance its goals. The mullahs' best interests lay in the eruption of a bloody war between Iraq and the Allies. Iraq would be eliminated from the regional balance of power, and the Arab members of the Allied coalition would lose credibility in the eyes of their own Muslim populace for relying on foreign powers. War meant Iran would have an opportunity to gain the upper hand. For this reason, the mullahs' policy was to push events toward an inevitable war.

Despite presenting themselves as neutral, in their private dealings with the Western countries the mullahs voiced their support for the Allied campaign and opposed the Iraqi occupation of Kuwait. Behind the scenes, they also told the Iraqis that should war break out, Iran would rally to their help with all its might. In an editorial in Iraq's *Al-Jumhuriya* newspaper, Editor in Chief Saad Al-Bazzaz revealed that throughout the Persian Gulf crisis, Rafsanjani had encouraged Baghdad to adopt a hardline stance:

> The top Iranian official said, "I have much more than what you have asked for ... We are on your side in the Kuwait affair. We request that you not take our official remarks as the only reflection of our stances. We stand beside Iraq and completely understand the circumstances and reasons for Iraq's position. Do not retreat from Kuwait. We will stand by you against America to the extent our strength allows and as much as we can."[12]

❖   ❖   ❖

Iran got the war it wanted in the Persian Gulf. When it ended, Tehran took advantage of the chaos in Iraq to dispatch thousands of Revolutionary Guards and agents to Iraqi cities, with the aim of establishing an Islamic Republic. At the same time, seven Iranian Guards Corps divisions and brigades attacked the bases and garrisons of the National Liberation Army (NLA) of Iran and the Mojahedin along the Iran-Iraq frontier.[13] The National Liberation Army, however, succeeded in repelling these attacks, inflicting thousands of casualties on the Guards forces and capturing a number of them.[14]

Although the mullahs' attempts to install a client regime in Iraq have failed again, they have not forgotten Iraq's unique characteristics or their own objective. For the foreseeable future, Iraq will remain an important target of the mullahs' policy of export of revolution and terrorism.   ❖

VII

Arms of the Octopus: Exporting Fundamentalism to Central Asia

The great nations of Azerbaijan, Turkmenistan, Uzbekistan, and Tadzhikistan are Muslims . . . Their credo is Islam and this shows the extent of Islam's influence.

—Ali Khamenei, April 4, 1992[1]

To realize their expansionist objectives, the Iranian mullahs have been following a step-by-step strategy to export revolution and fundamentalism. Their main targets have been Iraq and the Persian Gulf states. Although Tehran is still intervening in the Persian Gulf region, the collapse of the Soviet Union has opened a window of opportunity on Iran's northern frontier and convinced the Iranians to give priority to the new Asian republics. This temporary change in tactics has not in any way diminished Iran's strategic commitment to provide moral and material support for the fundamentalist forces in other parts of the Islamic world.

The mullahs' goal in Central Asia and the Caucasus republics is to create a powerful "Islamic" grouping, or as they put it, "the Union of Islamic Republics."[2] Such a "union" would obviously have enormous geopolitical implications in regional and international equations. To say the least, it would certainly strengthen Tehran's position vis-a-vis Iran's other neighbors and other nations within the Islamic world.

Ties of History and Culture
The republics of Azerbaijan, Turkmenistan, Uzbekistan, Tadzhikistan, Kyrgyzstan, and Kazakhstan were on Tehran's agenda long before they

gained independence. Common religion, history, and culture as well as strategic economic and military considerations made Central Asia and the Caucasus a tempting target for the mullahs.

Until tsarist Russia and Iran signed the treaties of Golestan and Turkmanchay in 1813 and 1829 respectively, annexing Azerbaijan, Armenia, and Georgia to the Russian Empire, the Caucasus was part of Iran. Several of the Central Asian republics were provinces of ancient Persia, and the region as a whole was heavily influenced by Persian culture, although most inhabitants were ethnically Turkic.[3] Two major cities of the ancient Persian region of Transoxania, Samarkand and Bukhara, are mentioned more often in classical Persian poetry and prose than are the names of Isfahan and Hamedan in present-day Iran. Transoxania and Azerbaijan are also considered a cradle of Iranian art and science, because many distinguished Iranian poets, scientists, and prose writers came from these areas. Transoxania was the home of Kharazmi, Abu-Rayhan Birouni, Avicinna, Rudaki, Farabi, and Daqiqi. Nezami Ganjavi and Khaqani Shirvani were from Azerbaijan and the Caucasus.

Iranian-Soviet Relations

The relations between Iran's fundamentalist regime and the former Soviet republics have gone through three different phases. In the first phase, before the Soviet Union's demise, Tehran tried to strengthen political and economic ties with the Eastern Bloc nations. Improved relations with the communist world were politically vital to the mullahs while their conflicts with the capitalist West continued.

As long as the Soviet Union was viable, the mullahs emphasized their relations with Moscow. Rafsanjani's trip to Moscow, only a few weeks after Khomeini's death in June 1989, was intended to bring about closer ties with the Soviets. He met with Mikhail Gorbachev and signed several major military and economic pacts with the Soviet officials. When the old guard tried to oust Gorbachev in August 1991, the mullahs remained tight-lipped. But they congratulated Gorbachev and Boris Yeltsin once Gorbachev returned to the Kremlin.

In the second phase, after the coup, as the Soviet Union began to unravel, the clerical regime stepped up its campaign in the newly independent Muslim republics. On the basis of a top-secret Supreme National Security Council policy decision made on September 3, 1991, Rafsanjani's government allocated an unlimited budget to expand its activities in Central Asia. As the first installment, the Iranian regime spent $130 million, adding $400 million in the next four months.[4]

But the pace of developments in the Soviet Union apparently caught Tehran by surprise. One of Rafsanjani's aides was quoted in the press as saying that the Iranians would need several months to decide how to approach the developments in the north.[5] At the same time, the Supreme National Security Council regularly convened under Rafsanjani's chairmanship to discuss the situation.

Iran's relations with the former Soviet bloc entered their third phase when the council finally decided to accelerate and expand relations with the already independent republics and those about to gain their independence, mustering all of its military and propaganda resources to catch up with developments. To this end, on September 22, 1991, the Badjgiran border crossing between Iran and Turkmenistan was reopened. Two weeks later, the president of Turkmenistan visited Iran and met with Rafsanjani. In a memorandum of understanding signed on October 5, Iran and Turkmenistan announced they would open consulates in Tehran and Ashkhabad. During his tour of Mashad (capital of the northeastern Iranian province of Khorassan), the president of Turkmenistan announced his government's readiness to extend the open border zone by forty-five kilometers to connect Mashad with Ashkhabad. During a visit to Iran in early October, religious leaders from Azerbaijan met with Rafsanjani. A delegation of Azerbaijani women also traveled to Tehran and met with Ahmad Khomeini. Subsequently, Foreign Minister Velayati toured the six republics to discuss bilateral relations and arrange scientific and cultural cooperation. In Tadzhikistan, the two countries announced they would open their embassies within one month. The mullahs' regime also transferred the headquarters of the Guards Corps Ansar Garrison (affiliated with the G.C. Qods Force) from Zahedan in the southeast to Khorassan, where it is now overseeing the Iranian regime's covert activities in the Central Asian republics. (See Chapter IX.)

After the Soviet Collapse

With the complete dismantling of the Soviet Union, Tehran pursued its policies in a more open, expanded, and aggressive manner. One internal document quoted a Foreign Ministry official as saying, "Some parts of [these republics] had been our own and we still feel a sense of belonging. This is the cause of concern for [the West . . .] Now that we have been expelled from Beirut, we would better find a footing here [in the former Soviet republics]." As one seasoned observer noted: "The Iranians are not just mischief-making in Central Asia like they have been in Lebanon. There is more to it than that. Iran is pursuing long-range political and military goals in the region."[6]

Initially, the mullahs opened embassies and diplomatic missions in all six republics. This provided a suitable and convenient cover for carrying out other activities. Top officials and senior clergy were given the mandate of establishing cultural ties with the people of the republics. The Organization for Islamic Propaganda became fully active, regularly dispatching preachers to the region. The mullahs' mission, as Ahmad Khomeini later explained, was to "create cultural resistance cells" and extend relations with "revolutionary Muslims" in these republics.[7]

Religion proved to be an important tool for the mullahs. Despite seventy years of communist rule in the Soviet Union, a time when religion was systematically suppressed, the population had deeply rooted religious feelings that made the republics susceptible to Iran's fundamentalism.[8] At the same time, phrases such as "the lost children of Islam are returning to the Islamic community" and "after seventy years of separation from Islam, our brothers in the Soviet Union find the opportunity for guidance" filled newspaper headlines in Iran. One Tehran daily commented, "If the people who have been educated by the Communist Party are left free, their choice would be an Islamic government."[9]

Tehran employed other means to advance its designs in the Central Asian republics as well. The republics were encouraged to expand trade and commercial ties with Iran as a way to stimulate their economies, an approach that had been successful in Lebanon.[10] In the mullahs' view, economic ties would enable them to "influence the republics' political inclinations."[11] Tehran proposed that Azerbaijan and five Central Asian republics join the Economic Cooperation Organization (ECO). To isolate Turkey and Pakistan, the mullahs also initiated the formation of the Tehran-based Organization of the Caspian Sea Countries that included Russia, Kazakhstan, Azerbaijan, and Turkmenistan.[12]

Azerbaijan: A Special Case

For the mullahs, Azerbaijan has special significance. The majority of the population are Shi'ite Muslims and speak the same dialect as the Iranian Azeris do. Once part of Iran, Azerbaijan has many families whose relatives live on the Iranian side of the border. Azerbaijan is also rich in oil and natural gas reserves. With the collapse of the Soviet Union, bilateral exchanges between Iran and Azerbaijan increased, as Tehran-Baku flights resumed and border crossings were reopened. The Iranian oil minister, Gholamreza Aqazadeh, traveled to Azerbaijan and signed several contracts. The Iranian minister of post, telegraph, and telephone also visited Azerbaijan to establish microwave communications between the two countries. The speaker of Azerbaijan's parliament met in Tehran with the leading clerical officials. The Azeri parliamentary speaker asked for Iran's support "to revive Azerbaijan's Islamic programs," and Velayati and his deputies visited Baku several times.[13] Delegations of fundamentalist clerics also went to Iran and met with senior Iranian mullahs to make arrangements for Tehran to supervise the trip by Azeri pilgrims to Mecca during the hajj.[14] Commentaries in Iran's state-run newspapers bring to light the mullahs' intentions about Azerbaijan and the Muslim-dominated republics in Central Asia: "It seems that the people of Chechen-Ingushetia have made up their decision to resist Moscow's pressures and keep up their struggle until the establishment of an Islamic republic in that land."[15]

Turkmenistan and Other Republics

Following ceremonies in 1992 to officially inaugurate border crossings between Turkmenistan and Iran, the vice president of Turkmenistan headed a delegation of four ministers and deputy ministers to Tehran, where they met and negotiated with Rafsanjani and other officials. The Turkmen president flew to Tehran to participate in an ECO meeting after his country became a member of the organization. There, he met Alireza Salari, president of ECO, and Muhammad-Hussein Adeli, governor of the Central Bank of Iran. The Iranian Central Bank subsequently announced that it had set aside a $50 million credit for exporters of goods to Turkmenistan. For the first time, a seminary began activities in that republic. Bearded Iranian mullahs, "driving Mercedes and Suzuki jeeps stacked with leaflets and books" became the new "missionaries" criss-crossing the open border. Turkmen youths were reported especially vulnerable to Tehran's fundamentalist propaganda.[16]

Essentially the same course of action was pursued in Kazakhstan, Tadzhikistan, Kyrgyzstan, and Uzbekistan. For example, Alma-Ata's clergy began publishing Kazakhstan's first Islamic newspaper, *Imam*. Tadzhikistan announced Farsi would be its official written language.

Muhammad Sharif, leader of the Islamic Movement Party of Tadzhikistan, visited the Iranian Foreign Ministry's Office of Political and International Studies. Tehran declared its readiness to send teachers to Tadzhikistan. After a visit to Tehran by a Tadzhik radio and television delegation, the mullahs' radio and television network agreed to produce the Tadzhik programs in Tehran. The Iranians suggested that a seminar of three Farsi-speaking nations, representing Iran, Tadzhikistan, and Afghan groups, convene in the Iranian capital. The formerly banned fundamentalist Islamic Revival Party opened an office in the Uzbek capital of Tashkent. The leader of the party, which claims one million members, later announced "Uzbekistan is an Islamic Republic."

Tehran's *Jomhouri Islami* editorial summed up the mullahs' strategy in the former Soviet republics. "As his Eminence the Imam Khomeini had stipulated, there are plenty of revolutionary forces in all the Muslim republics of Central Asia who have high potential and enormous love for revolutionary Islam. They must be strengthened through any possible means, and we must take advantage of this to win back more than 100 million Muslims living in the most sensitive regions of Asia."[17]

Afghanistan

In April 1992, the situation in Afghanistan was in total chaos. The pace of developments caught foreign governments and international observers by surprise. The Iranian minister of foreign affairs' Twelfth Bureau (responsible for Afghanistan, Pakistan, and Turkey) drew up a confidential report, in cooperation with the Guard Corps' Qods Force, for presentation to the Supreme National Security Council. It concluded in part, "The Islamic Republic of Iran can outplay its external rivals and can turn the situation in Afghanistan completely into its own favor by adopting a two-pronged policy concerning the developments there."[18] The report suggested that Tehran continue supporting the Afghan Shi'ite groups and adopt a more active policy to attract Farsi-speaking nationalities, including the Tadzhiks.

Consistent with those recommendations, the Iranians publicly endorsed the efforts by the United Nations secretary general's representative on Afghan affairs, Benon Sevan, to achieve a peaceful transfer of power to the Afghan mujahideen. Behind the scenes, however, Tehran was advancing a specific plan to gradually take control of the Afghan situation. Muhammad-Ibrahim Taherian, Iran's charge d'affaires in Kabul, had announced in January 1992 that "Najibullah must step aside. . . . Iran has decided to increase its influence in Afghanistan."[19]

The Guards Corps Qods Force was given the task of using Iranian-backed Shi'ite groups and Afghan refugees in Iran to expand its military network in Afghanistan and assist Afghan Shi'ite forces in the event of chaos. The Qods Force pursued this mission through Ansar Headquarters, located in Iran's northeastern city of Mashad. Radio intercepts of communication among Ansar forces stationed in the main headquarters, its tactical bases in Torbat-e-Jam and Taibad (on Iranian soil), and the Revolutionary Guards based in the Afghan city of Harat revealed the heavy transport of arms and troops into Afghanistan by the Revolutionary Guards. The Guards stationed in Harat also requested the command in Mashad to send "clergy and religious preachers."[20]

The intercepts further indicated that in their operations inside Afghan territory, the Guards Corps Qods forces were also using helicopters to ferry troops and equipment. On April 24, the counselor to Iran's minister of foreign affairs flew to Harat to take part in the city's Friday prayers. In his talks with Afghan parties and forces, he emphasized, "The future Afghan government must be an Islamic government."[21]

The Iranian government's current policy on Afghanistan has four major facets. First, the Iranian clerics are attempting to exploit the absence of a leadership acceptable to all nationalities and political and military groupings in Afghanistan. They see this situation as an opportunity to impose hegemony on that country. Tehran radio has broadcast messages of solidarity and declarations of *bei'at* (oath of allegiance) addressed to Khamenei by groups in Afghanistan such as the Afghan Hizbullah.[22] Ahmad Jannati, a senior cleric and leading member of the Council of Guardians, also spoke of Khamenei's leadership role: "To deal with the problems appropriately, our brothers in Afghanistan must accept [the leadership of] His Eminence Ayatollah Khamenei, the Muslims' Vali-e-faqih. This is in the interest of Islam and the dear people of Afghanistan."[23]

Second, Iran has given strong political and material support to the Afghan Shi'ites and the *Hezb-i-Vahdat-e-Islami* (Islamic Unionist Party), which was founded in Iran through the merger of nine Shi'ite groups amid the fast-changing developments in Afghanistan in 1992. Iran's state media give elaborate reports on "the victorious return of distinguished Afghan spiritual figures" from Iran and "the Afghan people's enthusiastic reception."[24] Upon their arrival in Kabul, the leaders of the Hezb-i-Vahdat-e-Islami declared that Shi'ites of Afghanistan comprised

25 percent of the population and demanded a share in power commensurate with that figure. The Iranians also supported that demand. To this end, Rafsanjani stressed "the Afghan people's need for our clerics" and ordered the dispatch of Iranian preachers to Afghanistan.[25]

Third, Tehran has relied on the Shi'ites as a primary base for its plans to interfere in Afghan affairs. Nevertheless, the Iranian clerics are also trying to take advantage of the ethnic aspirations and the cultural similarities of those Afghan nationalities who speak Farsi, particularly the two million Tadzhiks who have attained a more powerful stature in Afghan internal affairs since the fall of Najibullah. That is why the mullahs have taken actions such as sending a copy of *Shah-nameh* or other Farsi books along with every sack of flour provided in truckloads of food to the people in Afghanistan's western regions.[26]

In its radio propaganda, Tehran openly supports the northern Tadzhiks and Uzbeks against the Pashtus. General Rasheed Dostum, the controversial commander of the Uzbek paramilitary forces, said in an interview with Tehran radio: "If a reasonable and significant share in the Afghan government is not given to the National Islamic movement, this movement will take a different course of action."[27] He then added: "Alongside the Islamic Republic of Iran, Afghanistan and the new Central Asian states which share common cultural and religious backgrounds can create a vast geographic entity through strong and close ties."[28] Ironically, in August 1991, the Guards Corps Commander in Chief Mohsen Rezaii stated, "Afghanistan is a key bunker . . . Its addition to the countries in the region will turn it into a strong bastion. The resolution of this problem will strengthen Iran's position vis-a-vis the Central Asian Muslim republics, Pakistan, and one hundred million Muslims in India."[29]

The fourth facet of the Iranian policy in Afghanistan is to sow discord and add fuel to hostilities among different factions and groups. The goal is to weaken them and thereby pave the way for Iranian proxy groups to assume power. Reports of military clashes or political differences among groups that, prior to the fall of the communist government, were based in Pakistan were given prominent coverage by Iran's state media. Quoting the leaders of pro-Iranian groups, the Iranian media lashed out at the other factions and threatened the Governing Council. To cite but one example, from Tehran radio: "Mr. Mazari, a distinguished spiritual figure and the secretary general of the Hezb-i-Vahdat-e-Islami, stressed in an exclusive interview in Kabul with the Voice and Vision of the

Islamic Republic that unity among some groups in the north led to the liberation of Mazar Sharif and acceleration of the revolution and the victory of the mujahideen in Afghanistan. He added: 'Unfortunately, the demands of those groups who played an important role in this unity have not been met. If this situation were to continue, they will not remain silent.'"[30]

The mullahs' regime is pursuing this aspect of its policy both in Afghanistan and Tadzhikistan. Three million Farsi-speaking Tadzhiks live in the Republic of Tadzhikistan, in addition to the two million in northern Afghanistan. When large-scale demonstrations and protests against the government of Rahman Nabiyev and the conservative government left over from the communist period erupted in the Tadzhik capital, Dushanbe, Tehran immediately supported Nabiyev's opponents and welcomed the fall of the Tadzhik government on May 9, 1992.[31] Two days prior, in a fabricated report, Tehran had announced: "Tadzhikistan's President Rahman Nabiyev and his supporters have escaped from the capital, Dushanbe, and Muslims and other opponents have taken control of the city."[32]

The Islamic Revival Party (IRP), which has had the upper hand in the developments in Tadzhikistan, openly calls for an Islamic government and has very close ties with Iran. It was reported that the youths who staged a sit-in in May outside the Tadzhik Parliament were IRP members and received one thousand rubles a month from the mosques. Iranian diplomats in Dushanbe deny making direct payments to the demonstrators but acknowledge that they have generously given money to 100 mosques. The slogans of the protesters were "death to America, death to Russia, and long live the Islamic Republic." In May, the Tadzhik police was quoted as saying that an "Islamic fundamentalist group was stockpiling weapons."[33] Diplomats also said that in September 1991, Tehran covertly supported an uprising against a communist power grab in Dushanbe, allegedly paying demonstrators 100 rubles a day to lead Muslim prayers and demand the resignation of Tadzhik communist leaders.[34]

Many observers believe that Tehran's rulers have succeeded in expanding their influence over the Tadzhiks in Afghanistan and Tadzhikistan, thereby setting the stage for the establishment of a client government in Tadzhikistan and gradual control of power in Afghanistan.[35] Such a development would mean that the Iranian regime has acquired a suitable footing to export its fundamentalism beyond its northern frontiers. With Khomeiniism on the rise in these former Soviet republics, the Central Asian region—which also includes the Chinese region of Muslim-dominated Sinkiang, where the authorities have warned that Islamic fundamentalism is growing rapidly—is headed for an uncertain and turbulent future.

Pan-Islamism Versus Pan-Turkism?

Shortly after the Turkish Prime Minister Suleyman Demirel's much-publicized trip to Central Asian republics and Azerbaijan in April 1992 with a 144-member delegation of government officials and industrialists, Rafsanjani warned in a public speech that the rivalry to gain influence in that region had to be conducted "honestly."[36] Simultaneously, government newspapers in Tehran unleashed a barrage of virulent attacks against Turkey and its activities in the Muslim republics of the former Soviet Union. The Iranian daily *Kayhan*, for example, attacked Ankara's satellite broadcasting of its television programs into Central Asian republics, claiming such actions by Turkey came at a time when that country was under the influence of the West's loathsome and corrupt culture. *Kayan* added that Turkey was so alienated from the genuine Islamic and indigenous Eastern culture that its cultural identity was under question. By exploiting the pure sentiments of the people of these newly independent republics, *Kayan* continued, Turkey was trying to act as a springboard for its Western masters. *Kayan* went on to say Turkey did not consider itself an independent country alongside the newly independent Turkish-inhabited states of the former Soviet Union. Its officials had unequivocally referred to Turkey as the motherland for all Turks across the world—a serious cause for concern, *Kayan* said.

Hostile reactions by Tehran and Ankara to each others' meddling in the affairs of the Central Asian republics and the Caucasus have continued since the first signs of the Soviet Union's demise. In the intense rivalry to expand influence in the newly independent states with a population of fifty-three million, Turkey is counting on ethnic and language commonalities with most of the republics, promoting a kind of Pan-Turkism that stresses the unity of the Turkic nations from the coast of the Adriatic to Mongolia. Turkey is also recommending the creation of secular governments committed to a free market economy, modeled after its own political and economic system. The mullahs, on the other hand, pinpoint religious attachments and "Islamic" unity, at the same time underlining the republics' historical and cultural ties to Iran.

A number of Western countries, including the United States, have openly endorsed the Turkish option, reasoning that Turkey's influence in these republics impedes Tehran's efforts to export Khomeiniism and dominate the area. In a trip to several Central Asian republics, which coincided with the Economic Cooperation Organization (ECO) Summit meeting in Tehran, former U.S. Secretary of State James Baker said the establishment of "Islamic republics" in these countries would be a "historical mistake." During Demirel's trip to Washington, D.C., in February 1992, former U.S. President George Bush praised Turkey as the "symbol of stability" and a "model" for the newly independent states of Central Asia.

Islamic fundamentalism has, nevertheless, established itself as a serious alternative in all of Central Asia. This was acknowledged by Demirel during his trip to the United States: "After suffering from the Soviet Empire's years of pressure and oppression, the former Soviet republics must not come under the fundamentalists' pressures and oppression," the Turkish prime minister said.[37] The principal question, therefore, is whether Turkey can outplay Iran. Will Pan-Turkism or fundamentalism eventually fill the vacuum created by the collapse of the Soviet Union and Marxism?

The governments taking power immediately after independence consisted mainly of conservative ex-communist officials or secular political figures. The new governments were a cause for premature optimism from some Western observers who perceived them as an indication that fundamentalism would not make much headway in this region. Several months later, however, a more troubling reality came to the surface. One after the other, governments in Azerbaijan, Tadzhikistan, Uzbekistan, and Turkmenistan became engulfed in severe crises, during which it became apparent that Islamic fundamentalism was a powerful phenomenon threatening the status quo. These developments further demonstrated that in the Tehran-Ankara face-off, the mullahs will have the last word in Central Asia and the Caucasus, for several reasons.

Religious Appeal

Following several decades of religious oppression, the collapse of the Soviet Union has led to a wave of religious awakening in Central Asia and the Caucasus. The Central Asia correspondent of the Turkish daily *Cumhuriyet* has said of the republics: "The people are deeply religious, but at government and intellectual level, they have been trained by the former Communist Party." During the communist rule, out of 26,000 mosques and seminaries in these republics, only 400 mosques and 2 seminaries were allowed to operate. But today, throughout these republics one finds mosques being built or renovated. The London Sunday *Times* reported from Ashkhabad, the Turkmenistan capital, that after years of living under the communists' oppressive and antireligious rule, the youth in Turkmenistan now consider themselves to be, before anything else, Muslims.

In such a social setting, Tehran has a clear advantage. Parties advocating fundamentalist Islam have grown rapidly by taking advantage of the public's religious sentiments. In Tadzhikistan and Uzbekistan they are now the largest political organizations. Religion has become so important among the people of these republics that even secular politicians such as Azerbaijan's former President Ayaz Motalebov tried to pose as an advocate of Islam during election campaigns. Secular Turkey itself could not ignore this important element. Contrary to its vigorously secular constitution, Demirel's government sent 40,000 copies of the Quran in Turkish to these republics and dispatched representatives from the State Religion Organization. But the mullahs' "Islamic Republic" is in a much better position compared with Turkey to exploit this religious factor. It has used radio broadcasts, the dispatch of several thousand religious preachers, financial backing, and propaganda support for mosques and political and religious groups that are under its influence.

Common Borders

Iran has a 2,000-kilometer-long border with the Caucasian and Central Asian republics. Turkey, on the other hand, has a common border with the non-Muslim republic of Armenia and a few kilometers of border with the autonomous Nakhichevan republic, part of the Russian Republic. What is more, some of the largest and most populated Iranian provinces, such as Khorassan in the northeast, Mazandaran in the north, and Azerbaijan in the northwest, are neighbors to the new republics. Iran's geopolitical location is also important, because it can act as a bridge between Central Asia and the outside world. In a conference titled "The Collapse of the Soviet Union and its Effects on the Third World" held in Tehran in March 1992, an Iranian official said: "With the Soviet Union's collapse and the republics' independence, the regional and global maps have undergone changes. In place of one country that since the tsar's time was trying to reach the warm waters of the Persian

Gulf, fifteen republics have been established. By connecting them to the international waters and obtaining permission to use these republics' ground routes to the Black Sea and Europe, the interests of Iran and the republics could be served."

In May 1992, Rafsanjani spoke about rebuilding the Silk Road that in ancient times linked Iran to China via Central Asia.[38] Not only would such commercial routes increase Iran–Central Asia trade, they would also further attach these republics to Tehran. The Iranians are also strongly motivated to activate the transit route to Europe via the Caucasus and the Ukraine, thereby removing the Turkish monopoly on Iran's land access to Europe.

Historical Bonds

Whereas none of the Muslim republics of the former Soviet Union has ever been a part of Turkey or the Ottoman Empire, Iran enjoys ancient historical and cultural ties to these regions. While capitalizing on the religious and Islamic feelings, the Iranian clerics have also emphasized these historical bonds.

Mullah Abaii, Mashad Friday prayer leader, has said, "These Muslims are closer to us. The Treaty of Turkmanchay expired several years ago, and these countries are now parts of Iran." Government media systematically call for the abrogation of the Treaty of Golestan (1813) and Turkmanchay (1829), which gave Russia vast portions of Iranian territory in the Caucasus—inciting much irredentist sentiment. Some in the West argue that Central Asian Muslims will not become trouble-making allies of Iran because most of them speak Turkish and not Farsi, and having been just liberated from the yoke of communism, they reject revolutionary Islam.[39] This view ignores the fact that after many centuries, the new republics and Iran still have the same music and handicraft, and almost the same culture.[40] Moreover, Turkish is extensively spoken in northern Iran. Iran's Turks are among the most influential figures in Tehran and have dominated the armed forces for many centuries.

Economic Factors

Despite offering the new Central Asian republics a free market model, Turkey lacks sufficient economic capacity either to help start these republics' stagnant economies or absorb their new markets. It cannot compete with oil-rich Iran either. Vast segments of the Iranian economy have been devastated during the mullahs' rule, but Iran has considerable oil revenues. In countries such as Lebanon, the Iranians have demonstrated their readiness to spend extravagantly when it comes to "exporting revolution." Commenting on Tehran-Ankara economic competition in the former Soviet republics, the *London Observer* wrote that, plagued by a poor economy, high inflation, and large unemployment, Turkey cannot compete with Saudi Arabia or Iran, who spend cash. The Turks are aware that they cannot by themselves help reconstruct the economies of the former Soviet republics.[41] In short, as one analyst has noted, "Turkey cannot be counted on to block Iran's move. It is busy with its own problems."[42]

Discussing the increasing economic ties between Iran and the Central Asian republics, Alireza Sheikh-Attar, an Iranian official, said:

> After the war [with Iraq], economic prosperity [for Iran] is impossible without export markets. Our difficulties in export are the quality and high tariffs in the West which have denied us the chance to compete in the world markets. Now these republics are the best market for Iran, because the people's tastes are in harmony with Iranian products. The vast mineral resources of these republics can fulfill Iran's needs.[43]

By founding the Organization of the Caspian Sea Countries, the mullahs succeeded in bypassing Turkey and assuring direct relations with Azerbaijan, Kyrgyzstan, and Turkmenistan.

In the Tehran conference on the collapse of the Soviet Union, Iranian officials listed the activities the "Islamic Republic" of Iran would pursue to expand its relations with the Central Asian republics:

1. Setting up industrial and commercial exhibitions in Baku, Ashkhabad, Alma-Ata, Dushanbe, and Tashkent;
2. Facilitating traveling of citizens;
3. Allowing trucks from Azerbaijan to commute via Nakhichevan;
4. Establishing Islamic Republic Airlines offices in the republics' capitals;
5. Opening Iranian banks, joint production investments, and commercial centers;
6. Opening embassies and diplomatic representations;
7. Setting up Farsi language classes to spread the Farsi language;
8. Endorsing the Muslim republics' membership in international bodies such as the Islamic Conference Organization;

9. Providing assistance to increase the republics' economic potential and granting them export credits;
10. Reviving the Silk Road to China and Europe through construction of the Mashad-Sarakhs railway;
11. Offering help in renovating mosques and historical sites;
12. Creating the possibility of those countries' membership in the Economic Cooperation Organization (ECO).

Given the different historical, religious, political, economic, and cultural parameters, it must be concluded that Pan-Turkism cannot sweep aside the Pan-Islamism the mullahs are advocating in Central Asia and the Caucasus. If the situation is left on its own and fundamentalism is not eliminated in Iran, the Iranian clerics will take further steps toward dominating these republics. Turkey itself has been the target of Iranian-inspired fundamentalists.[44] It cannot itself compete with Iran.

Stressing that the Central Asian region "will turn into the most complex case of the transitional period," Henry Kissinger warned that fundamentalism seriously endangers the region.[45] It would be against the Russian and American interests for fundamentalist regimes to spread in these republics, he said.[46] That specter would affect the entire Middle East and would lead to a new tide of radicalism.[47]

A multitude of wide-ranging regional issues only complicates the situation in Central Asia and the Caucasus, from Kazakhstan's possession of intercontinental ballistic missiles with nuclear warheads to the bloody territorial conflict between Azerbaijan and Armenia. Indeed, with so much potential for instability and conflict, it is no surprise that some analysts have predicted that Central Asia will become a major crisis point before the turn of the century. The mullahs in Tehran, through their export of Khomeiniism to the republics, are making sure that prediction will come true.

VIII

Fundamentalism in the Arab World

*The third millennium belongs to Islam and the rule of Mus-
lims over the world.*

—Ali-Muhammad Besharati, Deputy Foreign Minister,
March 3, 1992[1]

Throughout the Arab world, from the arid, oil-rich deserts of Arabia to
the Atlantic coast of North Africa, the forces of Islamic fundamentalism
are on the rise. To what extent and in what ways are they dependent on
the Iranian regime?

Of all Arab countries, Iraq has been the most important target for the
clerical authorities in Iran. (See Chapter VI.) In addition, the mullahs'
regime is exporting its revolution to three specific regions in the Arab
world: the Eastern Mediterranean (the Levant), North Africa, and the
Persian Gulf states, including Saudi Arabia.

The Eastern Mediterranean

The question of Palestine and the occupied territories has such
political and psychological importance in the Islamic world that no
government can claim to lead the Muslim masses without being a key
player in the Arab-Israeli dispute.

Now that a new Middle East peace process has begun, the mullahs are
determined to establish themselves as the staunchest opponents of any
compromise. Tehran has invested heavily in the failure of the peace
conference, hoping to raise the stature of its fundamentalist alternative
in case the talks finally break down. (See Chapter XI.)

For these reasons, the Eastern Mediterranean region—Syria, Jordan,
Lebanon, Israel, and the occupied territories—is of critical importance

to the clerical regime's regional strategy. Tehran has a very high stake in Lebanon, with its large Shi'ite population and the presence of a multitude of proxy groups armed and financed by the Iranian government. Syria, the mullahs' sole ally in the Arab world, adds to the importance of this area for Tehran, even though the Algerian experience demonstrates that if the conditions were to become ripe for fundamentalists to take power in Syria, the mullahs would certainly drop their support for Hafez Assad.

Jordan and the Occupied Territories

The developments in Lebanon during 1991 and 1992, most notably the strengthening of the central government's authority and the decline of paramilitary forces, have seriously hampered the activities of the Iranian Revolutionary Guards' contingent in Lebanon and Iran's indigenous operatives—the Hizbullah. The Iranian leaders, therefore, are searching for a suitable replacement for Lebanon.

Its common borders with the occupied territories and Israel, Saudi Arabia, Iraq, and Syria, plus the presence of active Islamic fundamentalist elements and currents, make Jordan an ideal alternative.

Following the Persian Gulf War and before Tehran's resumption of diplomatic ties with Jordan in 1991, a high-ranking Iranian delegation visited the country. Its assessment, delivered to Iran's leadership in a confidential report, read in part:

> After Lebanon, Jordan is an excellent theater of activity for us. Albeit a small country, its strategic location carries great significance. The press there is relatively free and the setting for activities is quite suitable. A group of young men came to see us privately. They said that in the course of the [Iran-Iraq] War, they supported our stance. We must pay special attention to them, for people who were attracted to our viewpoints during the era of repression in Jordan are quite valuable to our cause. We must offer them direction and guidance to lead them to power. The ambassador who goes to Jordan, therefore, must be very capable and intimately involved in the Lebanese experience, so that we avoid making the same mistakes here as we did in Lebanon.

The opening of the Iranian Embassy in Amman in 1991 gave the mullahs a base to implement this policy. The leaders of the Muslim Brotherhood, which holds a third of the seats in the Jordanian Parliament, were invited to Tehran to attend the Conference to Support Palestine's Islamic Revolution, held simultaneously with the Madrid Peace Conference in October 1991.

The Iranian clerics believe that King Hussein is allowing the Muslim Brotherhood to participate in parliament at a time when the central government is weak in an attempt to use the Brotherhood's credibility to legitimize Hussein's government. In the mullahs' view, the king's authority to dissolve the parliament and his other extra-parliamentary powers are hindering any serious action by the Jordanian fundamentalists. The Iranian delegation to Jordan concluded: "The reality is that client regimes like Jordan will never tolerate such forces in the long run."[2]

Iran's leaders exercise great caution and sophistication in establishing contacts and offering guidance to Jordanian groups, because they are aware that the government will not hesitate to clamp down on fundamentalists in Jordan. In Tehran, the Jordanian government's temporary ban on *Al-Rabat* magazine, which had ties with the Brotherhood, was seen as "a step in the direction of restricting the activities of Islamic groups in Jordan."[3]

Upon instructions from the clerical regime, fundamentalists in Jordan test the situation carefully before taking any action. For instance, they hold rallies in small groups, and if threatened they immediately disperse. They hold their gatherings or speeches at night because "they know full well that any violent action in Jordan will ultimately serve the interests of the ruling government."[4] For example, 150 members of an underground group in Jordan went too far. They tried to kidnap one of King Hussein's sons on his way to school and were arrested. These individuals were previously active under the names of "Muhammad's Army" or "mujahideen in the path of God" and had received the necessary training in Afghanistan.[5]

Lebanon

The Islamic Revolutionary Guards Corps established its military presence in Lebanon in 1982, and the large local Shi'ite community provided the mullahs with a formidable background within which to operate. The presence of other Arab nationals in Lebanon also enabled Iran to strengthen its network by recruiting them. (See Chapter X.)

Iran continued to be directly involved in Lebanon after Khomeini's death in 1989. During his trip to Syria in April 1991, Rafsanjani personally intervened to prevent the mullahs' proxy groups from being disarmed. These groups operate in the Bekaa valley, near the Syrian border, and in South Lebanon, close to the areas under Israeli control. In previous years Rafsanjani had persistently aided and protected Iran's terrorist operatives in Lebanon. On February 1, 1992, Muhammad-Hussein Fadhlullah, a senior Hizbullah cleric, met with Rafsanjani and "gave him a report on the situation and issues relating to Muslims in Lebanon."[6]

Following the death of Hizbullah leader Abbas Moussavi in a helicopter attack in South Lebanon on February 16, 1992, the new leader, Seyyed Hassan Nasrullah, went to Tehran and met with Rafsanjani, Khamenei, and other officials of the regime to receive guidelines for his future course of action. Upon Nasrullah's return to Lebanon, an Israeli diplomat was assassinated in Turkey on March 7, and the Israeli Embassy in Buenos Aires was bombed on March 17. A U.S. official told Reuters news agency that his government's investigations showed that Tehran was directly behind the attack.

According to reports by Western and Middle Eastern intelligence sources, "the political training camps of the Popular Front for the Liberation of Palestine, led by Ahmed Jibril, are being transferred to Iran. The camps are believed to be in the area of Khorramabad and Kermanshah in southern and western Iran."[7]

The clerical regime has provided numerous facilities for terrorist groups in Lebanon. According to one report, "Imad Mugniyeh has been involved in many violent incidents against French and American forces in Lebanon. The hijacking of at least four planes and several bombings and killings are attributed to him. He has an Iranian diplomatic passport which facilitates his trips."[8]

Finally, the Revolutionary Guards continue their military presence in Lebanon. More than 1,500 Revolutionary Guards from the Guards' First Corps have been organized into "the Lebanon Corps." They have brought under their control areas of Lebanon, including the Bekaa Valley and Baalbek. Syria allows them to operate as part of its strategic cooperation with Iran.[9]

North Africa

For Tehran's rulers the export of fundamentalism to Iraq and the Persian Gulf states and especially Saudi Arabia has always had strategic priority in the Arab world. But for three main reasons the Arab countries of North Africa, including Algeria, Tunisia, and Sudan, have been given tactical priority: First, the domestic situation in the North African countries has made them much more vulnerable to the onslaught of Islamic fundamentalism. Second, the greater readiness and presence of the United States and its Western Allies in the Persian Gulf has sharply increased the risks for the mullahs in that region. Third, the Persian Gulf Arab states would be almost encircled by hostile states if North Africa fell into the hands of fundamentalist forces.

The mullahs believe that the scene is therefore set for a second phase of Islamic expansionism, this time in the Islamic hinterlands: the Arabian Peninsula, Mesopotamia, the Fertile Crescent, and Egypt. Unlike the wave of Islamisation that began in the seventh century, the current tide of what the mullahs call "reconversion" is moving in from the opposite direction: from the periphery to the center.[10]

The fundamentalists' rise to power in Sudan, their ascent in Algeria, and their serious threat to Tunisia, Egypt, and Morocco demonstrate that the mullahs may be proved right.

Algeria

As a result of close, long-term relations with Algeria, the mullahs succeeded in establishing extensive ties with that nation's indigenous fundamentalist groups and were able to infiltrate their ranks. The mullahs also counted on Algeria to serve as a springboard for the export of fundamentalism to its neighboring countries in North Africa, as well as to France, where millions of Muslims (mostly of North African extraction) reside. Iranian leaders were convinced that the fundamentalists' victory in Algeria would lead to the collapse of the Maghreb countries, as "Tunisia and Morocco cannot prevent this development through repressive measures."[11]

The regime's plans for export of revolution to Algeria can clearly be seen in the minutes of a confidential coordinating meeting among the representatives of Rafsanjani's office, Khamenei's office, the Foreign Ministry, and the Intelligence Ministry in July 1991. Parts of the conclusions are as follows:

> The principle raised by the leadership that Islam must continue to move forward in Algeria must remain on top of the agenda. Given the proximity of Algeria to Tunisia and Egypt, the impact of the Islamic movement goes beyond Algeria. Thus the pressure we are facing now in the Middle East region will ease if serious developments come about in North Africa. In addition to previous coordination with other North African countries, closer ties are necessary.

Later in the meeting, the status of Tehran's contacts in Algeria and those Algerians who had traveled to Iran were appraised as follows:

a. Contacts with the rest of those who had been briefed but not arrested must be maintained.
b. Previously established contacts should not arouse the sensitivity of the Algerian government. Caution must therefore be exercised.
c. Material assistance will from now on take on indirect form. The Ministry of Foreign Affairs will determine the third parties and contacts. The plan will be advanced by the Ministry through the Iranian Embassy in Algeria.

Ali Khamenei, the regime's spiritual leader, stressed in a meeting with the minister of education and a group of ministry officials, "We believe that the people of Algeria will finally attain their desired Islam and the rule of Islam."[12]

Tehran promised the fundamentalists that if a theocratic regime came to power in Algeria, Iran would provide Algiers with a $5 billion assistance package. Along with such economic incentives, the mullahs spared no efforts to incite the fundamentalist forces in Algeria. In a controversial speech, Khamenei emphasized, "The people of Algeria who chant '*Allah-o-Akbar*' ['God is Great'] from the rooftops have learned to do so from the Muslim and revolutionary people of Iran, because this nation has specifically taught Muslims throughout the world the path to struggle against the Arrogant West and the camp belonging to the enemies of humanity."[13] For their part, the Algerian fundamentalists reiterated that their prime objective was to establish an Islamic government in Algeria, modeled after "the Islamic Republic of Iran."[14]

Prior to the escalation of the crisis in Algeria, which led to the cancellation of elections in May 1991, the mullahs had taken some initial steps to export their revolution to that country. An internal document reveals that Tehran had dispatched in February 1990 some 100 Revolutionary Guards and Arabic-speaking students to Algeria. During local elections in Algeria, it "provided $3 million in campaign aid" to the fundamentalist forces,[15] who boasted of having an armed wing with direct connections to the Iranian religious center of Qom.[16]

Tunisia

The mullahs' activities in Tunisia were first exposed in 1987, when a group of local fundamentalists was arrested. These arrests followed the detention of an Iranian Embassy employee at the French-Swiss border. The employee carried documents revealing Iran's contacts with Tunisian fundamentalists and its other involvement in that country.

Subsequently, Iran's charge d'affaires in Tunisia, Ahmad Kan'ani, was declared persona non grata. In July 1987, a Tunisian named Lutfi, a former fundamentalist recruited and trained by the Iranians to join their network in Tunisia, was the target of an assassination attempt by the mullahs' terrorists after he provided the French police with detailed information on Tehran's activities and contacts in Tunisia. In a private meeting, Seyyed Hadi Khosrow-Shahi, the regime's ambassador to the Vatican, who was responsible for providing the necessary facilities for the regime's terrorists abroad and whose role has been extensively exposed by the media in Italy and Britain, expressed great dismay over the Tunisian developments: "In Tunisia they have arrested our good contacts on the charge of cooperating with Iran."

On March 23, 1992, an armed group calling itself the "Islamic Jihad" was uncovered by Tunisian security forces. The group's activities were overseen by one of the leaders of the An-Nahdha movement, which has very close links to Iran. One of the group's activists confessed during interrogations that he had received weapons training in Iran.[17]

Rachid Al-Ghannouchi, the leader of the An-Nahdha has regularly visited Tehran and carries a Sudanese passport given to him by Sudan at Iran's behest.[18] In a meeting on March 28, 1991, with Tehran University students visiting Algiers, he stressed, "Iranian youths' efforts inspired university students in Tunisia to resist Habib Bourguiba's rule. Our movement was in dire need of Islamic revolutionary ideals which marked a turning point in our movement."[19]

On September 1, 1991, a Tunisian magazine reported that "80 members of a secret Islamic movement were arrested in connection with Iran while trying to engage in subversive activities."[20] It has also been reported that in 1991, Tunisian security forces arrested 300 fundamentalists charged with plotting a coup.[21]

On January 15, 1992, an Iranian parliamentary delegation, headed by Ahmad Azizi, met the speaker of the Tunisian parliament in Tunis. The Tunisians reportedly criticized the Iranians sharply for their support for fundamentalists in the Maghreb region. The Tunisians were especially critical of Iran for supporting the An-Nahdha and its leader, Rachid Al-Ghannouchi, who had visited Iran upon official invitation of the mullahs. The Tunisian parliament's speaker told the visiting delegation: "As much as we are seeking to establish ties with Iran, we also demand Iran's noninterference in Tunisia's internal affairs."[22]

In light of the growing influence of Iranian-inspired fundamentalists in North Africa, Algeria, Morocco, and Tunisia signed a security pact in January 1992 in an attempt to adopt a uniform approach in their confrontation with fundamentalism.[23] The agreement came as Tunisia put its police and gendarmerie forces on full alert upon a directive issued by the Interior Minister.[24]

Sudan

Sudan's geopolitical position makes it an ideal base for export of fundamentalism to Africa.[25] As one of the continent's largest countries, it straddles the Arab north and the sub-Saharan heartland of Africa. Its long border with Egypt and its control of the western coastline of the Red Sea (putting it close to Saudi Arabia) give Sudan considerable leverage in the region. The Nile also gives Sudan great agricultural potential and its control of the river's flow is of vital concern to Egypt, which regards the Nile as its lifeline.

After the military assumed power in Sudan in June 1989, Tehran sharply increased its activities in that country. Many Sudanese students belonging to the National Islamic Front have gone to Iran, some to study in Qom, Mashad, and Tehran. In an interview, a Sudanese religious leader very close to the Iranian regime stated: "In the case of Iran, Islam emerged through a revolution, through military institution in the case of Sudan, and through the ballot box in Algeria."[26]

In December 1991, Rafsanjani paid an official visit to Sudan in the company of Intelligence Minister Ali Fallahian, Guards Corps Commander in Chief Mohsen Rezaii, and Defense Minister Ali Akbar Torkan, as well as more than 150 others. In a speech in Khartoum, Rafsanjani told his hosts: "Sudan can play a more important role in the new world order." During the trip, $17 million worth of financial assistance was given to Sudan. Iran also agreed to pay China $300 million for weapons it ordered for Sudan. In addition, Iran agreed to deliver one million tons of free oil to Sudan annually.

Following Rafsanjani's departure from Khartoum, two ships carrying oil, light weapons, and artillery shells sailed toward Sudanese ports. Soon thereafter, Sudan's military ruler, General Omar Al-Bashir, announced that Islamic laws would be put into effect in Sudan. The first order of business: Women would have to wear the veil in public places.

At about the same time, Western intelligence sources reported the dispatch to Sudan of a contingent of one to two thousand Iranian Revolutionary Guards. The Supreme Command of the Sudanese Armed

Forces stated that in meetings between Sudan's military commanders and Iranian Defense Minister Torkan "the two sides reviewed developments in military relations and cooperation and exchange of experts."[27] Subsequently reports on Sudan's attempts to establish a military unit similar to Iran's Revolutionary Guards Corps came to light.[28] The Sudanese leadership's foreign affairs counselor visited Tehran to get guidance on setting up such a force.[29] On March 31, 1992, the formation of the Popular Defense Forces (PDF) of Sudan was made public. As a Western journalist wrote: "Their khaki outfits made in Iran introduces these young troops who are ready to fight a *Jihad*, or holy war. The PDF forces trained to march with a gun and recite the Quran are part of Sudan's new Islamic forces. They are modeled after Iran's Revolutionary Guards and reported by some Western observers to be trained by Iranians."[30]

Reacting to these developments, the U.S. State Department announced, "It is obvious that very close political ties are developing between the Islamic Republic of Iran and Sudan's National Islamic Front which includes Iran's support for Sudan's paramilitary Popular Defense Forces."[31] Some American analysts expressed the view that "Sudan, which is being supported by Iranian money and know-how, will be another Lebanon very soon, becoming a base for the export of terrorism."[32] Because, as one expert put it, "Iran has tried in the past to export revolution, but Sudan is the first place where they have had a regime that is a willing supporter."[33]

Clear signs confirm this assessment: The mullahs have spent $20 million to build a main center in Khartoum and dispatched teams of Revolutionary Guards to Sudan for protection and security. The mullahs' top agent in Sudan, Majid Kamal, held the same post in Beirut during the 1980s and was active in the formation of the Hizbullah.[34] The Guards Corps contingent in Sudan was reported in May 1992 to be commanded by Husseinzadeh, a colonel in the Revolutionary Guards Corps.[35]

Iran is also trying to pursue a highly aggressive strategy in Sudan which encompasses not only Egypt but the south and central African Sahara as well. "Other indications, such as the presence of the leaders of some terrorist groups, aggravate the situation in Sudan,"[36] noted an American official.

A short while after Rafsanjani's return from Sudan, Egypt accused Sudan of training Islamic fundamentalists active in Egypt and charged that Sudan was the source of a vast illegal arms traffic to that country.

Reuters reported that "during two hours of talks in Cairo with Major General Al-Zubair Muhammad Saleh, Sudan's number two, Egyptian President Hosni Mubarak urged Sudan to distance itself from Muslim fundamentalist groups and explain its close links with Iran."[37] Meanwhile, Egyptian security forces reported "the arrest of a group of Muslim fundamentalists who were trained by Iranian groups based in Sudan."[38] The Egyptian press has contended that the man who in October 1990 assassinated Rifaat Mahgoub, the speaker of the Egyptian parliament, was trained in Khartoum. [39]

Following reports that the Sudanese Embassy in the United Arab Emirates had become a center for suspicious political activities, UAE officials expelled seven Sudanese diplomats, including Sudan's ambassador.[40] Tunisia also recalled its ambassador from Khartoum because Rachid Al-Ghonnouchi, leader of the An-Nahdha group, was given extensive facilities by the Sudanese, including a diplomatic passport. According to Egyptian and Tunisian intelligence sources, "Since May, Muslim extremists have been receiving training in about ten camps set up in Sudan with Iranians' cooperation. The camps are being used to train Islamic fundamentalists from Egypt, Algeria, Tunisia, and the Gulf states for subversion."[41]

As one Middle East analyst put it: "If Khomeini were alive, he would have been proud of his successors who succeeded in exporting fundamentalist Islamic revolution to the Horn of Africa. The Islamic Republic's activities began from Sudan and have now reached the Muslim communities in Kenya, Ethiopia, Somalia, and Djibouti."[42] Diplomatic visitors have reported a noticeable increase in Iranian activity in Mogadishu, the Somali capital.[43]

Egypt

Among the North African states, Egypt is considered the biggest prize for the mullahs. It is the most populous country in the region, and the Islamic fundamentalist movement has a long history there. One of the most important objectives of the Iranian regime's involvement in Sudan is to lay the groundwork for expanding its network among Egyptian fundamentalists. As an official from Rafsanjani's office said, "If developments in Algeria accelerate, the region will inevitably witness some movements in Tunisia, Egypt, and Sudan. We have forces in Egypt but do not want to lose them too quickly."[44]

In early 1992, the Iranian regime sent a skilled analyst by the name of Arefinia to Egypt in the company of its charge d'affaires, Ali-Asghar Muhammadi. He drew up a report concluding that Egypt was a fertile ground from which to recruit Islamic fundamentalist groups. He further stated that such groups could be quite effective militarily and would have to be assisted. Based on another top-secret document, Muhammadi, who had previously been commissioned to Lebanon, followed up these groups' activities in Egypt and began working with them.

Responding to Tehran's increasing support for fundamentalist forces, Cairo's Interior Minister Muhammad Abdel-Halim Moussa accused Rafsanjani's government of "exporting religious terrorism" to Egypt. He said Tehran was directly involved in acts of terror on Egyptian soil.[45]

The mullahs' actions to "export revolution" to Egypt and their support for fundamentalists there resulted in the closure of Iran's Interest Section in Cairo. Foreign Minister Velayati acknowledged that the Egyptian government's move was prompted by Iran's "contacts with Muslim groups in that country."[46] This coincided with Tehran's efforts to open an embassy in Cairo to "assist the people of Egypt."[47] Despite the diplomatic break, the mullahs have continued their efforts to bring about an "Islamic Revolution" in the Arab world's largest nation. Majlis deputy Abolqassem Sarhadizadeh said, "Currently the primary path to the salvation of Palestine passes through liberating Egypt from the clutches of reactionary [states] and the Arrogant [West]. The people of Egypt must repeat their past revolution and not allow the Arrogant West and reactionary forces to control their destiny."[48]

In February 1992, a group of thirty-five fundamentalists were arrested in Egypt. Ten of them belonged to the Jihad group supported by Tehran. Most of the thirty-five either carried weapons or were arrested while distributing leaflets.[49] After the arrest, Cairo announced that it had uncovered a plot against the government, reportedly backed by Iranian or Sudanese fundamentalists.[50] The government then arrested twenty-eight suspected Islamic activists, saying they were "part of an international network planning to overthrow the government." Egyptian security sources said the twenty-eight were arrested following the arrest of three men at a Cairo computer firm[51] that was a front for establishing ties with the regime in Iran.[52] At about the same time, Egyptian police arrested ninety fundamentalists from the Islamic Jihad in the wake of the murder of a police officer in the Al-Fayum region. Reacting to these developments, a senior Egyptian official said, "Egypt is monitoring with concern Iran's extensive activities on the African continent, particularly in the Nile region. Iran has signed agreements with African countries on the basis of which in exchange for opening embassies, consulates, and cultural centers, Iran will sell them oil with reduced prices."[53]

Morocco

Morocco's geographic proximity to Europe, its close ties with the West, and the existence of powerful fundamentalist currents make this country a priority on the mullahs' target list. In 1991 and '92, Morocco witnessed bloody confrontations between fundamentalist students and secular groups in the country's universities. Fundamentalist groups trained in Algeria and Sudan played an important role in these clashes. Tehran had high hopes that its embassy in Rabat, opened in spring 1991, gave the Iranian regime a greater opportunity to reach out to the fundamentalists and establish contacts with them, in the same way that links with the fundamentalists in Algeria were made and expanded.

On several occasions, the Moroccan government has warned against fundamentalist threats. During the Casablanca Summit in autumn 1991, the leaders of Tunisia, Morocco, Algeria, Libya, and Mauritania discussed "joint security measures to confront the fundamentalists."[54]

Saudi Arabia and the Persian Gulf States

When 200 armed men forcibly occupied the Great Mosque in Mecca, Islam's holiest spot, at the dawn prayers in November 1979, the world was shocked to see the fundamentalist challenge reach Saudi Arabia. Khomeini supported the fundamentalist raiders, and thus began a long, turbulent relationship between Tehran and Riyadh.

Saudi Arabia's immense wealth and its custody of Islam's holiest shrines made it an ideal target for the mullahs. They have even attacked Saudi Arabia's legitimacy, insisting the country change its name to *Najd and Hijaz*, and calling for the transfer of Mecca and Medina to international control.

Tehran's moves against Saudi Arabia have included smuggling large amounts of explosives and weapons into the country during the hajj pilgrimage. These activities reached their peak during the hajj riots in the holy city of Mecca in 1987. Rafsanjani later said of that incident:

> The martyrs' blood must be avenged by burning the roots of Saudi rulers in the region. The revenge for [the spilling of Iranians'] sacred blood [in Mecca rioting] will be to divest the control of the holy shrines and holy mosques from the

contaminated existence of the Wahhabis, these hooligans, these malignant people. The true revenge is to remove the colossal and precious wealth belonging to the Islamic world which lies under the soil of the Arabian Peninsula from the control of criminals, the agents of colonialism. The Saudi rulers have chosen an evil path, and we will send them to hell.[55]

Tehran is also trying to increase its leverage on Saudi Arabia by increasing its influence in North Africa, especially in Sudan. At the same time, the mullahs are feverishly competing with Saudi Arabia for ideological and political influence in Afghanistan and in the Central Asian republics.

Changes in the political landscape of the Persian Gulf region during and after the Persian Gulf crisis and war have compelled Tehran to tone down its official propaganda against Saudi Arabia, but the mullahs continue to foment trouble among the Shi'ite population of the Saudis' Eastern Province and support the fundamentalist surge in the country that has emerged since the Persian Gulf War. Through a number of proxy organizations based in Qom, the Khomeini regime is training Saudi nationals and returning them to the country. The state-run press occasionally carries the statements or declarations issued by such groups.

In Saudi Arabia itself, the fundamentalist challenge to the authorities has never been so vociferous. In a preemptive measure in January 1992, security forces arrested a large number of preachers and mosque prayer leaders who had accused the government in their sermons of violating the principles and laws of Islam and adopting pro-Western policies. Iranian officials and media strongly condemned these arrests. U.S. officials have expressed concern about the increased circulation of fundamentalist, antigovernment material in Saudi Arabia.[56] In addition, according to Western diplomats, the Saudis were particularly concerned about the increasing Iranian involvement in Saudi Arabia's southern neighbor, Yemen.[57]

When the Saudi government recognized Algeria's new government, a proxy group based in Tehran issued a statement denouncing the Saudi move: "Efforts by the rulers of *Hijaz* [Saudi Arabia] reflect this mercenary client regime's anti-Islamic objectives. Its only impact is to enlighten the Muslims throughout the world of the nature of such regimes."[58]

The Muslim World at Large

The mullahs' priority target areas for export of religious fundamentalism are by no means limited to Central Asia, the Arabian Peninsula, and

North Africa. African countries such as Nigeria, Tanzania, Senegal, and Mauritania, and Asian countries such as Indonesia, Malaysia, the Philippines, and the Indian subcontinent provide fertile ground for the growth of fundamentalist Islam. The mullahs regularly invite delegations of clergymen and preachers from these countries to Tehran to attend political and ideological conferences and ceremonies. In one such ceremony celebrating the 1992 anniversary of the "Islamic Revolution" in Iran, a Nigerian guest, Ibrahim Zakzaki, declared that "the emergence of Islam in Iran is a great triumph for the world's Muslims." Muhammad Kamal Adam, an Ethiopian, said, "Muslims must come to their senses and regain their Islamic thinking. To withstand the Arrogant West's assault and conspiracies, we must implement Islamic decrees and unite the Muslims." Sheikh Ahmad Tijansila, the prayer leader of Freetown, Sierra Leone's capital, stated, "The awakened Muslims will attain their righteous desire of assuming the reins of power." Abu-Bakr Ghailuli, head of the Congo's Islamic Group, said: "Whenever the people of the Congo want to speak about Godly and victorious uprisings, they refer to Iran's Islamic revolution as an example."

To advance their political designs in these countries, from Southern Africa to the Sahara and from the Horn of Africa to the western regions of the continent, Iran's clerics are trying to exploit any act of protest, most of which are the product of worsening economic conditions.

By the same token, Tehran intends to take advantage of the unrest and prevailing conflict in Kashmir. Addressing Western countries, Rafsanjani said, "Whereas you boast of human rights everywhere, why do you brand as terrorist the people of Kashmir who are being so brutally victimized?"[59] In a trip to Muzaffarabad in the Pakistani-controlled Kashmir, Mohsen Rezaii, the Guards Corps commander in chief, announced, "Iranians are prepared to go into battle alongside their brothers in Kashmir."[60]

Ali-Akbar Velayati, the foreign minister, said that India must allow the people of Kashmir to decide on their own future, and Iran cannot remain indifferent to the destiny of that region's Muslims. Khamenei, the regime's leader, stressed that Islamic nations must be aware that Kashmiri Muslims expect to be defended. "If the government of India believes that it can forever keep such large numbers of Muslims under pressure without any reaction by the Muslims in the world, it is undoubtedly mistaken," he said.[61]

An "International Islamic Army"

The existence of such an [international Islamic] army rules out the superpowers' interference in disputes among Muslim countries.

—Guards Corps Major General Mohsen Rezaii,
Commander in Chief of the Islamic Revolutionary Guards Corps,
August 6, 1991[1]

In the first few years of Khomeini's rule, while the doctrine of "export of revolution" was still in its infancy, the implementation of this policy went through different stages, gradually becoming more focused and sophisticated. Eventually, superior resources and the most veteran military commanders were assigned to carry out the policy.

The Revolutionary Guards Corps (also known as the *Pasdaran* [Guardians] of Islamic Revolution) was set up as a paramilitary force in the early months after the overthrow of the shah in 1979. Formed on Khomeini's order and made up largely of zealous supporters of the new theocratic state, the Guards Corps' original mandate was to maintain internal security. From the outset, it unleashed a brutal crackdown on democratic opposition forces, often attacking the rallies and ransacking the offices of political parties whose views were not necessarily in line with those of Khomeini. After the Guard Corps turned a peaceful demonstration of half a million Tehran residents into a bloodbath on June 20, 1981, the Guards Corps arrested tens of thousands of people. In the next few years, they executed 100,000 dissidents. Members of the Guards Corps became notorious for viciously torturing political detainees.

The Guards Corps also played a major role in the eight-year Iran-Iraq War, often using human-wave attacks that took the lives of one million

Iranians. The overwhelming majority were youngsters forcibly dispatched to the war fronts. In addition, the Revolutionary Guards Corps comprised the backbone of the Iranian regime's extraterritorial activities, planning and executing hundreds of terrorist attacks, bombings, hijackings, kidnappings, and assassinations of Iranian and foreign nationals. In a speech in late 1992 Rafsanjani stressed the role of the Guards Corps in helping the regime to stay in power: "The continuous readiness of these [Guards] forces at all times, their discipline, order, and widespread presence to defend the revolution are vital. In its organization, this force must always enjoy sufficient reserve and manpower."[2]

In 1979 the first organ within the Guards Corps responsible for directing terrorist operations and export of fundamentalism abroad was formed, the Liberation Movements Unit. It rapidly began to recruit and train fanatics attracted to Khomeini's ideology in different Muslim countries. The Liberation Movements Unit's primary objective was to establish client Islamic republics in Iraq and Persian Gulf states.

The regime, however, failed in its efforts to overthrow these governments, assassinate their rulers, or carry out "Islamic coups." Some of these countries arrested or expelled Tehran's *agents provocateurs*. Bahrain, for instance, expelled a Shi'ite cleric called Modaressi, while Kuwait forced mullah Mehri to leave the country and go to Iran. Both men were Khomeini's representatives and were incriminated in assassination and coup plots.

Mir-Hussein Moussavi, the mullahs' prime minister in the 1980s, elaborated on Iran's strategy in a 1985 interview: "Immediately after the revolution, we had our own vision of 'exporting revolution,' believing that the Islamic revolution would spread in the region within one year in a chain reaction. It seems, however, that we were mistaken in our initial assessment, which predicted a rapid spread of the revolution." [3]

As the acting commander in chief of the armed forces during the Iran-Iraq War, Rafsanjani reorganized the units and organizations involved in the export of revolution in two ways. First, he merged the Guards Corps Liberation Movements Unit with other groups that had sprung up, eliminating parallel organizations in a bid to streamline the export-of-Islam effort. Second, he strengthened the main units involved in the export of revolution to boost the efficiency and reduce the political independence of their activities.

Henceforth, the role of the Guards Corps' Intelligence Directorate increased and several new units were formed, including the Lebanon

Corps, the Ramadhan Headquarters (in charge of Iraqi affairs), and the Ansar Headquarters (in charge of Afghanistan, Pakistan, and Indian affairs.) Simultaneously, the regime drastically reduced the role of such organizations as the Martyrs Foundation and the Islamic Propaganda Organization, which had previously enjoyed some degree of autonomy in the export of revolution. The organizations' overseas operations were placed under the Guards Corps' supervision. Since the reorganization, the Guards Corps and three ministries—Foreign Affairs, Islamic Culture and Guidance, and Intelligence—have played key roles in the export of revolution.

Ministry of Foreign Affairs

Senior Iranian officials have repeatedly stressed in their public statements that "the Islamic Republic's diplomats must be devout Hizbullahis," that is, they must be dedicated to the spread of Islamic fundamentalism.[4] This requirement gives an important role to the Foreign Ministry and its diplomats in the export of revolution. A glance at the list of Tehran's Foreign Ministry officials and ambassadors and their past records reveals that this ministry is in fact a political-terrorist organ, and conventional diplomatic activities constitute only a part of its undertakings.

Hussein Sheikh ol-Islam, the deputy foreign minister for Arab and African Affairs; Muhammad-Hussein Mala'ek, the former ambassador to Switzerland; and Mehdi Ahari-Mostafavi, one of the ministry's director generals and the former ambassador to Germany, were among the leaders of the Students Following the Imam's Line. Closely linked to the Guards Corps, they played an active role in the 444-day seizure of the U.S. Embassy compound in Tehran. Hadi Najafabadi and Sirous Nasseri, the regime's ambassadors to Saudi Arabia and the European Headquarters of the United Nations, have had strong ties to the Guards Corps for many years. They were directly involved in the April 1990 assassination in Geneva of Kazem Rajavi, a leading critic of Tehran's human rights violations and the representative of the National Council of Resistance of Iran in Switzerland.

Manouchehr Mottaki, deputy foreign minister for international affairs, was a member of the Guards Corps before joining the diplomatic service. During his tenure as the regime's ambassador in Ankara, Mottaki was involved in at least two assassination attempts against the Mojahedin. Following protests by Turkish authorities, he was recalled to Tehran.

Kamal Kharrazi, the mullahs' permanent representative at the United Nations headquarters in New York, was one of the founders of the Guards Corps in 1979. For years, he was among the top decision makers pushing the regime's aggressive policies. Muhammad-Reza Baqeri, who replaced Mottaki as the ambassador to Turkey, was a member of the Guards Corps Intelligence Unit. Muhammad-Mehdi Akhundzadeh-Basti, Tehran's former charge d'affaires in London and the director general of international organizations at the Ministry of Foreign Affairs, was also previously active in the Guards Corps contingent in Gilan Province.

The tasks of the Ministry of Foreign Affairs have been defined by Iranian authorities as follows:

> Noting in particular the far-reaching and enormous objectives of the Islamic Republic with regards to the export of revolution and the liberation movements, social groups and even ordinary citizens, the Ministry of Foreign Affairs must adopt guidelines needed to coordinate the activities of different organs involved in the field of foreign policy.[5]

All political, propaganda, and subversive activities in any given country are carried out with the prior knowledge of the regime's embassy in that country and with the approval of the Ministry of Foreign Affairs. Exceptions to this rule need the approval of the Supreme National Security Council.

In Islamic countries, the regime's embassies have the additional task of establishing ties with indigenous fundamentalist Islamic forces. They provide these forces with pro-Iranian propaganda and gradually sustain them with financial support. After initial recruitment, these forces are sent to Iran for military training. Over the years, the mullahs' embassies have thoroughly implemented such a policy in Algeria, Sudan, Tunisia, Turkey, and above all, Lebanon. In 1988, Tunisia announced that it was severing ties with the Tehran regime because of the Iranian embassy's efforts to contact Tunisian fundamentalists and provide them with ideological indoctrination, training, and financial support.

Appraising Iran's activities abroad, the Supreme National Security Council concluded in the post–Persian Gulf War period that the policy of export of revolution was far less successful in countries where Iran had no embassy. A diplomatic delegation that had visited Jordan a few months prior to the opening of the regime's embassy in Amman concluded in a classified report: "There is much sympathy for our revolution in this country; we should open an embassy there and become active as soon as possible. We must compensate for the ten-year delay."[6]

The Foreign Ministry's Third and Fourth Political Bureaus attached to the Directorate for Arab and African Affairs are especially active in export of revolution. These bureaus are run by mullah Muhammad-Kazem Khansari, who has a long record in terrorist activities. Several key people work under Khansari's supervision:

■ Mahmoud Hashemi, Rafsanjani's younger brother and the head of the Third Political Bureau. He is also in charge of issues related to the Muslim Brotherhood.

■ Muhammad-Mehdi Pour-Muhammadi, head of the Fourth Political Bureau and in charge of the Algeria, Tunisia, Morocco, Libya, and Sudan desk. Muhammadi had spent time in Lebanon and was counselor at the Iranian Embassy in Syria in 1990.

In autumn 1991, the Ministry of Foreign Affairs established independent bureaus for the Central Asian republics, increasing its activities to facilitate the export of the Islamic revolution to those republics.

Ministry of Islamic Culture and Guidance

All official Iranian cultural centers abroad are affiliated with the Ministry of Islamic Culture and Guidance. In the mullahs' lexicon, cultural activity means laying the groundwork and recruiting agents for the export of Khomeiniism.

Muhammad Khatami, the minister of Islamic culture and guidance, was a major policy maker and a staunch advocate of the policy of "expansion of the Islamic Revolution" before being ousted for being "too liberal." Through Muhammad-Ali Taskhiri, a senior official at Khamenei's office, Khatami informed the regime's leader of the extraterritorial activities of the Ministry of Islamic Culture and Guidance. These activities are carried out under the supervision of the Ministry's International Directorate, headed by mullah Muhammad-Ali Abtahi. Sa'idi is the official in charge of the Arab Affairs Directorate.

The ministry's main task is to create places such as cultural centers or libraries where it will be easy for Tehran's agents to contact local sympathizers. Once contacted, recruited, and given basic indoctrination, local fundamentalists are sent to Iran or Lebanon for more training.

Pakistan offers a good example of the activities of Iran's cultural centers abroad. In December 1990, Sadeq Ganji, head of the Iran-Pakistan Cultural Center, was killed in a clash with Pakistanis. Investi-

101

gators said the killing was motivated by acts of sedition conducted by Ganji under the guise of cultural activities. Another member of the Cultural Center, who had been also shot, said: "Sadeq Ganji had turned the Cultural Center into a place for propagating revolutionary and Islamic culture. . . . He had greatly intimidated the Wahhabis, who are dependent on the Saudis and the Arrogant West. He was in close contact with all activist Shi'ite Islamic groups and had recently increased his links with their leaders."[7]

Ministry of Intelligence

Since its establishment some ten years ago, *Vezarat-e-Ettela'at* (the Ministry of Intelligence) has rapidly grown into one of the largest government institutions. Rafsanjani systematically oversees the ministry's operations through Ali Fallahian, the intelligence minister. A large number of the regime's assassination squads are affiliated with this ministry. The Intelligence Ministry also dispatches its special intelligence teams to various countries to reconnoiter the activities of the opposition, especially the Mojahedin, for the mullahs. In its routine contacts, the ministry offers intelligence assistance to help the Guards Corps carry out its special operations.

The intelligence minister, Fallahian, openly boasted of murdering the regime's opponents abroad in a press conference in August: "We track them [opposition groups] outside the country, too. We have them under surveillance. . . . We have succeeded in dealing blows to many of these grouplets outside the country and at the borders. . . . Last year, we succeeded in striking fundamental blows to their top members."[8]

The Qods Force

The Guards Corps' Special Qods (Jerusalem) Force is the most secret of the Iranian regime's numerous military organizations. Since its inception in 1990, the clerics have kept it under such secrecy that even many top officials in Tehran know nothing about the "Qods Force" except the name of its commander, Ahmad Vahidi. The new force, referred to as the "seed of the International Islamic Army" by its commanders, has now turned into the Guards Corps' most active, skilled, and elite unit. It includes the Corps' most experienced commanding officers and personnel. Its task is defined as "commanding, planning, and executing extraterritorial operations of the Islamic Revolutionary Guards Corps."[9] Its commander directly reports to the regime's leader, Khamenei. The Qods

Force directly supervises or at least coordinates all terrorist operations or activities related to the "export of the Islamic Revolution" to various countries. The Qods Force was established following a detailed appraisal by Iranian leaders of their extensive terrorist activities in the 1980s.

Prior to the formation of the Qods Force, the Guards Corps consisted of the army, the navy, the air force, and the *Bassij* (paramilitary urban security unit). Formed as an independent body, the Qods Force was placed under the command of the Guards Corps Central Headquarters. The Qods force commander, Vahidi, is a Guards Corps brigadier general and was formerly the commander of the Intelligence Directorate (a key department at the Guards Corps Central Headquarters). Once the Qods Force was formed, the Ramadhan and Ansar headquarters and the Lebanon Corps were placed under Vahidi's command. Despite numerous changes in the Guards Corps in recent years, Vahidi's position has remained unchanged. (See Appendix.)

Final coordination of the Qods Force's activities in a given country and provision of the appropriate diplomatic or other cover for its agents, the use of diplomatic facilities and immunities to get supplies and messages, and provision of arms and military equipment for terrorists fall within the responsibilities of the Ministry of Foreign Affairs and its embassies. The regime's embassies also gather detailed information on the activities of opposition groups and personalities. The Ministry of Foreign Affairs passes on the information to the Qods Force.

Organizational Structure

The most experienced Guards Corps commanders, particularly those active in extraterritorial operations, have been gathered in the General Staff of the Qods Force. In fact, there are no essential differences between members of the Qods Force Staff and the G.C. General Staff. The commanders of Intelligence, Operations, and Training directorates, for instance, are among the Qods Force's key commanders. Commander of the Qods Operations Directorate is G.C. Brigadier General Hussein Moslehi, the ex-commander of the Lebanon Corps. It was under his command that the U.S. Marine barracks in Beirut was blown up in 1983. Upon returning from Lebanon, Moslehi assumed command of the 1st Sarollah Corps, the G.C.'s most experienced and largest force in the Iran-Iraq War. The 1st Corps was made up of the Muhammad Rasulullah, Seyyed osh-Shohada, and Ali ibn Abi Talib divisions, which spearheaded the Khomeini regime's offensives in the Iran-Iraq War.

The commander of the Qods Force's Intelligence Directorate, Guards Corps Brigadier General Muhammad-Ja'far Sahraroudi, was previously the commander of Ramadhan Headquarters. He was the field commander involved in the assassination of Abdul-Rahman Qassemlou in Vienna in the summer of 1989 (see Chapter X). Carrying a fake passport with the name of Rahimi, Sahraroudi was arrested by the Austrian police. Following the regime's intervention, however, the Austrian government sent him to Tehran.

The commander of the Training Directorate is Guards Corps Brigadier General Shams. He was the ex-commander of a G.C. base in northwest Iran, subordinate to Ramadhan Headquarters. Subsequently, he headed the 9th Badr Division, comprising Iraqi POWs and nationals who joined the Iranian regime's forces. Shams commanded the regime's forces sent into Iraq in the aftermath of the Persian Gulf War. After the unrest in southern Iraq subsided, Shams became the commander of operations in northern Iraq. His deputy, Orouj, commands the Imam Ali training garrison in Tehran. Before his appointment to this post, Orouj was the commander of the Guards Corps Special Security Corps and in charge of Khamenei's bodyguard unit.

Another major section of the Qods Force is its Directorate of Finance, headed by Talebi. Because of the Qods Force's extraterritorial activities, the Directorate has been divided into two sections, one of which makes the financial arrangements for the forces sent abroad. Other key officers of the Qods Force include Manshavi, the head of the Commandant's Office, and Ahmad Salek, Khamenei's representative to the Force. Before the inception of the Qods Force, Manshavi commanded the extraterritorial forces of the G.C. General Staff. He also commanded the Sudanese nationals trained in Iran. Before being transferred to the Qods Force, mullah Salek was the commander in chief of the Islamic Revolutionary Komitehs, which later merged with the national police to form the State Security Forces. Salek is also the director of the Bureau of Islamic Movements in the Ministry of Foreign Affairs, a majlis deputy, and a member of the Assembly of Experts. He has played an instrumental role in the regime's terrorist actions abroad since 1979. He was also a key figure in the post–Persian Gulf War disturbances in Iraq. Salek attends a meeting with Khamenei every Tuesday.

In addition to the military staff, the Qods Force has a politically oriented staff called the General Staff for the Export of Revolution that handles the export of fundamentalism and terrorism to different countries. Specific assignments are surveyed and parceled out to different directorates of the Qods Force, including the directorates for:

1. Iraq
2. Palestine, Lebanon, and Jordan
3. Turkey
4. Afghanistan, Pakistan, and the Indian subcontinent
5. Western countries (Europe, United States)
6. North Africa (Egypt, Tunisia, Algeria, Sudan, and Morocco)
7. Arabian Peninsula
8. Republics of the former Soviet Union

According to a Qods Force official, the General Staff for the Export of Revolution was formed with the objective of "removing a fundamental weakness" of the regime's past policy of exporting of revolution. As he put it: "Despite our prior extensive military activities in these countries, the absence of a clear political superstructure did not allow us to reap the maximum benefit from these activities. Now, we are striving to have our own political groups or alternatives in each of these countries, so that our work will bear results."[10]

Each directorate of the General Staff for the Export of Revolution is responsible for establishing political ties with individuals and forces within the country under its jurisdiction to lure them to Khomeini's ideology. For instance, there have been large-scale efforts to forge relations with factions of the Muslim Brotherhood or other religious forces in the Arab countries. Meanwhile, the General Staff for the Export of Revolution has also been active against the regime's opponents. A close confidant of Rafsanjani describes these activities:

> The issue of the Mojahedin concerns the Qods Force. The Qods Force has different directorates for different countries. For example, there are directorates for Turkey, Iraq, Afghanistan, etc. If the Iranian nationals—the Mojahedin, the counter-revolutionaries, and so on—engage in some kind of activity against the Islamic Republic, these directorates handle their cases and make the appropriate decisions.[11]

Affiliated Units

The Qods Force has several command headquarters and bases across Iran where both Iranians and foreign nationals are recruited and trained before being sent abroad. The Qods Force's major training centers include the Imam Ali University, Shahid Kazemi, Beheshti, and Vali-e-asr garrisons. The Force also has special operational units stationed in safe houses in Tehran. They are subjected to rigid intelligence and security restrictions. This is to limit intelligence leaks on other members as well as on the objectives of the special units should any of them be captured in the target country.

The following Guard Corps units are under the command of the Qods Force: The 1st Corps (Ramadhan Headquarters), based in Kermanshah (western Iran); the 2nd (Lebanon) Corps; the 3rd (Hamzeh) Corps, based near Oroumieh, northwestern Iran; the 4th (Ansar) Corps, based in Mashad, northeastern Iran; Corps 5,000; Corps 6,000 (Africa Corps); the 7th Corps; the 8th Corps; and the 9th Badr Corps.

1st Corps, or Ramadhan Headquarters

The 1st Corps began its operations during the Iran-Iraq War and is charged with organizing and providing training and logistics for Kurdish and other small Iraqi groups, as well as gathering operational intelligence. Given its assignments, the organization of this Corps is different from any other G.C. headquarters. The 1st Corps carries out its tasks through five operational bases along the Iran-Iraq border and several tactical bases and posts at various sections of the northwestern, western, and southern fronts: Nasr Garrison in Naqadeh, Fatah Garrison in Sardasht, and Ra'd Garrison in Marivan in Iran's northwest; Zafar Garrison in Sarpol-Zahab in the west; and Fajr Garrison in Zaytoun Mahaleh in Ahwaz in the southwest.

Each of these garrisons has several affiliate command posts. For instance, the Nasr Garrison in Naqadeh has command posts in Piranshahr, Oshnavieh, Badinabad, and Ziveh. It also operates tactical posts in Galirash, Irbil, and Dohuk within Iraq. The 1st Corps' training centers are located in Sabetkhah Training Camp in Gilan-e-Gharb (west) and Ghayour Training Camp in Ahwaz (southwest). When necessary, this Corps coordinates with other bases to use their training camps. Among them are Montazeri Garrison in Kermanshah, Qods Training Camp in Hamedan, and Khatam ol-Anbia Training Camp in Tehran.

In 1991 and 1992, the 1st Corps devoted enormous energy to the assassination of Massoud Rajavi. It was also responsible for a car bomb outside the Sheraton Hotel in Baghdad in January 1992.

2nd (Lebanon) Corps

The command headquarters of the 2nd (Lebanon) Corps is in Damascus, and its forces are stationed in Lebanon's Bekaa Valley. Its main task in Tehran is to provide the Corps in Lebanon with adequate manpower and logistical support. Except for a limited number of permanent personnel, the core of the 2nd Corps' units are changed every three months.

3rd (Hamzeh) Corps

The Hamzeh Headquarters is under the direct supervision of the Guards Corps General Staff. It commands the Qods Force's logistics in northern Iraq and Turkey. The 3rd Corps also provides logistical support for the regime's forces in Turkey and northern Iraq that are connected with the Corps 5,000 (see below), as well as to the 1st Corps (Ramadhan Headquarters).

The 3rd Corps is commanded by G.C. Brigadier General Kamal Hedayat, who works under G. C. Commander in Chief Mohsen Rezaii. The 3rd Corps' activities in Turkey are reported to Ahmad Vahidi. The Golkhaneh Training Center in Oroumieh (northwest) is one of the 3rd Corps' training centers.

One of the most recent operations the 3rd Corps carried out in coordination with the Corps 5,000 was the assassination of a foreign diplomat in Ankara in March 1992. Javad Tale'i, a Qods Force Commander, directed this operation. Prior to the operation, a Tehran daily had warned Turkey that terrorist groups affiliated with the mullahs' regime would launch subversive operations against Ankara. "Iran must respond appropriately to the confiscation [of the Cape Males cargo ship carrying weapons for the mullahs' regime.] If that entails an eye for an eye, so be it," the daily said.[12]

4th (Ansar) Corps

The 4th Corps previously operated in the framework of the Ansar Headquarters and was charged with the Guards Corps activities in Afghanistan and Pakistan. After the Qods Force was formed, the 8th Samen ol-A'emmeh Corps was strengthened, reorganized, and renamed the 4th Ansar Corps, commanded by G.C. Brigadier General Isma'il Qa'ani, former commander of the G.C. 8th Corps.

The 4th Ansar Corps' main task has been to organize and provide logistics for the Shi'ite Afghan groups residing in Iran. It has also trained and dispatched terrorist squads to Pakistan to assassinate Iranian refugees and Mojahedin activists. Examples include the extensive attacks on the Mojahedin residences in Karachi and Quetta in July 1987. To carry out these tasks, the Ansar Corps has set up bases in Taibad, Zahedan, Zabol, and Birjand along Iran's eastern borders. Forces that are dispatched to Afghanistan, Pakistan, Kashmir, and India depart from these bases.

The disintegration of the former Soviet Union and the subsequent fall of the communist regime in Afghanistan suddenly placed great demands on the 4th Ansar Corps. New manpower and budget were infused into the Corps. Central Asia became its highest priority for export of revolution, dispatch of Islamic missionaries, and establishment of direct contacts with fundamentalist groups in the republics.

On February 11, 1992, five members of the Qods Force were arrested by Turkmen border guards while trying to enter the country illegally. They were armed with automatic rifles and grenades and planned to enter Turkmenistan via the Sarakhs border region. The 4th Ansar Corps has also set up a base in the border town of Maku to infiltrate its forces into the Azerbaijan Republic.

Corps 5,000

Corps 5,000 is more limited in numbers than other parts of the Qods Force, but it consists of highly experienced assassination and bombing squads. Their members are chiefly stationed in clandestine safe houses in Tehran and foreign countries. Their contacts are secret and their essential task is to put into action special operations in the target regions, especially Western countries, including Turkey. Foreign nationals are also members of this Corps. Corps 5,000 is responsible for all of Tehran's terrorist activities in Turkey. Receiving logistical support from the 3rd (Hamzeh) Corps, Corps 5,000 has its own independent bases in Iran's western frontier, including its operational headquarters located in Oroumieh, capital of the northwestern province of West-Azerbaijan. The Corps' central command is on Tehran's Pasdaran Street, near the Ministry of Intelligence.

Corps 5,000 planned and executed the regime's biggest terrorist operation in Turkey in the first half of 1992, against the People's Mojahedin Organization. On June 4, terrorist units kidnapped Ali-Akbar Ghorbani, a Mojahedin member, in the Shishli district of Istanbul. Ghorbani's mutilated body was found by the Turkish police on January

31 in Cinarcik, a suburb forty-five kilometers southeast of Istanbul. Interrogation of terrorists arrested for the car-bomb murder of Ugur Mumcu, a Turkish journalist, a few days earlier led to the discovery of Ghorbani's body. Before murdering him, the mullahs' terrorists had severely tortured him, pulling out his fingernails and slashing his genitals.[13] The Corps 5,000 also planted two 50-kilogram bombs in two Mojahedin cars on June 5. The subsequent explosions inflicted heavy damage to the neighboring areas.

The forces of the Malek Ashtar Brigade were transferred to Corps 5,000 after the Qods Force was formed. This brigade previously belonged to the Ramadhan Headquarters and took part in irregular warfare inside Iraq. The Malek Ashtar forces also held positions for some time at the Iran-Iraq southern front. After being incorporated into the Qods Force, this unit was organized in safe houses in Tehran. They were directly involved in the April 1990 assassination of Kazem Rajavi in Geneva.

Corps 5,000 has also sent assassination squads to Britain, Japan, Italy, Switzerland, Germany, and elsewhere. The Corps' operations include the murder of the Japanese translator of the *Satanic Verses* and an assassination attempt on the life of its Italian translator in summer 1991. It also assassinated Shapour Bakhtiar, the shah's last prime minister, in France in August 1991 in coordination with the 2nd (Lebanon) Corps. Corps 5,000 operational officers were also involved in the explosion of the Pan Am flight over Lockerbie, Scotland, as well as the March 1992 explosion at the Israeli Embassy in Buenos Aires.

A senior official of the mullahs' regime commented on the role of the Qods Force and its Corps 5,000 in assassinations abroad:

> The Qods Force does not operate in partisan methods. Neither does it get involved in the destruction of a garrison, a petrochemical base, or a bridge. Nor does it have a military target. The Qods Force wants its men to carry out operations abroad and return to the country, or reconnoiter individuals as subjects for operations by the special forces. These are the tasks of the Qods Force's Corps 5,000 and 6,000. That is what they do, and they are presently training their men for such purposes. A number of these people are stationed at the Guards Corps General Staff, and some of them have been distributed in Shahid Kazemi building, Imam Ali Garrison in north Tehran, and across the capital. They do not have any specific place. Some stay in houses we have rented for them in Tehran.... These operational units include expatriates from Islamic countries, like Lebanon and Syria.[14]

Corps 6,000

Corps 6,000 is entrusted with the task of exporting fundamentalism to African countries, with the Arab countries of North Africa enjoying top priority. The embassies and cultural centers affiliated with the Ministry of Islamic Culture and Guidance recruit the ideal individuals in each country. They are subsequently sent to Tehran to undergo political-ideological and military training. They thus acquire adequate preparations to implement their missions, including formation of resistance groups or carrying out terrorist acts, in their respective countries.

Sudan has been turned into the Qods Force's Headquarters in North Africa. The Force is currently centered in the Shambat and Koravi regions and is setting up more camps at the cost of $20 million. The instructional staff comes from the Force's Tehran headquarters. The commander of the base, Majid Kamal, spent the 1980s in Lebanon's Bekaa Valley, helping to organize the Hizbullah in Lebanon. The recruits trained in these bases come from North Africa (Tunisia, Morocco, Egypt, and Algeria), but there are some also from Saudi Arabia and other Arab countries. After receiving theoretical and practical training the recruits are taken to southern Sudan for real combat.

9th Badr Corps

The 9th Badr Corps, made up largely of Iraqi POWs, works closely with the 1st Corps (Ramadhan Headquarters) in training for activities inside Iraq's territory.

Training

The commander of the Training Directorate is G.C. Brigadier General Shams, whose deputy is Orouj. The Imam Ali University is the Qods Force's main training center. Located north of the former Sa'dabad Palace in northern Tehran (the headquarters for the shah's Imperial Guard Division), it serves as a terrorist training center for non-Iranian mercenaries. Courses in politics, ideology, demolition, explosives, shooting from a mobile position, weapons training, ambush and counter-ambush, pursuit and surveillance, fitness, and hand-to-hand combat are taught there.

Most of the instructors at the university have had a long record in extraterritorial operations. Orouj and Shams also offer instruction themselves. In cooperation with the Ministry of Foreign Affairs, the garrison's personnel department makes travel arrangements for expatriates due to arrive at the university for training. Kuwaiti nationals reportedly received training in the university's April–June 1991 term, and the recruits for the next term were from Kashmir. In a confidential report to the Qods Command in the wake of the assassination of Bakhtiar, an official of this university wrote: "Should we strengthen such training, it will provide us with suitable leverage around the world."[15]

The Qods Force also operates a college in Qom called *Beit ol-Moqaddas*. It is also known as the *Melal* (Nations) Training Center, because recruits come from different countries. The college offers ideological instructions which are quite different from the traditional teachings at Qom's seminaries. Eighteen Turkish nationals arrested for the car bomb murder of Turkish journalist Ugur Mumcu in Ankara in January 1993 told investigators that they had received training at this center.[16] Khatam and Qa'em centers operate under the jurisdiction of this college. The Khatam Center is in charge of identifying and recruiting forces abroad and the Qa'em Center handles the instructions.

The Beit ol-Moqaddas college offers a six-month curriculum. More than 100 Lebanese, a large number of Iraqis and Turkish nationals, and about 70 Afghan Shi'ites, as well as the 9th Badr Corps' battalion and more senior commanders, have taken the Qa'em training courses. Other instructional garrisons include Beheshti and Vali-e-asr garrisons in Tehran. Their training periods are from three to nine months.

X

Terrorism: Iran's Foreign Policy Instrument

If for every Palestinian martyred by Israeli mercenaries, five American or French citizens are murdered, they would no longer commit such crimes. . . . The Palestinians might say, In that case the world will call us terrorists. I say, however, do they not label you already?

—Hashemi-Rafsanjani, May 6, 1989[1]

Terrorism has been one of the primary tools of the mullahs' regime to spread fundamentalism and expand Iran's influence.

Most of the images that have come to symbolize terrorism over the past decade are tied closely to the Tehran regime's mercenaries: The 1986 street bombings in Paris, the corpse of an "executed" passenger thrown from a hijacked Kuwaiti plane in Cyprus, and the grim video-taped faces of hostages appealing to their governments.

Although not new to the past decade, terrorism has acquired qualitatively different dimensions since Khomeini and his Islamic fundamentalist government came to power in 1979. Indeed, today, Khomeini and his heirs can be considered the godfathers of terrorism.

Hallmarks of Terrorism

1. *State-sponsored terrorism.* Because terrorism has been one of the main instruments to advance the mullahs' foreign policy, decisions about terrorist operations have always been made at the highest levels of the

regime. Before he died, all decisions were made by Khomeini, who enjoyed the active advice of Khamenei, Rafsanjani, and other leaders.

In his letter of resignation to Khamenei in September 1988, Prime Minister Mir-Hussein Moussavi unequivocally stated that many terrorist activities were planned and carried out at the order of the highest echelons of the government and without his knowledge.[2] After surrendering to the French Police, a Tunisian national by the name of Lutfi, one of the Iranian regime's terrorist operatives in France, revealed that the 1986 bombings in France had been suggested to Khomeini by Ali Khamenei, the president at the time; Hashemi-Rafsanjani, then the majlis speaker; Mohsen Rafiqdoust, the head of the Foundation of the Deprived (at the time the minister of the Revolutionary Guards Corps); and Muhammad Muhammadi-Rayshahri, the then intelligence minister.[3] The bombings of shops and a café killed twelve people and wounded scores more.

When Khomeini was alive, Rafsanjani acted as the coordinator of the ministries of Foreign Affairs, Intelligence, Islamic Culture and Guidance, and the Guards Corps' units involved in terrorist activities. After Khomeini's death, Rafsanjani, as the country's president and the chairman of the Supreme National Security Council, has continued to make the final decisions on terrorist plans.

During the mullahs' fourteen-year rule, unlimited financial resources have been devoted to exporting terrorism. Tehran has also formed specific terrorist organs and institutions, and—as noted in Chapter IX—the Ministry of Foreign Affairs has played a key role in sponsoring terrorist activities.[4]

2. *Religious fanaticism.* The Tehran mullahs also exploit religion to legitimize acts of terror by calling them divine duties. The mullahs promise the perpetrators of such actions "a place in heaven." This religious factor generates intense hatred and catastrophic results. Some of the most devastating blows have been delivered through suicide missions. Shedding the blood of innocent people and ordinary citizens is easily justified as "a necessary price." In many cases, public places have been bombed at random—victimizing civilians and even children—merely to create fear. The fundamentalists' targets are determined by Tehran's political and propaganda interests.

3. *Handpicked targets.* The Iranian-sponsored terrorism has targeted a wide spectrum of victims during the past decade.

4. *Hostage taking.* The 444-day occupation of the United States

Embassy in Tehran, beginning on November 4, 1979, marked the start of the newly established clerical regime's experimentation with terrorism and provided a glimpse of what was yet to come.

In 1986, when the departure of an Iranian cargo ship from an Italian port was delayed for a few days because an Iranian sailor had requested political asylum, Tehran retaliated by preventing Italian nationals, including diplomats, from leaving Iran. Rafsanjani had this to say about the incident: "They delayed our ship. We spoke with them with humane language. It was to no avail. Yesterday we ordered several Italians not to leave Iran. [The authorities] returned them from the airport."[5]

In March 1992, when relations between Berne and Tehran soured over the arrest of a top Iranian terrorist in Switzerland, a Swiss businessman disappeared in Tehran without any trace. Several days later, it became clear that the Swiss national had been taken hostage.

The tragic saga of the Western hostages held captive by Tehran's proxies in Lebanon was the very essence of Iranian-sponsored terrorism. In the words of Rafsanjani, "If the oppressed people of Lebanon do not take hostages, then what else can they do?"[6] Rafsanjani tried to delay the hostages' release to gain the maximum concessions. Sheikh Muhammad-Hussein Fadhlullah, a Hizbullah leader, acknowledged in March 1991 that holding the Western hostages had become a liability: "If it were left to us, we would release them this very day. But Rafsanjani believes that the Americans are not yet ready to step forward and accept Iran's demands."[7] Consequently, Tehran agreed to the freedom of the Western hostages only when the region's political landscape had been totally reshaped in the aftermath of the Persian Gulf War.

5. *Hijacking.* Another method often employed by the mullahs' regime in recent years has been the hijacking of passenger airliners. In August 1983, an Air France Boeing 737 was commandeered as it left Vienna and forced to go to Tehran. Its cockpit was blown up on the tarmac of Mehrabad Airport by the hijackers. In June 1985, a TWA Boeing 727 was hijacked while en route to Rome from Athens. An American navy diver was murdered while the plane was parked on the tarmac of Beirut Airport. An Air Afrique DC–10 airliner was hijacked in July 1987 by Iranian-backed terrorists who killed a French passenger at the Geneva Airport. The Swiss president revealed in an interview at the time that the government of Iran was responsible for the affair. On April 5, 1988, a Kuwaiti airliner 747 jumbo jet was hijacked in Bangkok and forced to land in the northeastern Iranian city of Mashad. A leading Lebanese

terrorist boarded the plane to control the operation. After fifteen days, the episode ended in Algiers, but not before two passengers were murdered by the terrorists.

6. *Bombings in public places.* In September 1986 a wave of bombings shook Paris. Fuad Ali Saleh, accused of killing twelve people and injuring hundreds in these incidents, was arrested while carrying explosives into a car in Paris in March 1987. A student of theology in Qom, Saleh confessed that he had been commissioned by Tehran. Bomb blasts in two beach-side restaurants in Kuwait City in 1985 left ten people dead and eighty wounded. During the 1989 hajj in Mecca, three bombs went off around the Grand Mosque, injuring scores of pilgrims. Terrorist agents who claimed responsibility for the explosions were captured and stated in their confessions several months later that they had been trained by the Iranian regime. In August 1986, a number of Iranian diplomat-terrorists were arrested in Jiddah Airport carrying large quantities of explosives.[8]

7. *Suicide missions, car and truck bombs.* In April 1983, a bomb-laden truck exploded in front of the American Embassy in Beirut, killing 61 and wounding 120 persons. The Emir of Kuwait was wounded in a suicide attack on his motorcade in May 1985 that was linked to Iran. Car bombs were used to assassinate Saudi diplomats in Turkey and Thailand. In March 1992, a powerful bomb exploded in the Argentine capital, Buenos Aires, destroying the Israeli Embassy.[9] Two months later, a senior official at the U.S. State Department said, "The United States has uncovered strong indications that Iranian diplomats helped plan the March 17 bombing."[10] According to these reports, several other foreign embassies in Latin American countries had been identified for similar terrorist attacks.

Rafsanjani and other senior Iranian officials have repeatedly and officially accepted the responsibility for terrorist actions by their operatives in Lebanon and elsewhere. Three years after the explosion of the U.S. Marine barracks near Beirut, Rafsanjani said, "They hold us accountable for the blow the Americans received and the humiliation they suffered in Lebanon. We are indeed responsible [for it.]"[11] Brigadier General Mohsen Rafiqdoust, the former Guards Corps minister and Rafsanjani's brother-in-law, stated, "Both the TNT and the ideology which in one blast sent to hell 400 officers, NCOs, and soldiers at the Marine Headquarters had been provided by Iran."[12]

8. *Assassinations of foreign nationals and Iranian oppositionists.* The most

publicized example of the mullahs' terrorism against foreign nationals was Khomeini's decree in 1989 ordering the execution of the Indian-born British author, Salman Rushdie. Despite a wave of international condemnation and appeals to annul the decree, Rafsanjani and other high-ranking officials have stressed its irrevocability. In reply to a question on the subject, Rafsanjani said:

> The fact that the entire power of the Arrogant West is defeated in relation to a blasphemous book provides a clear path to materialize the Imam's [Khomeini's] thoughts. The Imam's decree on the execution of Salman Rushdie is the decree of Islam; it remains in force and will be subject to no changes.[13]

In November 1992, mullah Hassan Sane'i, a top cleric and the head of the state-run Panzdah Khordad Foundation, issued a statement, confirming an increase in the $2 million reward for killing Salman Rushdie.[14] In a January 31, 1993, press conference in Tehran, Rafsanjani told foreign journalists, "Nothing can change this [the verdict] because, the leader [Khomeini] is dead, . . ."[15] The following month, Khamenei added, "The Imam [Khomeini] fired an arrow toward this brazen apostate. The arrow has left the bow and is moving toward its target and will sooner or later strike it. This sentence must definitely be carried out and it will be carried out."[16]

In addition, the mullahs' terrorists have so far set several libraries and bookstores on fire for carrying Rushdie's book. They also wounded the Italian translator of the book and murdered its Japanese translator.

In March 1990, a famous Turkish journalist working for the daily *Hurriyet* and his driver were shot and killed in Istanbul.[17] According to *Hurriyet*, the police concluded that the murderers had received their orders from Iran. An Iranian diplomat named Aqiqi, who is also a member of the Intelligence Ministry, was involved in the murder. He is now working at the Iranian Embassy in Vienna. On January 15, 1992, Mustapha Geha, a Shi'ite Lebanese author who had written anti-Khomeini commentaries in Beirut's newspapers, was murdered in the Sabtiyeh district of Beirut.[18]

On January 24, 1993, Ugur Mumcu, a renowned Turkish journalist, was killed as a powerful bomb exploded in the car he was driving in Istanbul. He was a staunch critic of the mullahs' fundamentalism. In a related development, a prominent Turkish industrialist escaped assassination on January 27, when his bodyguards exchanged gunfire with four armed men who stopped his car as he was driving to work.[19]

The clearest evidence of the terrorist nature of the mullahs' regime, however, is its extensive and vigorous campaign to assassinate its Iranian opponents abroad. A glance at the list of such victims indicates that during Rafsanjani's first four years as president, and despite his "moderate" reputation, the number of Iranian dissidents murdered by Tehran's terrorist squads exceeded the number of those assassinated during Khomeini's rule. (See Appendix.)

The most notable of these assassinations was the murder of Professor Kazem Rajavi, the elder brother of the Iranian Resistance's leader, Massoud Rajavi. Ordered by Rafsanjani, it required enormous resources, extensive planning, and coordination among several of the regime's organizations. On April 24, 1990, a terrorist squad killed Rajavi, the representative of the National Council of Resistance of Iran to the United Nations and Switzerland, near his home in a Geneva suburb. Because of his international endeavors to defend human rights in Iran, Rajavi was a distinguished personality. Sirous Nasseri, Tehran's ambassador to the United Nations Office in Geneva, on two occasions personally threatened to murder him. After extensive investigations, Roland Chatelain, the Swiss magistrate in charge of the case, and Swiss judicial and police officials confirmed the role of Rafsanjani's government and the participation of thirteen official agents of the Iranian regime who had used "service passports" to enter Switzerland for their plot.[20]

On July 13, 1989, Abdul-Rahman Qassemlou, the secretary general of the Democratic Party of Iranian Kurdistan; Abdullah Qaderi, a member of the Party's Central Committee; and a Kurdish middleman were gunned down by a team from the Revolutionary Guards Corps who were negotiating with them in Vienna on behalf of the mullahs' regime. The person commanding the attack was Muhammad-Ja'far Sahraroudi, chief of the Intelligence Directorate of the Guard Corps Qods Force.[21] Police arrested Sahraroudi, who had gone to Austria under the assumed name of Rahimi, but released him quickly, enabling him to return to Iran at once. On August 6, 1991, Shapour Bakhtiar, the shah's last prime minister, and his personal secretary, Soroush Katibeh, were stabbed to death in Paris by the mullahs' terrorists.

On September 17, 1992, Farsi-speaking gunmen charged into a Greek restaurant in Berlin and murdered Sadegh Sharafkandi and two other Iranian Kurdish nationals.[22] Sharafkandi had succeeded Abdul-Rahman Qassemlou, the leader of the Iranian Kurdish Democratic Party.

Prior to the killings in Berlin, Iranian agents stabbed to death Fereidoon Farrokhzad, an Iranian entertainer, at his home in Bonn in August 1992.[23]

An International Terrorist Network

To carry out bombings, hijackings, and assassinations, the Iranian clerics have established a vast network of agents and centers throughout the world.

Switzerland

In recent years, the mullahs' regime has turned Switzerland into one of its major terrorist centers in Europe. The regime's embassy in Berne and its consulate in Geneva coordinate, oversee, and direct Tehran's terrorist operations throughout Europe. Berne and Geneva also act as the command and logistic bases for terrorism in Cologne, Paris, Vienna, and other important European cities. The assassination of Kazem Rajavi in Switzerland; the attempt on the life of Kamal Rezaii, the Mojahedin spokesman in Germany, on May 28, 1990; the attempt to murder an Iranian Kurdish dissident on September 6, 1990, in Sweden; and assassinations of Iranian refugees in 1990 and 1991 in Paris were carried out under the supervision of Berne and Geneva.

From 1986 to early 1992 Muhammad-Hussein Mala'ek, Tehran's former ambassador to Switzerland and one of the students involved in occupying the American Embassy in Tehran, oversaw these operations.[24] Later this task was given to Muhammad-Reza Alborzi, the new ambassador in Berne, and Sirous Nasseri in Geneva.

Another of the regime's diplomat-terrorists is Seyyed-e-Razi, who met in December 1991 with Hamid Naqashan to coordinate the terrorist plans in Zurich. Hamid Naqashan was the commander in chief of intelligence and operations of the Guards Corps' Liberation Movements Unit, which was incorporated into the Special Qods Force commanded by Ahmad Vahidi.

Tehran's terrorist contacts in Switzerland also played an important role in the August 1991 murder in Paris of Shapour Bakhtiar, carried out under the supervision of the Qods Force. Moussa Kowsari (passport name of Vakili-Rad), and Muhammad Azadi, commander of the hit squad, were members of the Qods Force. Vakili-Rad was arrested by the Swiss police and extradited to France, but Azadi succeeded in leaving Switzerland for Turkey on September 4, after Mala'ek gave him refuge on August 22, 1991, in the Iranian Embassy in Berne. Another key terrorist operative in Switzerland is Mustafa Sadeqi-Meibodi, stationed at the regime's consulate in Geneva. He directs all the Intelligence Ministry's affairs throughout Europe. Zein ol-Abedin Sarhaddi, who was arrested in Switzerland in 1992, is a special VEVAK agent who played an active role in coordinating and implementing Bakhtiar's murder.[25] He also has valuable information on the details of Rajavi's assassination. In addition to an embassy and representative offices in Switzerland, the regime's terrorists have other facilities, such as a headquarters in the Gonche region of Geneva that is used for support and logistic purposes.

Germany

Germany is particularly important for the mullahs' terrorist efforts because of the high level of political and economic relations between the two countries. These provide Tehran with enormous freedom of action that has been exploited to establish numerous logistics, supply, and intelligence centers and bases in Germany.[26] The presence of many Iranian opposition groups and large Muslim communities, mostly composed of immigrant Turks, has encouraged the Iranian regime to intensify its terrorist activities and to recruit agents from among the Muslims residing in Germany.

The Iranian Embassy in Bonn is a command center, and the *Khaneh Behdasht-e-Iran* in Cologne is another logistics headquarters for the regime's terrorist operations in Europe.[27] The regime's top officials in Germany are chosen from among those who have previous background and experience in terrorist activities. Mehdi Ahari-Mostafavi, Tehran's former ambassador to Bonn, was one of the students who occupied the American Embassy in Tehran. He also shaped Iran's terrorist network in Austria. Hassan Khosrojerdi, director of the House of Iran, a cultural center, was involved in terrorism in Syria and Lebanon. Ahmad Kan'ani, who preceded Khosrojerdi in that post, was also the Guards Corps commander in Lebanon.

France

From 1981 to 1986, when the Iranian Resistance's leader, Massoud Rajavi, was headquartered in a Paris suburb, the Tehran regime devoted a vast terrorist network to attempting to assassinate him. On several occasions, plans were discovered. Iranian agents either escaped or were expelled from France.

As in Germany, the mullahs are seeking to recruit agents for terrorist purposes from among local Muslims, several million of whom reside in France, most from North Africa. One of the clerical regime's important recruitment centers is *Ahl al-Beit al-Islamiah* which is disguised as a cultural center.[28] A 45-year-old Kuwaiti national by the name of Haj Ibrahim, who runs an Islamic library, is in charge of the Ahl al-Beit center, which publishes the *Ahl al-Beit* magazine to lure new members. During the Iran-Iraq War, France was the target of the mullahs' terrorism in return for what Tehran said was that country's support for Iraq.

On September 19, 1991, the French police arrested Massoud Hindizadeh, one of the regime's diplomats in Paris. Prior to his arrest, Hindizadeh was in charge of the Iranian radio and television operations in France. His terrorist background had been revealed by the People's Mojahedin. He was arrested along with eleven other terrorists. Hindizadeh subsequently confessed to the involvement of the leaders of the Iranian regime in several assassinations in Paris. On October 12, the French police arrested another regime agent working undercover as the head of Iran Air's cargo department at the Orly Airport. Following these arrests, the French Justice Ministry issued an international arrest warrant for Hussein Sheikh-Attar, the adviser to the Iranian minister of post, telegraph, and telephone. A Paris court on March 11, 1992, handed out five-year jail sentences to two Iranian intelligence agents convicted of illegally transporting arms. Nasser Daryaei and Mahmoud Sheyzari were tried in absentia after they fled Paris in February 1986.[29]

Turkey

A neighbor of Iran to the northwest, Turkey has also been a hotbed of terrorism for the mullahs who want to blackmail Turkey and gain political and economic concessions.[30] Members and supporters of the People's Mojahedin have been regular targets of Tehran's terrorists in Turkey. Istanbul is home to one of the mullahs' most active Intelligence Ministry centers outside Iran. There, Tehran's agents forge documents and passports and establish contacts with its terrorist squads before sending them on missions to Europe. The Intelligence Ministry's operational units move about in absolute secrecy and do not have any contacts with Tehran's embassies and official representative centers. Many of the terrorists use refugee passports to cover their traces.

Nariman Shah-Ibrahim has been one of the senior officers of the Intelligence Ministry in Turkey for several years. Before receiving the assignment for Turkey, he had the task of maintaining control over foreign guests at hotels, eavesdropping, photographing their documents, and searching rooms in their absence. In Turkey, he had a hand in the assassination of Colonel Hamid Farzaneh, an Iranian army officer, and the explosion of the Saudi Airline offices in Istanbul and in Karachi, Pakistan. Shah-Ibrahim has a refugee passport from Denmark under his real name. His contacts at the Intelligence Ministry in Tehran are Reza Nouri and Ali Saber. Two Intelligence Ministry agents working under his command are Hamid Farsi and Faramarz Farahani.

Cyprus

Tehran uses Cyprus to provide weapons and supplies to terrorists, and to establish contacts and gather information. Many meetings between terrorist teams in Europe and their Iranian supervisors are held there. Until the mid-1980s, the mullahs' regime used a canned-food company in Spain—which has convenient access to France—to stockpile large quantities of weapons, including rocket launchers, machine guns, and grenades. These were to be used in a large-scale terrorist attack against Massoud Rajavi. With the discovery of the facilities in Spain, the Tehran regime transferred its weapons storage to Cyprus.

Lebanon

Because of its large Shi'ite population and its proximity to Israel, Lebanon has been one of the regime's prime targets for the export of fundamentalism and terrorism since the beginning of Khomeini's rule. In mid-1982, the Guards Corps' Muhammad Rasulullah brigade was dispatched to Lebanon. Two thousand Revolutionary Guards stayed in Lebanon when the brigade returned to Iran. In addition, the Guards Corps' organization was restructured to include a "Lebanon Corps," to provide manpower, training, and logistical support to the regime's forces in Lebanon. The Guards Corps based its forces in the city of Baalbek in the Bekaa Valley in eastern Lebanon, where a large enclave of Shi'ites live. Baalbek thus became the center where the Guards and the Khomeini regime's indigenous supporters were settled, trained, and subsequently dispatched on terrorist missions. The Guard Corps has many bases in the Bekaa Valley. The Sheikh Abdullah or Sakaneh Imam Ali base (also known as the Baalbek base) is the largest of these bases and plays a central role in such activities. The Guards Corps has also established many bases in townships around Baalbek to exert control over the area it holds. In 1992 senior Iranian government officials reportedly ordered their terrorist units in Lebanon to prepare for major operations all over the Middle East. They expanded command, control, and communications systems and sent personnel to sites in Sudan. According to one expert, "Sudan is an ideal position for launching attacks on Egypt, Israel, and Saudi Arabia."[31]

Kuwait

Tehran has long used its embassy as well as Iranian schools and other facilities in Kuwait to find recruits for terrorism. The Iranian mullahs have been able to recruit from among the large Shi'ite minority in Kuwait and take them to Tehran for training at the Guards Corps bases. After the Iraqi occupation of Kuwait in August 1990, tens of thousands of Kuwaiti-Iranians returned to Iran. The mullahs' intelligence and Guards Corps forces became very active in locating suitable candidates. Currently, the regime is trying to expand its influence in Kuwait through those Iranians who return to Kuwait and by taking advantage of the chaotic situation there after the Persian Gulf War.

Pakistan

The presence of a large Shi'ite population, the Afghanistan problem, violent clashes between pro-Saudi groups and pro-Iranian forces, and especially the possibility of carrying out terrorist attacks against the Mojahedin's supporters, have turned Pakistan into a center for the mullahs' terrorism. Pakistan's close relations with Iran, in particular, give the mullahs enormous room to maneuver and expand their activities. Tehran's embassy in Islamabad coordinates terrorist actions in Pakistan and oversees the work of the following terrorist centers: the Iranian consulates in Karachi and Lahore; the Islamic societies in Lahore, Karachi, and Peshawar; and Iran's cultural houses in Karachi and Quetta. In addition, the Intelligence Ministry and the Guard Corps employ many of their operatives in Karachi and Lahore in the guise of restaurateurs and shopowners.

Prospects

The long arm of Iran's terrorists stretches to Turkey, Pakistan, and India in Asia; Lebanon, Saudi Arabia, and Kuwait in the Middle East;

Belgium, France, Austria, Sweden, Italy, Cyprus, Spain, Germany, Switzerland, the United Kingdom, and Greece in Europe; and Argentina in Latin America. The extent to which the mullahs enjoy a free rein to maneuver and operate—whether in the framework of diplomatic institutions or business facilities or other suitable cover in any given country—is directly correlated to the frequency and the number of terrorist activities in those countries. One can certainly say that the mullahs' regime is neither inclined nor able to abandon terrorism as one of the primary instruments of its foreign policy.[32] One Tehran-based foreign diplomat noted, "The difference between now and before is that they do not want to get caught."[33] The mullahs may try to exercise more caution in pursuing their terrorism, but terrorism will remain intertwined with the mullahs' foreign policy. ■

XI

The Mullahs and Middle East Peace

The Muslims' fury and hatred will burn the heart of Washington some day and America will be responsible for its repercussions. . . . The day will come when, like Salman Rushdie, the Jews will not find a place to live anywhere in the world.

—Guards Corps Major General Mohsen Rezaii,
Commander in Chief of the Islamic Revolutionary Guards Corps,
October 21, 1991[1]

Since the peace talks between Israel and its neighbors began in 1991, Tehran has spared no effort to undermine the Middle East peace process. "We must endeavor to defeat this conference, and we know that this conference is a sham,"[2] Rafsanjani said shortly after the talks opened. The regime's leader, Khamenei, also voiced his objection, saying, "In the present circumstances, we must oppose this ominous peace conference to the extent we can. The active presence of the people and mujahideen of Palestine as well as a political and public relations campaign will defeat the Arrogant West's conspiracy."[3] State-controlled media have devoted a significant portion of their political commentaries and programs to lambasting the talks, sometimes issuing death decrees for those taking part and urging "zealous Muslims" to murder the negotiators for committing "treacheries." Calls to take "immediate practical measures" (tantamount to terrorism in the mullahs' lexicon) abound in the government press. A typical report said:

The world has realized that the liberation of Palestine constitutes a strategic ideal for the Islamic Revolution . . . Practical support for Palestine's Islamic

Revolution in all financial, political, intelligence, and military domains represents inevitable necessities at this historical juncture. . . . The Muslims must pay attention to the directives of His Eminence, the Leader, to fully understand these fateful moments in todays' Islamic world and take immediate practical measures.[4]

The mullahs' regime opposes the trend toward peace in the Middle East, because continued tensions serve its interests. Since coming to power in 1979, the Iranian clerics have devoted enormous energy to the Palestinian issue. Cognizant of the depth of the attachments of Muslims and particularly Arab masses toward Palestine and Qods (Jerusalem), Khomeini justified the war with Iraq, a neighboring Muslim state, with the slogan of "liberating Qods through Karbala." He also tried to gain influence among Muslims and Arabs through propaganda moves such as "the International Qods Day" and the "twenty-million-member army to free Qods." Moreover, the Palestinian issue and the universal attention it commands in the Middle East diverted attention from Iran's internal affairs, notably the brutal clampdown there on liberties and democratic freedoms.

But the most important factor motivating Khomeini's heirs to oppose the peace process is the very nature of the velayat-e-faqih regime. The clerics fear and openly acknowledge that if peace were to take hold in the region, they will be "the next target" for scrutiny. Khamenei himself warned: "If the Palestinian problem were resolved forever, America will prepare herself for her principal task, namely to fight Islamic movements." The regime's leaders also believe that the establishment of peace in the Middle East will further aggravate their international isolation. Muhammad Yazdi, the head of the judiciary, explained: "Organizing such a [Middle East peace] conference is consistent with the efforts of America and other Western states to isolate Islam."[5]

In his speech to the Conference to Support Palestine's Islamic Revolution in Tehran in late 1991, Rafsanjani said: "Without doubt, no issue bears greater significance for us than Palestine. . . . We are presently involved in such problems as Kashmir, Afghanistan, Lebanon, Iraq, India, Africa, and Muslims in the Soviet Union. . . . But the Palestinian issue is first and foremost and our most important task is to address it."[6] Elsewhere, Rafsanjani warned against "a new fire the peace conference has set ablaze."[7] His ambassador in Damascus, Muhammad-Hassan Akhtari, cautioned that this conference aims to "uproot Islamic movements throughout the entire Muslim world."[8]

In the "strategic ideal of liberating Palestine," Tehran is in fact searching for its own "strategic survival." Mohsen Rezaii, the Guards Corps commander in chief has said, "If we lose on the Palestinian issue today, other issues will also be lost."[9] Indeed, the peace process is interwoven with the fate of the Iranian regime and constitutes its "pivotal" problem.[10] Thus, in the words of Ahmad Khomeini, "Despite their differences on minor issues, the country's officials have no disagreements whatsoever on the Palestinian problem, neither concerning the goal nor the means to achieve it."[11] In the words of Khamenei, "The Palestinian nation has only one path to salvation—a violent and selfless struggle which must be conducted inside and outside occupied lands. This is an Islamic struggle which all Muslims are dutybound to help."[12] To this end, Rafsanjani also boasted, "As the chief executive of the Islamic Republic, I declare that we are ready to contribute to alleviate the needs of Palestine. We are even prepared to send troops to help the Palestinians."[13]

Reaffirming his rejection of the Middle East peace process in January 1993, Khamenei said, "The government of Israel is a usurper [government] and must be annihilated. . . . This is a fundamental issue on the basis of which we are opposed to any action which would run counter to this goal."[14] Five days later, Rafsanjani echoed the same theme during a press conference with foreign journalists in Tehran: "We believe Israel is an illegitimate government . . . As such, we will be against these [Arab-Israeli] peace talks."[15] ◈

XII

Armed to the Teeth

*Since the enemy has atomic facilities, Islamic countries must
be armed with the same capacity.*

—Ata'ollah Mohajerani, Iranian Vice President, October 1991[1]

Following the 1988 Iran-Iraq ceasefire, Western observers argued that
Iran would immediately embark upon rebuilding its economy, devastat-
ed after eight years of war, or at least give reconstruction top priority.
Tehran's boisterous propaganda echoed this theme.

But not only did the mullahs fail to revive the crippled economy, they
continued to give precedence to upgrading their war machine. Iranian
leaders began a major and rapid military procurement program, including
an ambitious effort to acquire nuclear weapons.

Rafsanjani's 1989 five-year economic plan allocated some $50 billion
to military expenditures. By 1992, Iran's military spending was 40
percent more than it had been at the peak of the Iran-Iraq War.[2]

The mullahs' military hardware buying binge goes far beyond their
defense needs. According to *Jane's Defense Weekly*, "There are at least
240 major, state-owned plants producing military equipment and an
estimated 12,000 privately owned workshops manufacturing military
related products."[3] Informed analysts and sources say that in expanding
its military-industrial base, the regime in Tehran "has been assisted by
the former Soviet Union, North Korea, China, Pakistan, Argentina,
Brazil, and Germany."[4] Other major suppliers of arms to Iran include
Belgium, Sweden, Taiwan, Italy, India, Poland, Yugoslavia, Bulgaria,
and Romania.

Tehran has aimed its arms spree in three directions: conventional
arms, chemical and biological weapons, and nuclear technology.

Conventional Weapons

During the past three years the Iranian regime has bought $3 billion in arms from North Korea. In October and November 1991 alone it "purchased 150 Scud missiles from that country."[5] The North Koreans also delivered 170 more advanced Scud-B and C missiles.[6] China has also been indispensable in developing Iran's missile production capabilities.[7] As part of a $5 billion weapons agreement in 1989, China agreed to sell Tehran parts that could be used for medium-range ballistic missiles.[8] In addition, the Iranians are to receive from Syria 170 Scud-D missiles, with a range of 1,200 kilometers.[9] The Chinese have reportedly sold Tehran M-11 missiles with a range of 1,000 kilometers. The Defense Ministry announced in January 1992 that the defense industries would begin mass producing long-range surface-to-surface missiles with high destructive power. The missiles are reported to be an upgraded SS-1 'Scud-B' with extra fuel tanks and a reduced warhead payload.[10]

The former Soviet Union and China have also provided Tehran with advanced fighters and bombers, including 72 F-7 fighters, 25 SU-24 bombers and 30 top-of-the-line MiG-29s.[11] Presently, the Guards Corps is using a $14 million credit with China to obtain spare parts for 500 BMP-1 armored fighting vehicles.

The collapse of the former Soviet Union has prompted Tehran to obtain various types of weapons for the lowest possible prices from Soviet successor states. Following his trip to Russia in December 1991, Foreign Minister Velayati returned with a suitcase full of contracts for weapons purchases.[12] For example, the Russian Federation has a $4 billion contract to deliver to Iran 48 MiG-29 fighters, 500 T-72 main battle tanks, and other types of weapons, including SA-5 surface-to-air missiles and 122mm howitzer and the 130mm gun.[13] The Associated Press reported that "the Soviet Union and its successor states transferred more than a billion dollars worth of military equipment to Iran in 1991. It is expected that there will be more than a billion dollars worth of deliveries in 1992."[14] In addition, Russia is to provide Iran with spare parts, armaments, and operating manuals for the estimated 115 Iraqi jets that flew to Iran during the Gulf War.[15] A number of Iranian pilots received MiG-29 and Sukhoi training in Russia.

According to an agreement signed with the Russian Federation in March 1992, another 400 advanced T-72 tanks worth $720 million were to be delivered to the Revolutionary Guards Corps. Furthermore, the Guards Corps has agreed to pay $175 million for 500 BMP-2 armored fighting vehicles equipped with laser-guided antitank missiles. Officials from the Russian Federation have also reportedly visited Tehran to assure the Iranians of their cooperation in transferring the technology to build and assemble T-72 tanks. Iran's T-72 version will include some of the weaponry and equipment of the more modern Soviet T-80 main battle tank, such as the night vision system and the reactive armor.[16] This contract is said to be worth $9 billion, stretching over several years. The mullahs have bought another 1,500 T-55 tanks from Poland,[17] and 15,000 DCA rocket launchers and 2,000 surface-to-air missile launch pads from Bulgaria.[18]

Tehran is also aiming to revitalize its naval force, devastated during the eight-year war with Iraq. Separate deals with China and Russia will give Iran its first attack submarines and fast-moving warships equipped with antiship missiles. The Russians have agreed to deliver two Kilo-class diesel-powered submarines valued at about $600 million.[19] The crews for the boats are training in a Russian-controlled naval base in Latvia.[20] In addition to an option to buy a third Kilo submarine, Tehran has negotiated a deal to purchase five 400-ton minisubmarines from Moscow. In late 1992, the Iranians also discussed with Russia the purchase of two additional Kilo-class diesel submarines. The defense minister, Akbar Torkan, began negotiations for more submarines after completing payment for three Kilos ordered earlier.[21] Reports in the Iranian media indicate that the vessels will be based at the southern port of Chah Bahar along the Gulf of Oman.[22] The mullahs have not restricted their buying spree to the Chinese, the North Koreans, or the former Eastern Bloc. According to *Defense Week*, "a contract with Brazil for 15 military cargo aircraft and 15 Tucanos was fulfilled in 1991."[23] In fact, Iran has replaced Iraq as Brazil's main Middle East customer for arms.[24]

Chemical and Biological Weapons

In addition to its vast conventional weapons procurement program, Tehran has actively sought to produce chemical and biological weapons. Rafsanjani has acknowledged: "We must fully equip ourselves with chemical, biological, and radioactive weapons."[25] Procurement and stockpiling of chemical weapons has been on the agenda of the Revolutionary Guards Corps. In 1991, German intelligence services reported that Iran was in possession of a blueprint the Germans used to build the Rabata chemical arms factory in Libya. Experts believe that Tehran will produce modern chemical weapons in the late 1990s.[26]

Recent reports on the hitherto undisclosed aspects of the mullahs' efforts to procure biological and chemical weapons show that with foreign assistance, the Tehran regime has made very dangerous advances in these areas. In cooperation with foreign governments in such countries as China and North Korea and a number of European—including German—firms, the Guards Corps is now able to produce chemical weapons, nerve gases, and biological weapons. It has stockpiled large quantities of such weapons of mass destruction. The Guards Corps also possesses the technology to mount chemical warheads on long-range Scud missiles. Currently, the regime has set up chemical plants in four regions of the country and is training the Revolutionary Guards on how to use chemical weapons.[27]

■　■　■

In 1992, the Guards Corps expanded its chemical weapons sites. The strictly confidential nature of the program has meant that only a limited number of people are aware of them. Rafsanjani has appointed his close confidants to supervise these plans, and they report to him directly.

Karaj Program

The Guards Corps, Ministry of Defense, and Engineering Research Center of *Jahad-e-Sazandegi* (the Construction Crusade) are working together on a chemical weapons complex on a site fourteen kilometers west of Tehran, near the Tehran-Karaj Highway. The Engineering Research Center of the Construction Crusade oversees the main production sites of chemical materials in the country.

The Karaj program is highly confidential, and Chinese experts supervise the progress of the work. A large number of Chinese engineers and military experts cooperate with the Guards Corps on the site. The regime intends to transfer its best experts to this location.

Razi Serum and Vaccine Production Center

A special team is working secretly at the Razi Serum and Vaccine Production Center in Karaj. The center is situated on the Qazvin-Hessarak Highway. The team is carrying out its research on biological weapons under the supervision of the Guards Corps.

Razi Chemical Corporation

All the laboratories and experts of this corporation work under the supervision of the Revolutionary Guards Corps' Chemical Warfare Unit. Since the days of the Iran-Iraq War, the corporation has been producing materials needed by the Guards' Chemical Warfare Unit.

The corporation's main production facility is situated in Bandar-Khomeini in southwest Iran. The corporation's central offices are located in the building of the Oil Ministry's Petrochemical Industries Establishment. The corporation works independently of the Oil Ministry.

Marvdasht Center

The center is involved specifically in the production of mustard gas for the Guards Corps. There are also research facilities and large laboratories. A big fire broke out in the center in 1987, leaving 400 dead. It is situated in Marvdasht, in Fars Province in southern Iran.

Poly-Acryl Corporation

The corporation operates ostensibly as an ordinary commercial venture administered by the *Bonyad-e-Mostaz'afin* (Foundation for the Deprived), but is, in fact, one of the principal chemical gas production facilities of the Guards Corps.

The production center is forty-five kilometers from Isfahan on the Isfahan-Mobarakeh Highway. There are offices on Isfahan's Seyyed Alikhan Street, and the central office is on Tehran's Gandhi Street.

Nuclear Weapons

Nuclear arms, in the mullahs' view, are "the most strategic guarantee" for their survival in the future of the region. In 1991, Ata'ollah Mohajerani, one of Rafsanjani's deputies, also laid emphasis on the need to obtain atomic weapons. "Since the enemy has atomic facilities," he said, "Islamic countries must be armed with the same capacity." As the majlis speaker in 1989, Rafsanjani underscored the need to obtain an atomic arsenal, stressing that Iran cannot ignore the reality of the modern world's atomic weapons.

The efforts by the mullahs' regime to develop a nuclear arsenal date back to 1985, when Tehran revived the nuclear program that was abandoned with the fall of the shah in 1979. A special section within the Revolutionary Guards Corps was assigned the task of overseeing scientific research and of securing nuclear technology for military use.[28] To that end, the facilities of Iran's Atomic Energy Organization (IAEO) were placed under the control of the Guards Corps, whose first order of business was to set up new installations hidden from the view of international observers.

The mullahs reached agreement with Argentina in 1987 to obtain a supply of 20-percent enriched uranium to be used in Tehran's Amirabad research center, which has a five-megawatt nuclear reactor. They also struck deals with both Argentina and Pakistan for the training of nuclear specialists.[29] In 1988, when the regime reluctantly accepted the ceasefire in the Iran-Iraq War, the Guards Corps accelerated the IAEO's activities. It launched a top-secret project code-named the "Great Plan." Its initial budget was $200 million, and the project has been extensively funded ever since.[30] In 1992, they allocated $800 million to the project. In addition, a department in the Ministry of Defense was put in charge of acquiring nuclear-related technology from abroad. Two Iranian nuclear experts supervised the project.

Following Khomeini's death in 1989, Rafsanjani aggressively pursued the development of Iran's nuclear capabilities, attempting to attract nuclear scientists and specialists back to Iran by offering them substantial salaries. He also sought to secure nuclear equipment and technology from foreign countries. Nevertheless, the Guards Corps encountered serious difficulties because the efforts to obtain fuel and technology made little progress. Subsequently, a meeting was held in early 1990 between Rafsanjani, Mohsen Rezaii, the Guards Corps commander in chief, and other senior officials involved in the nuclear project, to assess the progress and prospects of Iran's nuclear program. Afterward, Rafsanjani issued directives to step up the efforts to obtain technology and other necessary equipment from a variety of countries, including China, Pakistan, Argentina, and France.

In the aftermath of the Persian Gulf War, when Germany informed Tehran that it would no longer continue its nuclear assistance to the mullahs' regime, Rafsanjani intervened personally. He vowed in public that the Islamic Republic would pursue its bid to acquire nuclear technology and warned Germany of losing Iran's markets.

In 1992, Rafsanjani met with a visiting official from China's Council of Science and Technology, the Chinese organization responsible for nuclear programs. Subsequently, a ten-year pact was signed between the two countries for scientific cooperation and the transfer of military technology.[31] Trusted Iranian experts were also dispatched to Europe and elsewhere to infiltrate nuclear research institutions and later repatriate their knowledge to Iran.[32] By mid-1992, Tehran had succeeded in signing an agreement with the Russian Federation to obtain two 440-megawatt nuclear reactors and buying a Calutron-type uranium-enrichment device from China. It also obtained a Cyclotron from the Belgian firm Ion Beam Applications. Although the company maintains that the equipment is generally used in medical research, nuclear industry experts say that "it could be adapted to enrich uranium."[33]

On his trip to China in September 1992, Rafsanjani took along ten Iranian nuclear experts. These experts have been undergoing training since. In addition, another twenty specialists are completing their training in China.

The primary objective of this trip was to obtain greater Chinese cooperation on technology and equipment and the dispatch of more Chinese nuclear experts to Iran. Rafsanjani's key nuclear goal during this trip and meetings with the Chinese president and officials was to speed up the completion of a nuclear center in southern Iran called the Darkhovin Site. On September 10, the regime's officials signed an extensive secret nuclear cooperation pact with China, only parts of which were revealed.

Tehran has also been seeking to hire foreign experts. At least fifty-four experts from foreign nations, including China, have been hired. The actual number of experts, however, is much greater. Dozens of Chinese and Russian experts also regularly travel to and from Iran. These experts are engaged in nuclear research, training Iranian specialists, supervising the construction of facilities, and setting up nuclear reactors.

In addition to the foreign nuclear experts mentioned above, the regime has managed to engage—at very high salaries—two Russian scholars, one expert from Kazakhstan, and one specialist from Turkmenistan to work in the training and research department of the Atomic Energy Organization in Tehran. These individuals are involved in research to speed up the "Great Plan." In addition, three specialists from Hungary are working in the GAMA Energy Center in Banab in northeastern Iran.

To keep the nuclear program a secret, several parallel but independent and self-sufficient installations, including laboratories, workshops, and plants, are already under way in different parts of the country.

The Isfahan Project

The Isfahan Project is currently the centerpiece of the "Great Plan" to gain nuclear weapons and has been given priority in Rafsanjani's five-year economic program, for two reasons. Its geographical location in central Iran makes Isfahan relatively secure from any foreign military attack of the kind that destroyed the nuclear site in the southern city of Bushehr during the Iran-Iraq War. Second, unlike the already cramped Amirabad installation in Tehran, the Isfahan plant has much greater potential for expansion.

The Isfahan Project will consist of a full-cycle program, focusing on nuclear technology research and production of nuclear weapons. The complex is located on a mountainside, forty kilometers from Isfahan. Some of the buildings are camouflaged, and others are constructed underground. A small nuclear reactor is presently in use there, but Tehran is working to obtain a larger one. A starter device known as a "neutron sparker" has been purchased from the Chinese. Experts at this facility, which is 40 percent complete, have received training in China.

The Karaj Project

The secret Karaj Project is similar to the one in Isfahan. It is a small city constructed under the cover of a medical and hospital complex. Chinese and Russian experts are involved in completing different phases of the project. The installation of the Chinese-supplied Calutron and the Cyclotron accelerator purchased from Belgium at the site is near completion, but the rest of the complex is only 35 percent completed.

The Gorgan Project

One of the largest nuclear sites in Iran, the Gorgan Project is located northeast of Gorgan, on the shores of the Caspian Sea. It is supervised by Mansour Haj Azim, deputy director of the IAEO. Specialists from Russia and other former Soviet republics were hired to work on the project. They have completed preliminary earthquake studies to assess the feasibility of installing large reactors at the site.

The Darkhovin Project

Referred to as the "Karoun Plan," the Darkhovin Project is located at a Guards Corps garrison fifty kilometers northeast of Abadan, on the Ahw az-Abadan Highway in southwest Iran. During the October 1991 meeting between Chinese President Yang Shang Kun and Rafsanjani, China agreed to provide technical and assessment assistance to complete the project, which was abandoned after the Iranian revolution in 1979. Chinese experts pay frequent visits to the Darkhovin complex.

The Mo'alem Kelayeh Project

Also known as the "Alamout Plan," the Mo'alem Kelayeh Project is located at an industrial complex in northern Qazvin, 120 kilometers northwest of Tehran. The Guards Corps relocated the local inhabitants to clear the area for construction of this site. To keep the project totally secret, Tehran did not seek the assistance of foreign experts and technicians in building the facility.

The Yazd Project

One of the most recently built nuclear sites is located in the vicinity of the city of Yazd in central Iran, close to a uranium mine in the nearby Sarghand desert.

The Yazd complex has been established over the past three years. Its existence is a tightly kept secret, and the entire facility, taking up several thousand square meters, has been built underground. In summer 1992, a complete video report on the progress of the nuclear site was prepared for Khamenei. In November, Hashemi-Rafsanjani visited the site. Accompanied by Mansour Haj Azim, the deputy director of Iran's Atomic Energy Organization, Rafsanjani was evaluating the progress of the center.[34]

The Bushehr Project

Code-named the Qods (Jerusalem) Project, this complex was originally constructed by German firms during the reign of the shah. The site was heavily damaged during the eight-year Iran-Iraq War. The German refusal to resume work on the project after the war created a diplomatic crisis between Germany and the Khomeini regime. With help from China and Pakistan, the Guards Corps has rebuilt major parts of this multibillion-dollar facility. Rafsanjani paid a visit to the site in February 1993 to assess the progress of the project.[35]

The Bandar Abbas Project

Located near Bandar Abbas on the Strait of Hormuz, the Bandar Abbas Project is the site of Iran's ballistic missile production facilities. It is supervised by a special Guards Corps unit. The Revolutionary Guards Corps has taken over all the industrial installations dealing with medium- and long-range missile production.

For the past five years, the Iranians have been trying to modify the Silkworm short-range missile into a long-range missile. The tests were made possible with equipment bought from the German MBB Corporation.[36] The Iranians have already produced a missile with a range of 400 kilometers and are working on a ballistic missile with the range of 1,500 kilometers. The Bandar Abbas Project also includes work on arming the ballistic missiles with nuclear warheads. The navy commander, Rear Admiral Ali Shamkhani, and his deputy, Rear Admiral Abbas Mohtaj, oversee this operation.

China, Pakistan, and Argentina are the main suppliers of equipment and material for Tehran's nuclear program. Tehran and Islamabad want to engage in joint ventures in the field of nuclear technology. During the visit by General Assif Nawaz, Pakistan's army commander in chief, to Iran in November 1991, an agreement was signed between the two countries, stipulating that both Pakistan and Iran will pursue their atomic programs with the assistance of the People's Republic of China. Iran is to allocate $5 billion for the joint atomic venture.[37]

Nuclear aid was also the "secret topic heading the agenda during the October visit to Tehran of the Chinese President," according to one Western report.[38] Chinese experts have been sent to Iran, and Iranian technicians have been trained in China as part of the cooperation between the two countries on nuclear weapons.

Presently a shortage of enriched uranium prevents the mullahs from achieving the nuclear goals. A shareholder in the French-led Eurodif conglomerate, Iran has refused to forfeit her right of access to enriched uranium.[39] With the Soviet Union's collapse, Iran saw a window of opportunity to realize its long-held nuclear dream. Several senior IAEO officials traveled to the former Soviet republics to persuade nuclear scientists to go to Tehran. Reza Amrollahi, the IAEO president, paid several visits to the Ukraine and Kazakhstan to explore the possibility of acquiring nuclear technology, nuclear warheads, and enriched uranium.

Western experts viewed Velayati's visit in mid-December 1991 to Tadzhikistan—which has large uranium reserves and is the site of the former Soviet Union's uranium-enrichment plants—as an attempt to purchase enriched uranium. The cash-strapped Kazakhstan has been more inclined to cooperate.

According to intelligence reports from within the mullahs' regime, Tehran has purchased four nuclear warheads from the Central Asian republic of Kazakhstan. The first round of discussions about the sale were held when Kazakhstan's minister of transportation visited Tehran in April 1992. Subsequently, a group of Iranian officials, including several from the Ministry of Defense, traveled to Alma Ata in August. Revolutionary Guards Corps Brigadier General Vahid Dastjerdi, the commander of logistics for the Ministry of Defense, and Brigadier General Bake Muhammad-Doust, in charge of the ministry's industrial purchasing, were members of the delegation headed by the Defense Minister Ali Akbar Torkan. Tehran has paid in full for the four warheads, but they have not yet been delivered.

◆   ◆   ◆

A glance at the mullahs' weapons procurement program and their high military budget shows that Tehran's arms purchases far exceed its defense needs. The arms buildup is motivated by Iran's enormous domestic political and economic crises. "They are in rather desperate shape, and the answer is to look outside aggressively," said one Western expert.[40] The offensive nature of the arms buildup, in light of the clerics' continuing efforts to export fundamentalism, is a source of grave concern for regional and global peace. Western analysts worry that "Iran is conspiring to build a strategic strike capability."[41]

Tehran's stockpiling of weapons has already changed the regional balance of power; the situation can only get worse if no international action is taken to ban arms sales to Iran. The mullahs' renewed assertiveness in bilateral relations with their neighbors—including their intimidating treatment of the United Arab Emirates on the ownership of a Persian Gulf island—is an ominous sign that more trouble lies ahead. ◆

XIII

Crisis from All Sides: Inside the Mullahs' Regime

We are now passing through the most difficult stage of our [political] life. In other countries, whoever chooses this path, it results in changing several administrations. . . . Those who make these decisions themselves will be sacrificed in the process.

—Hashemi-Rafsanjani, May 28 ,1992[1]

This book has primarily focused on the Iranian regime's foreign policy and export of fundamentalism. But what about the domestic scene? An examination of Iran's internal politics shows that the theocratic state is inherently unstable. The mullahs export ideological fundamentalism and terrorism because they cannot rule without crises.

In August 1988, when the eight-year Iran-Iraq War ended with Khomeini's acceptance of a ceasefire, observers expected that Iran would swiftly move towards economic reconstruction. Ten months later, when Khomeini died, these expectations were revived with the added hope that the mullahs would moderate their domestic and foreign policies. More than four years later, it has become clear that such expectations were unfounded.

Unable to respond to the growing needs of Iranian society, the absolutist velayat-e-faqih regime is today beset by internal crises. This situation has compelled the regime to cling ever tighter to Khomeini's spirit and to stage hollow shows of force to cover up its intrinsic weaknesses. The mullahs have stepped up repression at home and done their best to generate crises abroad.

Political Repression

The mullahs have made a few cosmetic changes, such as hosting an Islamic human rights seminar, appointing a presidential adviser for women's affairs, and registering a few progovernment associations. But overall the political situation in Iran has deteriorated. According to reports compiled from the regime's official press, the Rafsanjani administration's security forces in 1991 arrested 300,000 people whose "crimes" included improper veiling, addiction, wearing blue jeans, and possessing video recordings, cassette tapes of pop singers, or a pack of playing cards.[2]

Meanwhile, the suppression of women took on new dimensions of brutality. In 1992, officials acknowledged, 113,000 women were arrested in Tehran for "improper veiling" and "moral corruption." Scores of pregnant women were reportedly flogged in public on the same charge. Despite prevalent state censorship, the press reported several cases of stoning and beheading in public.

The number of officially announced executions in 1991 was three times the total for 1990.[3] After his third visit to Iran, Reynaldo Galindo Pohl, the United Nations Special Rapporteur on the human rights situation in Iran, reported weekly increases in executions, continued suppression of religious minorities, a general atmosphere of intimidation of journalists, and self-censorship in fear of government reprisal. After two years of recommendations, Galindo Pohl concluded in his 1992 report to the Commission on Human Rights that the Iranian regime had made "no appreciable progress towards improved compliance with human rights."[4]

Bodies suspended from gallows are a routine sight in Iranian cities. No political party or group outside the narrow spectrum of officially sanctioned "Islamic" ideology is allowed to operate. During the elections for the Fourth Majlis, the Council of Guardians screened all the candidates both before and after the elections to verify their loyalty to the clerical establishment. At least thirty political opponents have been assassinated abroad since Khomeini's death, including Kazem Rajavi, the outstanding advocate of human rights in Iran.[5]

In June 1992, the mullahs' regime began a series of officially announced summary executions in different Iranian cities in retaliation for extensive antigovernment demonstrations. On the orders of emergency Islamic Revolutionary Courts in Mashad, Arak, Shiraz, and several other Iranian cities, scores of demonstrators and Mojahedin supporters were hanged. The mass executions provoked an international outcry and were condemned by, among others, the European Parliament and Amnesty International. Rafsanjani and the other leaders of the regime publicly endorsed the executions and called for harsher measures against oppositionists.

In December 1992, the United Nations General Assembly adopted its strongest-ever resolution, condemning continuing human rights abuses, including summary execution, the use of torture, and suppression of women.[6]

Edging Toward Bankruptcy

Majlis deputies admit that today, some 70 to 80 percent of Iran's populace[7] and 90 percent of its state employees live below the poverty line.[8] Out of every eight Iranians only one has a job earning income.[9] Only five million Iranians are fully employed out of a work force of twenty-four million.[10] Young people are leaving the country by the thousands to search for jobs, mostly illegal, in foreign countries such as Japan. Twenty-five million people are without homes.[11] A 50 percent inflation rate and sky-high prices weigh heavily on the public.[12] The monthly rent for an ordinary apartment exceeds a month's salary of a government employee.[13] During the winter of 1991–'92, heating oil and fuel shortages and high prices brought yet another crisis, and many lost their lives in the freezing cold. Gasoline prices soared 70 percent last year, although oil is the main source of government revenues and is the most plentiful commodity in Iran.

During Rafsanjani's four-year tenure, the nation's foreign debts have risen from $12 billion to $35 billion. There is a shortage of fifteen million homes, at least 150,000 classrooms and 120,000 teachers.

The instability of the clerical regime and lack of confidence in its future have frustrated the government's efforts to attract foreign investments.[14] As for industry, gross and private investments dropped 3.5 and 9.2 percent respectively last year.[15] One majlis deputy said that the share of industry in Iran's gross national product (GNP) is less than that of the least developed countries in Africa.[16]

The prospects are equally grim for agriculture. The area of land under cultivation has continuously decreased, and the country's forests and pastures are being destroyed.[17] Forty percent of the villages, the traditional centers of agriculture and animal husbandry, have been abandoned.[18] Out of fifty-one million hectares of cultivatable land, thirty-two million are unusable.

Statistics on the reconstruction of the war-stricken areas show that only 250,000 of Iran's four million war refugees have returned to their home towns.[19] Most did so unwillingly and live in terrible conditions. These regions still do not have running water or electricity and lack minimum health and educational facilities.[20] Houses remain devastated and areas are infested with uncleared mines. According to the report of the U.N. secretary general, 90 percent of what has been done for reconstruction is of a temporary nature and must be redone.[21] In 1992, only $980 million, or one-fifteenth of the defense budget, was earmarked for restoring the war-stricken regions.

Mounting Protests

A new wave of popular protests has emerged since the cease-fire in the Iran-Iraq War and Khomeini's death. Although the Persian Gulf War retarded the general outpouring of discontent for a year, it has become obvious that even the enormous windfall of the mullahs during the Gulf crisis did not last long.

Until the 1988 cease-fire, followed by Khomeini's death, Iran's domestic social crises were exported abroad via war and terrorist operations. These crises, however, were bound to surface again, particularly because Rafsanjani has not been able to implement any serious economic plans in the past four years. This has in turn aggravated the living conditions, putting far more economic pressure on the public than in wartime. Since July 1991, some 1,000 demonstrations, protests, strikes, and clashes have erupted in different Iranian cities. Tehran alone has been the scene of over 200 acts of protest. Khuzistan, Azerbaijan, Kermanshah, Isfahan, Fars, Hamedan, Mazandaran, Khorassan, and Gilan provinces each witnessed some ten to thirty-five demonstrations and protests in the same period. These incidents ranged across all sectors of society. There were fifty blue-collar strikes, forty-six by students and educators, and thirty-five white-collar and government employees strikes. The rest involved other groups.

The forms of protests also varied widely, from simple slogan writing and distribution of fliers, to well-organized strikes, to violence that included the torching of government vehicles and buildings. The latter, in particular, are indicative of Iranian society's volatile state and the public's deeply rooted hatred of the clerics and willingness to take risks.

Large-scale demonstrations have erupted in several provincial capitals. On April 15, 1992 thousands of people demonstrated in Shiraz, the capital of the southern Fars Province. The protesters clashed with the security forces during the biggest antigovernment protest in that city in a decade. Shiraz residents attacked government offices, banks, and gas stations, setting many of them on fire.[22] On May 5, the town of Arak, the Central Province's capital, was the scene of widespread antigovernment demonstrations. Thousands of people came out onto the streets to protest the policies of the Rafsanjani government. A state of martial law was declared and at least 200 people were arrested.[23] On May 31, tens of thousands of people in Mashad, the capital of the northeastern province of Khorassan, took part in the largest antigovernment protest in the city in the past eleven years. The regime acknowledged that at least 100 government buildings, banks, and corporations, 28 municipality cars and 7 buses were destroyed or burned. Angry residents clashed with security forces and wounded a number of them. More than 3,000 people were arrested and 20 protesters swiftly executed.

The government blamed the Mojahedin for organizing these protests. In Mashad, for example, the mayor acknowledged that the "Mojahedin" took part in the protest "in an organized way."[24] Perhaps the most telling characteristic of the growing trend of protests is the government's inability to stop them, despite a brutal clampdown and widespread arrests and executions.[25]

The following account by a reporter from the *Economist* shows how concerned the regime was about the Mojahedin's role in the Mashad protests: "'Did you meet with any members of the Mujahideen when in Mashad?' the army officer kept asking. On the way home from a visit to Mashhad, where the riots had exploded on May 30th, your correspondent was arrested, strip-searched and interrogated for ten hours. The questions concentrated on the People's Mujahideen, the armed Iranian opposition quartered in Iraq . . ."[26]

During the elections for the Fourth Majlis in April and May 1992, the overwhelming majority of Iranians stayed away, registering their resounding rejection of the ruling regime. Although officials had lowered the minimum age to 15, boosting the number of eligible voters to 30 million during the first round in April, only 4.5 million (or 15 percent) went to the polls. During the second round in May only 2.5 million (or 8 percent) voted. Those who voted did so to get the election stamp on their identity cards, vital for everything from leaving the country to gaining admittance to the university.[27]

The election results were interpreted by some abroad as a clear-cut victory for Rafsanjani's "moderate policies." But the nationwide boycott demonstrated that for the average citizen in the street, the differences between the ruling factions have to do more with style than substance. Khomeini's son, Ahmad, was quite unequivocal on this matter during an audience with a group of majlis deputies. "At the Council for the Determination of the Exigencies of the State and at the Supreme National Security Council, I personally witness that the greater majority of the views and votes of both currents are the same," he said.[28]

Far from being a choice between reform-minded leaders and the old guard, the majlis elections marked an end to the power-sharing arrangement Khomeini had so delicately knitted. Unable to maintain the tenuous balance of power that his mentor so skillfully manipulated, Rafsanjani had no choice but to deny his allies a share of power. It was as if he had to amputate one of the two legs upon which the entire system was standing. The elections, therefore, weakened the regime as a whole because the losing side no longer felt compelled to safeguard or respect the political process from which it was so mercilessly excluded. What is more, in the months ahead, as social unrest and economic perils heighten, Rafsanjani will have no one to blame. For the first time during his four-year tenure, he has to personally shoulder the responsibility for his failures.

When Khomeini "drank the chalice of the poison of the cease-fire" in 1988, he deprived his regime of a very effective scapegoat upon which he blamed the country's entire problems: the war. Ironically, it seems that four years after Khomeini, his protege has found himself facing much the same predicament: to purge the so-called radical faction, also known as the Imam's Line, and thereby deprive the entire regime of one of its major components, or accept the status quo and the daily infightings which have crippled both the cabinet and the majlis.

The Crisis Continues

As the events of subsequent months demonstrated, the purging of the "hard liners" from the majlis did not have any impact on growing popular discontent. The unrest in Mashad in late May 1992 gave new impetus to eruption of protests elsewhere throughout the country. Although these have to a large extent been smaller, they are frequent. An irreversible trend has begun, which the mullahs take very seriously as a warning of things to come.

On June 28, some 30,000 people demonstrated in Tabriz, capital of the northwestern province of Azerbaijan, to protest the razing of their homes. Clashes with security forces led to the arrests of more than 100 people. On July 23, more than 1,000 teachers and students in the city of Javanrood, in western Kermanshah Province, disrupted a speech by the city's majlis deputy and clashed with security forces.[29] On July 5, huge explosions rocked ammunition depots at the Allaho-Akbar barracks near Kermanshah, killing hundreds of Guard Corps members.[30]

The atmosphere has also been reported tense in Isfahan in central Iran, where a de facto curfew is in effect in many districts in the evenings. The situation is also tense in Rasht in northern Iran, where people have frequently clashed with the police. Demonstrations and clashes erupted in July in south Tehran townships of Golshahr, Islamshahr, Safarabad, Moussa-Abad, Robat Karim, and Khalij. The appearance of demolition crews usually sparked the clashes, yet in none of these incidents did the story end there; chants of "death to Rafsanjani" and "death to Khamenei" soon followed.

One of the regime's officials warned in a confidential report that Tehran's suburbs, especially Islamshahr, are a "hotbed of protests." The official described potential uprisings as "more important than those in Mashad." "Tehran is different from other cities, and [whatever happens there] would bear grave consequences," he noted. Despite the transfer of two Guards Corps divisions to Tehran and a state of full alert in the capital's barracks, officials are concerned that "if unrest simultaneously breaks out in several parts of the capital, the number of available forces is not sufficient to control the situation." To counter the spreading wave of protests, the regime has formed antiriot battalions and brigades and staged numerous urban maneuvers in Tehran and other cities.

Khamenei and Rafsanjani have both emphasized in unambiguous terms the need for an active and continued presence of the Bassij forces in "all scenes," as well as the need for the Bassij "to be entrusted with maintaining the national security." Rafsanjani called upon the repressive forces to protect the security of "streets and borders," and to "undertake, as an integrated and concentrated force, their momentous task of protecting the security and welfare of the society."[31] Stressing the need for further clampdown, Khamenei said: "The offenses in question are not those of individuals. The worst offenses are those which destabilize the foundations of the state . . . Youths are covertly dragged into corruption as grouplets under the enemy's direction. This is vice, moral vice, political vice, and economic vice."[32]

Brutal crackdown, however, has failed to quell antigovernment demonstrations and protests throughout the country, in the cities, factories, schools, businesses, the military, and so on. The People's Mojahedin Command Headquarters inside Iran recorded at least 114 protests in August and September 1992 alone, 47 of which occurred in Tehran. In October, three bombs heavily damaged Khomeini's tomb[33] and a powerful bomb destroyed several buildings of the Guards Corps Command Headquarters in Afsarieh district in east Tehran.[34] For three consecutive days in November, residents in the industrial city of Arak (central Iran) staged antigovernment demonstrations and clashed with security forces. In December, hundreds of workers of Mobarakeh Steel Industries in Isfahan went on strike to protest low wages and dismal living conditions. On February 18, 1993, 3,000 workers in Tabriz Tractor Manufacturing Complex in the northwestern Azerbaijan Province went on strike, protesting the deteriorating living conditions and increasing pressures and intimidation by the regime. A series of explosions and fires erupted in Iran's southern oilfields in Khuzistan Province, prompting Ali Fallahian, the minister of intelligence, to dismiss the province's intelligence chief and personally visit the oilfields in late February.[35] These follow strikes a few months earlier by some 100,000 oil industry workers in Tehran, Isfahan, and Abadan refineries. The state-controlled media on occasions reported some of these protests, although in a distorted manner.

The mullahs have blamed the Mojahedin for organizing these activities. In a stark revelation and a sharp departure from a long-standing policy of news black-out on the Mojahedin, Rafsanjani said during a Friday prayer sermon in June in Tehran, "We still have an enemy both inside the country and abroad. . . . We have an organized enemy abroad and they have contacts with each other [at home and abroad]; they have organizational or periodic and single contacts both [in Iran and abroad]."[36]

Before the Fourth Majlis elections in April, Rafsanjani blamed his failures on the rival factions. Since the April purge, however, the entire responsibility for the catastrophic economic situation rests squarely on his own shoulders. Time is finally running out on Khomeini's heirs, who are engulfed in crises from all sides. Arrests, harassment, and other repressive measures cannot reverse the trend that has already begun. As the old Iranian saying goes: "Floodwater never returns to the stream." ◘

XIV

The Search for a Solution

*If the war you are talking about today had been dealt with
from the beginning through reason and logic and without
excitement, it would not have grown so in dimension or
ferocity.*

—Thucydides, *The Peloponnesian War*

Looking at the volatile political problems of today's Middle East, one
wonders if solutions can be found. The editorial pages of Western
newspapers reveal that both governments and independent Middle East
experts are puzzled by the phenomenon of "Islamic fundamentalism"—
the dynamics of its growth and its prospects. This chapter will address
three traditional alternatives to religious fundamentalism in the region—nationalism, liberalism, and Marxism—and examine the reasons
for their failures.

Nationalism

For most Middle Eastern countries—except those, such as Iran, that
had a distinct and independent geographical and historical identity—
the "nation state" is a relatively recent phenomenon which came into
being when these countries gained independence in the early decades of
the twentieth century, after the fall of the Ottoman Empire. Arab
nationalism began with Arab movements seeking independence from
foreign occupation near the end of the nineteenth century and grew with
the writings of that century's renowned Muslim writers, such as Rafi'at
Tahtawi, Nadim, and Muhammad Abdoh.

In successive decades, nationalism played an important role in all the region's countries and was the guiding principle of the ideology of many ruling or powerful parties in the Middle East. A wide spectrum of governments, including that of Gamal Abdel Nasser in Egypt, Dr. Muhammad Mossadeq in Iran, Mustafa Kemal (Ataturk) in Turkey, and the Ba'ath parties in Iraq and Syria, adopted nationalism as the ideological basis of their rule. Regional and international developments, however, have gradually reduced the power of nationalism in the Arab world and the Middle East. Never have the ranks of the Arab states been so divided; never has the ideal of Arab unity seemed so remote.

This weakening of a fundamental ingredient of Arab politics created an opportunity for the growth of nationalism's traditional, but hitherto subordinate, rival in these countries, Islamic fundamentalism. Although the fundamentalists had always lagged behind nationalist movements at critical junctures in the region's modern history, such as the oil nationalization movement in Iran in 1950–53, the Suez Canal crisis in 1956, and the Bangladesh War in 1971, the picture is now changing dramatically.

Liberalism

As a social institution, democracy is another new arrival to the Middle East. Vast areas of this region remained for centuries under the despotic rule of the Ottoman sultans. Those countries not under Ottoman rule were under monarchic dictatorships. Even the 1906 Constitutional Revolution in Iran did little to democratize that country.

Among the various factors sociologists cite in explaining this lack of democracy, the most important is the social and economic underdevelopment of the middle class. Since most of these societies were originally feudal and at the same time subject to colonial rule or domination, the bourgeoisie in Middle Eastern societies were essentially traders and merchants, unlike European capitalists, many of whom were the owners of industries. Dependent on the goodwill of large landowners and the traditional, conservative clergy, the Middle East middle class was unable to represent the advanced demands of the liberal bourgeoisie or to aspire to realize them.

The birth of the bourgeoisie in these societies therefore miscarried, resulting in the creation of middle classes that, unlike their European counterparts, had no strong representatives to defend their rights and values. The entrepreneurial class that did emerge almost always allied itself with, or acquiesced to, dictatorships. In Iran, whether under the shah or during Khomeini's rule, this social group has always acted as an appendage of the ruling regime. The primary victims of this lack of an autonomous, enlightened, and distinct middle class were democratic and parliamentary institutions.

Common factors such as cultural stagnation, rampant illiteracy, and the tradition of blind submission to authority aggravated this situation. The periodic crises of Western democracies (the emergence of Fascism and Nazism in the 1930s and the reluctance of some Western powers to adapt themselves to the realities of the postcolonial era in the 1960s) had a significant impact. Consequently, liberal trends in Muslim countries were generally discredited. This may explain why, when the status quo collapsed in Eastern Europe, societies there have moved in the direction of parliamentarism and democracy, whereas when the old order begins to crumble in the Middle East, no society begins building democratic structures.

Despite the traditional lack of democracy, however, the yearning for freedom has persisted among the people of the Middle East. Whenever an opportunity for revolt against despotic rulers has presented itself, the people have spared nothing, not even their lives, to attain their ideals. The 1906 Constitutional Revolution in Iran and similar political upheavals in other Middle Eastern countries attest to this reality.

Some countries, including Iran, Egypt, Turkey, and Pakistan, have nevertheless experienced periods of relative liberalism during this century; but the sociopolitical weaknesses of democracy's advocates have led to the failure of almost all of these experiences. Ironically, these very weaknesses have allowed the Muslim fundamentalists to expand their sphere of influence among the impoverished, traditional urban dwellers. Had the liberal nationalists been capable of establishing durable democratic institutions, improving political awareness, and guaranteeing such essential rights as freedom of speech and association, they could have reversed the trend, limiting the fundamentalists' appeal to small, uneducated, and ultratraditionalist sectors. But due to their fundamental shortcomings, indigenous liberals in the Middle East have been and remain incapable of and disinclined to introduce a genuine democratic alternative that could realize democracy and freedom.

Marxism

From the very beginning, the political forces allied with the Communist Bloc and the former Soviet Union never inspired much enthusiasm among the people, primarily due to the region's profound religious beliefs and sentiments. The limited advances that Marxist-oriented political forces made in some countries during the 1960s and '70s were reversed when the shah fell and an Islamic fundamentalist regime took power in Iran. As fundamentalists began to rise, the Marxists declined. Ultimately, the Soviet Union's disintegration virtually ended their social and political influence.

Although Marxism was essentially unappealing to the masses, political parties that looked to Moscow for inspiration played an active role in some countries from the Second World War until the 1980s, because of the increasing role the Soviet Union played in Middle Eastern politics. In Iran, the communist *Tudeh* (masses) Party offered its complete support to the "anti-Imperialist Imam Khomeini," officially sanctioning the execution and suppression of the Mojahedin, collaborating with repressive organizations such as the Guards Corps, and spying on the Mojahedin.

For all its attempts at currying favor with the mullahs, however, the Tudeh Party never became a serious contender in post-shah Iran. After the revolution, the Mojahedin emerged as the largest opposition party in the country. The Tudeh Party was unable to shake off its image as a hated and powerless appendage in Iranian politics, particularly as the Mojahedin exposed its treacherous policies, past and present. The Tudeh consequently never got off the ground, and no one mourned the party's political death in 1983, when all its leaders surrendered to the regime.

During the 1980s, governments in the region dependent on the Soviet Bloc gradually changed their orientation. For example, South Yemen, the sole Marxist government in the Arab world, successfully merged with North Yemen and accepted the economic system of its neighbor and longtime rival.

The demise of communist-influenced parties and regimes created a vacuum at one end of the Middle East's political spectrum: the segment that had traditionally acted as a focal point for dissident intellectuals, students, and impoverished blue- and white-collar workers. Had democratic alternatives existed, they could have easily attracted these social forces and become the cornerstones of consensus governments. In the absence of such alternatives, however, the reactionaries and Islamic fundamentalists became de facto winners after Eastern Europe's collapse and communism's demise.

Fundamentalism Misinterpreted

In summing up, it is appropriate to point to two misinterpretations of Islamic fundamentalism in the West. Some contend that the emergence of fundamentalism is merely a by-product of poverty and the unequal distribution of wealth. They argue, therefore, that social and political reforms can curb and even eliminate fundamentalism. Without question, fundamentalists take full advantage of social deprivation. But at least in this part of the world, fundamentalism should not be viewed merely as a function of economic factors. All of the elements contributing to the crises that plague the region, such as poverty and bureaucratic corruption, were in place in the 1970s. Prior to the mullahs' coming to power in Iran and their export of fundamentalism, however, fundamentalist groups had never developed beyond isolated religious sects. The historical, social, and cultural roots of this phenomenon must not be overlooked.

Without confronting fundamentalism in political and cultural terms—and that means first of all coming face-to-face with the mullahs' regime in Tehran—not much can be achieved. In recent years, the mullahs' rise to power in Iran has played a key role in opening the way for fundamentalism's expansion. Khomeini swept into power on a genuine wave of popular religious sentiments and revived religious demagogy.

Another erroneous perception, sometimes encountered in the West, is the suggestion that the Islamic fundamentalists' rise to power is not necessarily a negative development; it could be a step in Islamic society's progress toward democracy. This interpretation, beyond being ethnocentric, is extremely dangerous because the logical next step is appeasement of the fundamentalists. It further reveals a profound misunderstanding of the religious nature of Khomeini and is equivalent to suggesting that Fascism and Nazism in Europe in the 1930s "contributed" to Europe's progress toward democracy. Perhaps, but only after a world war, millions of victims, and the greatest catastrophe in human history. To argue that fundamentalism is "natural" to Middle Eastern development is an insult to the dignity and history of the Middle Eastern peoples.

Islamic fundamentalism is based upon a medieval and totalitarian ideology. It interferes in the most trivial personal matters of the citizenry, imposing a repressive system that eliminates all avenues for free political, social, and economic activities. Furthermore, owing to its nature, this ideology recognizes no geographic boundaries and, therefore, elevates the export of revolution, crisis, and disruption of all norms of international relations to the top of its agenda.

Has not the experience of the mullahs' regime—which continues executions and torture after fourteen years in power, and which uses any opportunity to export terrorism and fundamentalism and to undermine all peace initiatives in the region—been sufficient? ◾

Modern, Democratic Islam: Antithesis to Fundamentalism

*The reason Khomeini so interferes in all the minute details of
people's lives and leaves them no room to breathe is because
the world of this demon and his heirs is comprised of vengeance, obsession, and hatred. . . . In contrast, we must go
among our people with a spirit of compassion and openness.
Let them be free. Let them step forward to vote and elect
freely. Let a spirit of mutual understanding, forgiveness, love
of construction, and national unity take the place of spite and
vengeance. Let the scars left by Khomeini on the body of this
nation be healed.*

—Maryam Rajavi, September 6, 1991[1]

With the words quoted above, Maryam Rajavi strikes at the heart of the
profound differences and ideological antagonism that pitted the Mojahedin's Islam against Khomeini's. Beyond words and theoretical discussions, the very presence and position of Maryam Rajavi symbolizes the
chasm separating the two ideologies. The Mojahedin and the mullahs'
regime both call themselves Shi'ite Muslims. But within the Mojahedin
movement, women attain the highest positions of leadership and command as well as equal rights with men. The mullahs deny women their
most rudimentary rights and treat them as subhuman. As the secretary
general of the Mojahedin Organization and deputy commander in chief
of the National Liberation Army of Iran, Maryam Rajavi leads a move-

ment half of whose military commanders and political officials are women, as are one-third of its rank and file.

In telling contrast, women are the objects of Rafsanjani's ridicule: "The differences in height, sturdiness, voice, growth, muscular structure, and physical strength, endurance of hardships and illness in women and men show that men are stronger and more capable in all of these matters. . . . Men heed reasoning and logic, whereas most women tend to be emotional . . . These differences affect the delegation of responsibilities, duties, and rights."[2] In the early years of Khomeini's rule, a leading official was equally candid in remarks to the Assembly of Experts: "Who says just because a woman can change a baby's diaper, clean and nurse him, she is qualified to become president or prime minister? Let's say a woman became prime minister. Imagine the disgrace if one morning we went to the prime ministry only to find it closed because the prime minister had given birth the night before."[3]

The contrasts between the Mojahedin and the mullahs are not limited to their outlooks on women. In all areas, from interpreting the Quran and the *Sunnah* (tradition), the Prophet, and the Imams, to social and economic policies, an all-out, unabated, and bloody confrontation is being waged between Khomeiniism and the Mojahedin. This war has raged relentlessly over the past fourteen years on ideological, political, social, and military fronts, resulting in the executions of at least 100,000 Mojahedin.

Khomeini well understood that the Mojahedin were the main enemy of his regime and ideology. When, on June 12, 1980, an attack by armed Pasdaran on a rally of 300,000 Mojahedin supporters in Tehran's Amjadieh soccer stadium aroused a wave of protests by the country's political forces and figures, Khomeini replied, "Our enemy is not in the United States, nor in the Soviet Union, nor in Kurdistan, but right here, right in front of our noses, in Tehran."[4]

More than a decade later, none of the scores of traditional nationalist, Marxist, or liberal parties and groups who surfaced in Iran's post-shah political landscape remain. One by one, they were eliminated, forced to acquiesce or to surrender outright by Khomeini, as he exploited the masses' religious beliefs. Although the Mojahedin have been the primary target of the mullahs' repression and terror during the past decade, they have established themselves as the only viable and powerful alternative to the mullahs.

The Khomeini-Mojahedin confrontation and the latter's views and outlooks are intrinsic to the discussion of fundamentalism. This confrontation pits Khomeini's fundamentalist fanaticism against democratic, modern Islam. The outcome will have profound implications beyond Iran's borders, because it will strike at the heart of the spread of fundamentalism in the Muslim world. The choice then is not just between freedom or repression within Iran: the triumph of the anti-fundamentalist Mojahedin would be a victory for peace, tranquility, and understanding in the Middle East and the Islamic world. Conversely, the continued reign in Iran of the velayat-e-faqih, the principle of absolute theocratic rule, will only result in greater instability, anarchy, and fanaticism in Muslim territories.

The Antithesis of Fundamentalist Islam

The People's Mojahedin Organization of Iran was founded in 1965 by Muhammad Hanifnejad, a leader of the opposition movement in Iranian universities after the fall of Dr. Muhammad Mossadeq's government. The Mojahedin's objective was to overthrow the shah's dictatorship and establish democracy in Iran.

At the time, political movements against the shah fell into three broad categories: nationalists, Marxists, and fundamentalists. Mossadeq's once powerful party, the National Front, represented the secular opposition. But after Mossadeq's fall from power, the Front was taken over by politicians totally out of step with the society's needs who advocated a passive "wait and see" attitude. They had no specific political agenda and no real platform. Their only political capital was Mossadeq's popular appeal. Banished to his native village of Ahmadabad by the shah, Mossadeq distanced himself from them, telling visitors that Iran had to rely on the "energetic, dynamic younger generation" to topple the shah and bring about democracy.

The second group of opposition forces were the Marxists, who included a spectrum of widely divergent and sometimes contradictory political viewpoints, from the pro-Moscow Tudeh Party to small factions inspired by communist Albania.[5] The Marxists were united, however, by their inability to penetrate Iranian society and inspire mass support. This was primarily due to the populace's strong attachment to Islam, but the Marxists' own serious deficiencies—especially splits and ideological feuds—were also to blame. They remained basically confined to intellectual circles and the university campuses, a hotbed of the anti-shah movement.

The third group of anti-shah dissidents were the Muslim fundamentalists. Until the 1960s, the *Feda'ian-e-Islam*, a virulently dogmatic and fanatical group best remembered for its terrorist activities in the 1950s, dominated this wing. After Khomeini's expulsion to Iraq in 1963, he began to be regarded as the leader of the fundamentalist opposition to the shah, primarily because of his strong objections to land reform and women's suffrage.

The Mojahedin's Hanifnejad and his fellow activists, like the vast majority of Iranians, were Shi'ite Muslims. They might have been expected to join the secular National Front or the "Shi'ite" pro-Khomeini opposition; they did neither. Recognizing the rich history of Islam as a force for social change, Hanifnejad and his colleagues began six years of research into the various aspects of Islamic teachings in order to distinguish the genuine Islam of Muhammad from the views espoused by fanatics. This was in essence a declaration of war on fundamentalism, which had until then dominated all that was done in the name of Islam.

Thus, in the midst of the anti-shah political struggle began a more formidable, ideological battle against religious fundamentalism. From the outset, the Mojahedin emphasized the dangers of fundamentalism and endeavored to draw a distinction between Islam and reactionism. They produced a treatise on questions of existence, history, man, and economy; and they presented their own interpretation of Islam's holy book, the Quran, of the *Nahj ol-Balagha*, and of current political issues.[6] Massoud Rajavi was instrumental in these efforts, which he continued from prison following his arrest in 1971, and later after the 1979 revolution.

In 1971, the shah's secret police (SAVAK) arrested Muhammad Hanifnejad and other Mojahedin leaders, including Rajavi. On May 25, 1972, after months of brutal torture, Hanifnejad was executed. Rajavi was also sentenced to die. International activities and pressure by political personalities and human rights advocates, particularly by Rajavi's elder brother, could only commute Massoud Rajavi's death sentence to life imprisonment. Rajavi subsequently undertook the Mojahedin's leadership.

The execution of the Mojahedin's founders, their heroism under torture, and their commitment to genuine Islam generated tremendous support for the organization. By the early 1970s, the organization had assumed the leadership of the anti-shah movement. This popularity compelled some pro-Khomeini clerics to declare their support for the

Mojahedin. Many, like Rafsanjani, later occupied key positions within Khomeini's regime. Exiled to Iraq, Khomeini, however, never agreed to endorse the Mojahedin in spite of his followers' persistent appeals that to do so would increase his own popularity. Khomeini could see, even at that early stage, his own demise in the Mojahedin's version of Islam, and he considered them "anticlerical." Under intense pressure, he finally issued a decree allocating a portion of *sahm-e-Imam* (religious funds) to "the families of imprisoned young Muslims," a veiled reference to the Mojahedin.

In 1975, however, a group of communists staged a coup within the Mojahedin, murdered its leaders who were still outside SAVAK's prisons, and shattered the organization. The fundamentalist mullahs, hitherto overshadowed both socially and politically by the Mojahedin, saw an opportunity. Inside the prisons and in society at large, they engaged in hysterical anti-Mojahedin propaganda and finally collaborated with SAVAK.

Behind the walls of SAVAK's prisons, Massoud Rajavi began in 1975 to revive the Mojahedin Organization. Rajavi focused on distinguishing democratic Islam from all other ideologies. Four years before Khomeini seized power in Iran, Rajavi singled out fundamentalism as the principal threat waiting in the wings: "We believe this [backward religious] current is the antithesis of, and the principal threat to, all groups who struggle in the name of Islam," he said.[7]

In a compilation of his discussions, later published in 1979, he elaborated on this statement:

> Ideologically speaking, our relations with the backward religious current are antagonistic in nature, i.e., the relation between two opposites. The proof of one depends on the other's denial. According to Imam Ali (the first Imam of the Shi'ah), fundamentalist Islam turns every truth into falsehood and every falsehood into truth. Therefore, there are not and cannot be any similarities between the two.[8]

After 1975, the religious fundamentalists led by Khomeini took advantage of the Mojahedin Organization's disintegration to seize the leadership in the anti-shah movement. A unique combination of international conditions helped them to assume power in Iran in 1979. But a major political, social, and military confrontation soon broke out, pitting the Mojahedin against Khomeini. In the course of this conflict, the Mojahedin had to make great sacrifices, but stood firm on the principles of democratic Islam. All of the Mojahedin's activities and political positions during the first two and a half years of Khomeini 's reign were focused on exposing the backward ruling regime and acquainting the people with democratic Islam. Rajavi commented on this process in an interview:

> From the Mojahedin's point of view, the Khomeini regime—in its entirety and with all of its institutions—was illegitimate to begin with, because it had usurped the leadership of the revolution. The Khomeini regime is incapable of resolving any of our people's basic problems—whether political freedoms or economic, social, and cultural needs. This regime is historically illegitimate. Our formal cooperation or participation in its executive organs, was, therefore, inappropriate unless we could at one point or another break the regime's backward framework and impose our own conditions from a position of strength. . . . [9]

The early postrevolutionary ruling regime was made up of two factions, one a Khomeini-led fundamentalist grouping of mullahs such as Beheshti and Rafsanjani, and the other made up of religious liberals such as Bazargan and his Freedom Movement. In their approach to this incongruous coupling, the Mojahedin focused the brunt of their criticism on Khomeini and his supporters, insisting that the main threat was fundamentalism. The Mojahedin therefore also opposed the pro-Moscow, Communist Tudeh Party. The Tudeh Party argued that liberals were the "indigenous agents of imperialism" and the main enemy of the people of Iran. It was the liberals within the regime who should be denounced, not the clerics, the Tudeh Party said. As a result, they moved closer and closer to Khomeini and the fundamentalist mullahs, becoming de facto allies. The Mojahedin's opposition to Khomeini thus led the Tudeh Party to brand the Mojahedin lackeys of imperialism. Eventually, the Tudeh ended up collaborating with the Revolutionary Guards in the execution, torture, and imprisonment of Mojahedin supporters. In 1981, when Massoud Rajavi flew to France, the Tudeh Party demanded his extradition to the Khomeini regime.[10]

One of the Mojahedin's most important actions against fundamentalism was their refusal to vote for the Khomeini regime's constitution establishing the velayat-e-faqih in 1979. In Rajavi's words:

> We have already proven that we are not content with rhetoric, and stand by our commitments, however heavy the price or whatever the sacrifice. This is how we have time and again broken out of a deadlock and opened the way, as on the day when we said "no" to velayat-e-faqih knowing that we would consequently

be denied the right to take part in the presidential elections and their benefits; and on the day when our chants of "death to Khomeini" echoed throughout the country, when nobody else dared to even offend "Mr. Khomeini."

A review of the confrontation between the Mojahedin and Khomeini is not complete without mention of Ayatollah Seyyed Mahmoud Taleqani, the prominent interpreter of the Quran. Ayatollah Taleqani played an important role in the 1979 anti-shah revolution, and his popularity rivaled Khomeini's. Although a bitter opponent of religious fundamentalism, he was appointed to the ruling Assembly of Experts. Because the mullahs did not want to alienate Taleqani or his supporters, they did not incorporate the velayat-e-faqih into the constitution until after Taleqani's death in September 1979.

To counter Khomeini's interpretation of Islam, Rajavi gave a series of lectures on Islamic philosophy and modern Islamic thought at one of Iran's largest universities, Sharif University of Technology, in 1979. Ten thousand people attended the weekly lectures. Hundreds of thousands of published transcripts as well as video recordings of the lectures were distributed in Tehran and other cities, providing a huge audience with its first real exposure to Islam as a modern, democratic religion, a very different version than what mullahs historically presented. Lecturing on comparative Islamic philosophy, the Mojahedin leader also presented a detailed critique of the fundamentalist approach to Islam, as well as atheistic, agnostic, and materialistic philosophies.

Alarmed by the popularity of Rajavi's lectures, Khomeini presided over a number of televised classes in which he interpreted verses of the Quran. His monotonous and overly reactionary lectures soon became a subject of national ridicule. Khomeini abruptly ended the sessions.

Having failed to win the argument, Khomeini's regime turned to force as the only way to stop the open debate. In April 1980, armed gangs acting on government orders rampaged through the nation's campuses, killing and wounding students and destroying buildings, libraries, and dormitories under the pretext of the "Islamic Cultural Revolution." All universities were closed down, and a group called the "Supreme Islamic Cultural Revolutionary Council" was set up to purge universities and institutes of higher education of all students harboring any sympathy for the Mojahedin.

Attacks by Khomeini's operatives on any opposition political activity also made it difficult for the Mojahedin to continue their political campaign. From 1979 to 1981, at least 100 Mojahedin members and supporters were stabbed, clubbed, or shot to death by Khomeini's agents. Two thousand Mojahedin prisoners were tortured. Throughout this period, the Mojahedin continued to pursue their political activities peacefully, a far more complex and difficult task than the one facing them during the shah's reign. In Rajavi's words:

> Consistent with the mood of the majority of Iranians, we believed that the Khomeini regime and its institutions enjoyed temporary political and social legitimacy. Until June 1981, therefore, we neither picked up arms nor violated the mullahs' own constitution. In other words, whereas the regime was, in an absolute sense, devoid of ideological legitimacy, in relative terms and owing to the desires of the majority of Iranians, its legal institutions still remained to be tested.[11]

In the months preceding June 1981, the mullahs mobilized gangs of club-wielders who routinely attacked the Mojahedin's rallies, centers, and offices throughout the country in a bid to provoke the organization into armed action. The Mojahedin, however, refused to respond in kind to avoid any premature confrontation with the regime. Under Rajavi's instructions, they were determined to use every opportunity to carry on their lawful political activities.

The Mojahedin organized a peaceful demonstration of half a million Tehran residents on June 20, 1981. Mojahedin leaders reasoned that if Khomeini's government retained even a slight commitment to the rule of law, the clerics would leave some breathing space, albeit small, for political parties to engage in nonviolent political activity. Khomeini, however, had already concluded that absolute repression was his regime's only chance for survival. The brutal clampdown of the peaceful march eliminated the last vestiges of peaceful political activities. Khomeini had declared war on the Mojahedin. Arbitrary arrests and summary executions immediately followed.

A Glance at the Mojahedin's Basic Viewpoints

In comparing Khomeini's fundamentalism to the Mojahedin's modernism, such fundamental issues as the country's future political system, democracy, and human rights are especially important. Commenting on the intrinsic differences between the Mojahedin and Khomeini, Massoud Rajavi has said:

When Khomeini became the leader and the Imam, as a first step words were sacrificed and left empty of substance and meaning. Such noble words as "Islam," "freedom,'" "republic," etc., were systematically debased and cheapened. They called the most savage tortures "religious punishment." They mutilated prisoners' bodies, gouged out their eyes, and stoned people to death under the banner of religion.[12]

Democracy and Government

The totalitarian principle of velayat-e-faqih is the basis upon which Khomeiniism stands. In contrast, for the Mojahedin democracy is indispensable to Islam. Their vision of Islam tolerates its opponents and treats them fairly. Islam blossoms only in a spirit of freedom and truthfulness, and therefore cannot trample upon the legitimate rights of the people. Power and governance do not constitute the ends of Islam, the Mojahedin believe. It is committed to certain inviolable moral principles which cannot be ignored under any circumstances.

In accordance with this spirit, all member personalities and organizations of the National Council of Resistance, including the Mojahedin and other opponents of the mullahs' regime, regardless of their numerical strength, political status, and so forth, have an equal vote. In the decision-making process, therefore, the Mojahedin, though a nationwide political party with a considerable following, has only one vote, like every other organization and personality in the council. The NCR President, Massoud Rajavi, has repeatedly emphasized that such a council constitutes a historic democratic experience for Iran, a nation that has suffered under the dictatorships of the shah and Khomeini for seventy years.[13]

In accordance with the council's program, after the overthrow of the mullahs' regime, a provisional government headed by Massoud Rajavi will be in power for a maximum of six months, its main task being to hold free elections for a National Legislative and Constituent Assembly. Afterwards, the provisional government will submit its resignation to the parliament. The people's elected representatives will then determine the country's mode of government and the new republic's constitution.

The program of the National Council of Resistance and the provisional government emphasizes "recognizing the people's right to make decisions and determine their own destiny" and regards the attainment of national sovereignty, rather than clerical sovereignty, as "the most valuable achievement of the just Resistance of the people of Iran." The program underscores complete freedom of belief and expression and a ban on censorship and inquisition; complete freedom of the press, parties, assemblies, political associations, and various unions, societies, and councils; and the right to dissent at all civil and military levels and positions.[14]

Democracy and the "popular vote as the source of legitimacy to govern" are among the most fundamental differences between the Mojahedin's and Khomeini's ideologies. Khomeini frequently remarked that the vali-e-faqih, the absolute ruler, had a divine right to rule, whereas the Mojahedin have insisted that only the popular vote is the determining factor. In Rajavi's words:

> The Mojahedin profoundly believe that to avoid the deviations that beset contemporary revolutions throughout the world, they must remain wholeheartedly committed to the will of the public and democracy. If they are to act as a leading organization, before all else the populace must give them a mandate in a free and fair election. It is not enough to have gone through the trials of repression, imprisonment, torture, and executions under the shah and the mullahs. The Mojahedin must also pass the test of general elections. If the Mojahedin were to choose to compensate for the lack of popular mandate by relying on their past sacrifices or organizational prowess, or arms, their resilient, lively, and democratic organization would soon become a hollow, rotten bureaucracy.... If the people don't vote for us (after we have overthrown the mullahs' regime), we shall remain in the opposition, holding firmly to our principles.[15]

Rajavi's emphasis on the need for a popular mandate to govern and his rejection of the fundamentalists' claim of "divine legitimacy " is not unique in Islamic history. There are important precedents set by Muslim clerics and laymen who argued passionately against the notion that elections have no place in an "Islamic" rule. Years before Khomeini came to power, respected clergymen like Ayatollah Mirza Hussein Na'ini and Ayatollah Taleqani warned against the danger of religious tyranny. Ayatollah Na'ini stressed this in his writings at the time of the Iranian Constitutional Revolution at the turn of the century:

> Among the forces safeguarding despotism are the religious tyrants. They adopt certain words and components of religion to appear appealing to the naive. They deceive the ordinary people, unfamiliar with the principles and basics of the

religion and the essence of the Prophets' mission. They make these people obey their rule. They claim to safeguard the religion and to be looking after the interests of the religion, but in fact they spread the shadow of Satan over the public and keep them under this ominous shadow of ignorance and wretchedness.

Because they manipulate the pure emotions of the people and take cover behind the strong fortifications of religion, they are much more dangerous and harder to repel. Although religious tyranny differs from political tyranny in appearance, in essence they act similarly and lead in the same direction. Both utilize the financial and spiritual resources of the people to preserve power. As stipulated in the Quran, obedience to them constitutes dualism.[16]

Tolerance of Opponents

The Iranian clerics used the slogan "the only party is the Party of God [Hizbullah]" to crack down on their political opponents and suppress freedoms. During the early years of Khomeini's rule, organized gangs chanted that slogan as they raided meetings and ransacked the headquarters of political organizations, bookstores, publishing houses, newspapers, and so forth.

The Quran, on the other hand, says to Muslims: "Allah forbiddeth you not those who warred not against you on account of religion and drove you not out from your homes, that ye should show them kindness and deal justly with them. Lo! Allah loveth the just dealers."[17] Although many companions of Imam Ali urged him to act decisively against the Kharijites in the seventh century, or at least restrict their freedom and political activities, Ali replied, "So long as they do not harm us, we will not take any action against them. If they debate with us, we will do likewise. We will continue to pay them their share of the treasury. We will allow them to go to the mosques to pray. Only if they resort to violence and killing will we reluctantly fight them."

The Mojahedin have been profoundly influenced by such teachings of the Prophet and Imam Ali. In 1980, the Mojahedin formally asked the Khomeini regime's judiciary to refrain from executing the leaders of a coup that shattered the Mojahedin Organization. In 1983, the Mojahedin denounced the torture, harassment, and detention without trials of the Tudeh Party leaders, although the latter caused the imprisonment and subsequent execution of hundreds of Mojahedin supporters and sympathizers by turning them over to the security forces.

The program of the National Council of Resistance and the provisional government guarantees the individual's right to dissent and freedom from persecution in the future Iran. It specifies that there are no limits to any individual's or group's political activities short of armed rebellion against the government. The program also states: "Our rich heritage of Islam, contrary to Khomeini's [fundamentalism], does not draw its rightfulness and legitimacy (including political legitimacy) from coercion and compulsion. We firmly believe that Islam can only flourish in the absence of any discrimination, privilege, or social or political coercion."[18]

Religious Tolerance

Islam's early history abounds in examples of fair, humane, and equitable treatment of adherents to other faiths. When Imam Ali appointed Muhammad ibn Abu Bakr as the governor of Egypt, he impressed upon him the need to treat non-Muslims with fairness, to restore the rights of the oppressed, and to deal harshly with the oppressors. Upon hearing that a Jewish girl's jewelry had been forcibly taken away by people acting in the name of Islam, Ali said that he would understand if a Muslim felt so much pain and sorrow over such an injustice that he died of grief.[19] Inspired by such examples, the Mojahedin have shown their firm belief in legal equality, unity, and fraternity for all, religious or nonreligious, Muslim, Christian, Jewish, or a follower of any other religion or school of thought. The Declaration of the National Council of Resistance on the Relations of the Provisional Government with Religion and Denomination, declares:

1. All forms of discrimination against the followers of various religions and denominations in the enjoyment of their individual and social rights are prohibited. No citizens shall enjoy any privileges or be subject to any deprivations in respect of nomination for election, suffrage, employment, education, becoming a judge, or any other individual or social rights, for reason of belief or nonbelief in a particular religion or denomination.
2. Any form of compulsory religious or ideological teaching and any compulsion to practice or not practice religious rituals and customs is forbidden. The right of all religions and denominations to teach, proselytize, and freely perform their rituals and traditions, and the respect and security of all places belonging to them, are guaranteed.
3. Jurisdiction of judicial authorities is not based upon their religious or ideological status, and laws not formulated within the legislative institution of the land will have no authority or validity. Together with the abrogation of the rules of *qessas* (retaliation), *hudud* (religious punishments), *ta'zirat* (corporal punishment), and *diyat* (penalties) imposed by Khomeini's inhu-

man regime, and with the dissolution of the so-called revolutionary courts and prosecutors' offices, and the *Shari'ah* courts, all included in the Provisional Government's immediate tasks, judicial processes will take place within the unified judicial order of the Republic, on the basis of universally recognized legal principles and in accordance with the law.

4. Religious, denominational, and ideological inquisition by the government or any of its agencies in any form is prohibited.

Human Rights

"The history of human rights in Iran is being written in blood, the blood of those striving for freedom," commented the late Kazem Rajavi in an interview a few years before he was gunned down by assassins sent by the mullahs. His remark aptly describes the Mojahedin's commitment to human rights. Islam as understood by the Mojahedin teaches the responsibility and free will of man, and places great emphasis on the independent character of every human being. Each individual is a world unto himself and represents the verity of all mankind. In the words of the Quran: ". . . if any one slew a person—unless it be for murder or for spreading mischief in the land— it would be as if he slew the whole people. And if any one saved a life, it would be as if he saved the life of the whole people."[20]

The program of the National Council of Resistance of Iran recognizes the "individual and social rights of all citizens as stressed in the Universal Declaration of Human Rights." It guarantees general freedoms, including freedom of association, thought and speech, the media, parties, unions, councils, faiths and religions, and professions. The NCR program also calls for "the abolishment of military and extraordinary tribunals, the investigation of political offenses in civil courts with juries present," and guarantees the "right of the accused to defense and to the choice of the defense counsel, and the right to appeal." It emphasizes "the banning of torture under any pretext," and stresses "the judicial and professional security for all citizens and abolishment of Komitehs and the Guards Corps."

Grace and Compassion Versus Violence and Vengeance

"Humans, whether they want it or not, are brethren . . . Reconciliation between two persons is better than all prayers and fasts . . . Religion is good behavior." These are the words of Muhammad, the Prophet of Islam. The Quran says: ". . . but do thou good, as God has been good to thee."[21] "Speak with humility to the people . . ."[22] "God commands justice, the doing of good and liberality to kith."[23]

Imam Ali's life embodied his commitment to the teachings of grace, compassion, and love in place of vengeance and violence. When the Battle of Jamal ended, Ali pardoned all those who had waged war on him. "He who forgives one who has oppressed and is merciful to one who has denied him kindness" was Ali's model of an honorable human being.

In this sense as well, the Mojahedin are inspired by the teachings of Islam. In the words of Maryam Rajavi, "The Mojahedin represent an Islam in which love, compassion, and liberty are the genuine values. Khomeini, on the other hand, always promoted vengeance and brutality. Did anyone ever see Khomeini utter a word of kindness?"[24]

Women's Rights

Nowhere is the fundamentalists' backward frame of mind more apparent than in their treatment of women. For Khomeinists, women have no place in society; a woman's place is in the home, where she must be an obedient wife, caring mother, and no more. Under the pretext of its self-styled crime of "improper veiling," the Khomeini regime viciously humiliates Iranian women, flogging and torturing the violators. Morteza Moqtada'i, Head of the Supreme Court, announced, "Women appearing in public without traditionally defined veiling will be sentenced to up to seventy-four lashes."[25]

The clerical regime does not recognize women as fully human. A woman described her plight thus: "Is it a sin to be a woman? The Tehran branch of the Islamic Free University announced some time ago that it was hiring professors. Since I had a master's degree in Persian literature, I approached the university. Although I was perfectly qualified, they openly told me that because I am a woman, they could not hire me."[26]

The mullahs also try to segregate men and women in any possible place, on the streets, in classes, on buses, and at the beach. The director of public transportation in Tehran announced, "As of December 10, 1988, the plan for sexual segregation of bus passengers will be carried out on all the double-decked buses. The sisters [women] will accordingly board buses from the rear door and put their tickets in a box next to it. The upper deck and part of the lower deck are assigned to brother [men] passengers, whose tickets will be collected by the conductor."[27]

These and thousands of other rules and regulations show the medieval dogmas of the fundamentalist rulers of Iran in action.

The Mojahedin, on the other hand, fully recognize the rights and freedoms of women. Women comprise more than half of the Mojahedin Executive Committee presided over by Secretary General Maryam Rajavi. In October 1991, the Mojahedin's parliamentary body—the 837-member Central Council—unanimously elected a woman, Fahimeh Arvani, as the organization's deputy secretary general. She also presides over the Mojahedin's Central Council.[28]

In April 1987, the National Council of Resistance adopted a Declaration on the Freedoms and Rights of Iranian Women. The document underscores the need to abolish all forms of coercion, suppression, and discrimination endured by women in Iran. The declaration maintains that such practices are unjust and violate human dignity. To realize the full rights of women, the NCR contends, such a plan is essential. It will serve as a guideline for the provisional government's policies in this respect. It emphasizes women's right to hold any government position, including the presidency and a judgeship—a right denied by the mullahs' constitution. Women's right to freely choose their clothing, to file for divorce, to choose their spouse, to receive equal pay for equal work, and to enroll in any educational establishment has also been guaranteed. The declaration calls for "the full equality of women and men in the social, political, cultural, and economic spheres." Women have made up a majority of the NCR's membership since its expansion to 150 members in December 1992.

❖ ❖ ❖

Human evolution has been described as an unrelenting passage from the realm of necessity to the realm of freedom. In this context, the Mojahedin-mullah confrontation in Iran is the struggle between a reactionary perversion of Islam and true Islam, which advocates freedom and awareness; an ideological duel between the forces of ignorance and the proponents of liberty. If Iran is to emerge from the clutches of Khomeini's terrorist-religious tyranny, the Mojahedin are the only solution. Democratic, liberating Islam will doubtless triumph. Massoud Rajavi's words offer a glimpse of what Iran will become when the mullahs are overthrown:

> We shall live in peace and coexistence with our neighbors. Democratic Iran will not recognize any place for vengeance, blind hatred, or Khomeini's tribunals or

brand of anarchy. We are responsible enough not to be involved in internal and international adventurism. We do not want an antidemocratic theocracy like Khomeini's. Instead of "exporting the revolution," we shall invite our country's experts to return to Iran. In democratic Iran no one will be persecuted for his ideology or religion. Tomorrow's Iran will be free of repression and religious hypocrisy. Women, workers, peasants, religious and ethnic minorities will not be oppressed. Kurds, Turks, Jews, Muslims, Armenians, Christians, Zoroastrians, and non-Muslims will enjoy equal rights. Iran will become a symbol of peace, stability, and friendship in the Middle East.[29]

Notes

CHAPTER I

1. *The Glorious Qur'an*, translation and commentary by A. Yusuf Ali (USA: American Trust Publications, 1987), *Sura II: Baqara*, Verse 256, p. 103.

2. *Rahmaton lil a'lamin*, or "Mercy for the Worlds," is a popular Muslim reference to Prophet Muhammad.

3. "*Al-Islam huwal-hal*" ("Islam Is the Solution") was a ubiquitous slogan of Algerian fundamentalists.

4. The People's Mojahedin Organization of Iran *(Sazeman-e Mojahedin-e Khalq-e Iran)* was founded on September 6, 1965, by Muhammad Hanifnejad and two other like-minded intellectuals, Sa'id Mohsen and Ali-Asghar Badi'zadegan. Islamic, democratic, and nationalist, the Mojahedin were at the forefront of the anti-shah movement which resulted in the 1979 revolution.

5. Daniel Pipes, *In the Path of God* (New York: Basic Books, 1983), p. 65.

6. Ali ibn Abi Taleb, *Nahj ol-Balagha*, translation and commentary by Haj Alinaqi Faiz ol-Islam (Tehran: Faiz ol-Islam Publications, 1972), sermon 40, pp. 125–126.

7. Richard P. Mitchel, *The Society of Muslim Brothers* (London: 1969), p. 32.

8. H. A. R. Gibb, *Civilization of Islam*, pp. 142–143.

9. Ibn Taymiyeh (Taqi od-Din Abu al-Abbas Ahmad), *Menhaj as-Sunna an-Nabawya (The Ways and Traditions of the Prophet)*, First Volume (Cairo: 1962), p. 371.

10. Bernard Lewis, "Politics and War," in *The Legacy of Islam*, 2d ed., ed. Joseph Schacht and C. E. Bosworth (Oxford: Oxford University Press, 1974), p. 163.

11. A. P. Petroshevsky, *Eslam Dar Iran (Islam in Iran)*, (Tehran: Marvi Publishing, 1975).

12. Hamilton A. R. Gibb, "Religion and Politics in Christianity and Islam," in *Islam and International Relations*, ed. J. Harris Proctor (London: Pall Mall, 1965), p.10.

13. Abu Bakr Al-Baghlani, *Al-Tamheed*, p. 186.

14. *Al-Rasa'il (Letters)*, Third Volume, *Political Philosophy of Ikhwan as-Safa (Brethren of Purity)*, series of articles on Islamic thought (Tehran: 1977), pp. 25–49.

15. Morteza Ravandi, *Tarikh-e-Ejtema'iy-e Iran (Social History of Iran)*, Third Volume (Tehran: 1978), p. 512.

16. Hassan Ayat, *Chehreye Vaghei-ye Mossadeq ol-Saltaneh (The True Visage of Mossadeq ol-Saltaneh)* (Qom: Islamic Publications, 1981), p. 3.

17. Ibid., p. 20.

18. Ayatollah Seyyed Mahmoud Taleqani was a long-time activist against the shah and a highly respected religious leader. His endeavors in defense of the people's fundamental rights began against the oppressive rule of the shah's father, Reza shah, in the 1930s. He was a staunch supporter of Iran's nationalist leader, Dr.

Muhammad Mossadeq. Between the coup that ousted Mossadeq in August 1953 and the 1979 revolution, Taleqani was active in the anti-shah movement and was arrested and tortured on several occasions by the SAVAK. Soon after the fall of the shah, relations between Taleqani and the ruling mullahs soured. He passed away on September 10, 1979, at the age of 69.

19. Al-Kawakibi, *Tabaye' ol-Istibdad (Characteristics of Despotism)*, (Tehran: 1905), p. 12.

20. Ibid., p. 22.

21. Ibid., p. 182.

CHAPTER II

1. *Ressalat*, Tehran, 7 January 1988. (See Appendix.)

2. Ruhollah Moussavi Khomeini, *Velayat-e-faqih* (Najaf: 1971), p. 63.

3. Khamenei Friday prayer sermon, Tehran radio, 1 January 1988.

4. *Ressalat*, Tehran, 7 January 1988.

5. Khomeini, op. cit., p. 65.

6. Associated Press, dispatch from Paris, 7 November 1978.

7. United Press International, dispatch from Paris, 8 November 1978.

8. Massoud Rajavi is the leader of the Iranian Resistance. He joined the Mojahedin in 1966, soon becoming a member of the organization's Leadership Committee. Until 1971, when he was arrested by the shah's secret police (SAVAK), Rajavi served along with the Mojahedin's founder, Hanifnejad, formulating the organization's ideological perspectives and course of action. When the Mojahedin's leaders were sentenced to death by a shah's military tribunal, Rajavi's sentence was commuted to life imprisonment due to international pressure. Professor Kazem Rajavi, Massoud's elder brother, who was assassinated in Geneva in April 1990, played a major role in organizing a worldwide campaign to save Massoud Rajavi's life. Rajavi remained in prison until 1979 and was among the last group of political prisoners released a week after the shah fled the country. From the beginning, Rajavi emphasized that the new regime must respect the people's fundamental rights. Under his leadership, the Mojahedin emerged as the focal point of the democratic opposition to Khomeini. In June 1981, Rajavi organized the nationwide Resistance and in July 1981 formed the National Council of Resistance in Tehran. Rajavi left Tehran for Paris in July 1981, on board an Iranian Air Force Boeing jet piloted by veteran air force officers sympathetic to the Mojahedin, to enlist international support for the political alternative to clerical rule. In June 1986, Rajavi left France for Iraq to form the National Liberation Army of Iran, the Resistance's military arm.

9. Immediately following the demonstration, the regime began widespread arrests of the protesters or anyone suspected of being a Mojahedin sympathizer. As dusk fell, hundreds of detainees were sent before the firing squads in summary fashion in Evin and other prisons. In the first week after June 20, government media reported the execution of more than 700 people. Some were shot even without their identities being established. The regime printed the victims' pictures in Tehran dailies, asking the parents of those executed to go to prisons to identify their children. (See Appendix.)

10. In 1979, under Khomeini's auspices, Muhammad-Hussein Beheshti, Ali-Akbar

Hashemi-Rafsanjani, Ali Khamenei, and Hassan Ayat founded the Islamic Republic Party. The IRP gradually monopolized power within the regime. Beheshti became the Party's Secretary General and was replaced by Khamenei after he was killed in June 1981. On June 2, 1987, upon Khomeini's personal order, the IRP was dissolved "to avoid further factionalization within the government."

11. Mehdi Bazargan, head of *Nehzat-e Azadi-e Iran* (Iran's Freedom Movement), was Khomeini's hand-picked premier for the provisional government following the overthrow of the shah. His government collapsed after the American Embassy takeover in Tehran in November 1979. Despite Bazargan's endorsement of the clerics' policies, the Rafsanjani administration banned his movement from engaging in any activity.

12. *Constitution of the Islamic Republic of Iran* (Qom: Center for Islamic Publications, 1979), p. 9.

13. Ibid., p. 17.

14. *Ressalat*, Tehran, 15 August 1988.

15. *Ressalat*, Tehran, 20 August 1988.

16. *Ressalat*, Tehran, 18 August 1988.

17. *Ressalat*, Tehran, 13 November 1988.

CHAPTER III

1. Hashemi-Rafsanjani Friday prayer sermon, Tehran radio, 10 October 1991.

2. On March 28, 1989, Khomeini officially ousted Montazeri as his would-be successor. Montazeri, who was chosen as Khomeini's heir apparent in 1985, had expressed a different opinion on Khomeini's order for massacre of political prisoners following the cease-fire in the Iran-Iraq War in summer 1988. Khomeini relegated Montazeri to the position of preacher in the Qom's theological school.

3. Hussein-Ali Montazeri's confidential letters to judicial officials, 15 August 1988, and to Khomeini, 31 July 1988. Copies of the letters were obtained by the People's Mojahedin Organization of Iran. (See Appendix.)

4. Ahmad Azari-Qomi, *Ressalat*, Tehran, 5 June 1989.

5. Abolqassem Khaz'ali interview, in *Ressalat*, Tehran, 5 June 1989.

6. Tehran radio, 25 June 1989.

7. Tehran radio, 14 February 1992.

8. Shabestari interview, in *Ressalat*, Tehran, 24 February 1992.

9. Raja'i-Khorassani interview, in *Ressalat*, Tehran, 8 January 1992.

10. Constitution of the Islamic Republic of Iran, including the revisions made by the Council for Constitutional Revision (Tehran: 1989) .

11. Reuters, dispatch from Istanbul, Turkey, 1 May 1992.

12. Tehran radio, 3 August 1989.

13. Muhammad-Hussein Beheshti, president of the Supreme Judicial Council, was killed in June 1981. At the time, his power was second only to Khomeini's.

14. Representatives of the International Committee of the Red Cross were reported in March 1992 to have been expelled from Iran. Neither the regime nor the Red Cross officials concealed the fact that the reason for a halt to the Red Cross's

activities in Iran was the emergence of "sensitive" problems and issues with regard to the political prisoners. The decision for expulsion of the Red Cross was made in a meeting of the Supreme National Security Council headed by Rafsanjani. Afterward, Muhammad Yazdi, head of the judiciary, accused the Red Cross of espionage, and the state-run newspapers launched a smear campaign against the ICRC.

15. Anushiravan Ehteshami, "The Structure of Power in Post-Khomeini Iran" (unpublished paper, January 1991), p.18.

CHAPTER IV

1. Larijani interview, in *Ressalat*, Tehran, 7 August 1989.
2. Larijani interview, in *Ressalat*, Tehran, 2 August 1989.
3. Larijani interview, in *Ressalat*, Tehran, 29 July 1989.
4. The roundtable discussion was attended by Muhammad Khatami, Muhammad-Javad Larijani, and Morteza Nabavi, the editor of *Ressalat* newspaper and former minister of post, telegraph, and telephone. Excerpts of this discussion appeared in a two-page article in *Ressalat*, Tehran, 2 August 1991.
5. *Ressalat*, Tehran, 7 July 1991.
6. Rafsanjani made these remarks while addressing the Global Hizbullah Conference in Tehran, Tehran radio, 22 May 1990.
7. *Ressalat*, Tehran, 8 January 1992.
8. *Ressalat*, Tehran, 7 July 1991.
9. Gerald Seib, "Iran Is Re-Emerging as a Mideast Power as Iraqi Threat Fades," *Wall Street Journal*, 18 March 1992.
10. *Ressalat*, Tehran, 7 July 1991.
11. Manouchehr Muhammadi, *Principles of Foreign Policy of the Islamic Republic of Iran* (Tehran: Amirkabir Publishing House, 1987), p. 37.

CHAPTER V

1. *Kayhan*, Tehran, 11 January 1992.
2. Tehran radio, 14 December 1991.
3. A classified policy paper prepared by experts of the Iranian government's Supreme National Security Council in January 1991. A copy of the paper was obtained by the People's Mojahedin Organization of Iran.
4. Ernest Gellner, *Muslim Society* (Cambridge: Cambridge University Press, 1981), p. 99.
5. Muhammad Hanifnejad is the founder of the People's Mojahedin Organization of Iran. An agricultural engineer, Hanifnejad was born in 1938 in Tabriz, capital of the northwestern province of East Azerbaijan. As a Muslim intellectual, he had been politically active against the shah's dictatorship and was imprisoned in 1963. After his release, he founded the Mojahedin in 1965 based on Islamic ideology and nationalist policies. From 1965 until 1971, he concentrated on expanding the organizational network across Iran and formulating the movement's ideology, tactics, and strategy. In September 1971, the shah's dreaded secret police, SAVAK, arrested the organization's leaders, including Hanifnejad.

After months of brutal tortures, all but one of the members of the Leadership Committee, Massoud Rajavi, were executed. Hanifnejad was executed on May 25, 1972.

6. Daniel Pipes, *In the Path of God* (New York: Basic Books, 1983), p. 284.

7. Hassan Pirnia and Abbas Iqbal Ashtiani, *Tarikh-e Iran (History of Iran)*, 3rd ed. (Tehran: Kayyam Publishing House, 1973), p. 51.

8. Ibid, p. 223.

9. The four Shi'ite source books written in the ninth and tenth centuries on Hadith are *Kafi (Sufficient)* by Kolayni, *Tahzib (Purification)* and *Estebsar (Quest for Knowledge)* by Sheikh-e Toussi, and *Man La Yahzor ol-Faqih (In the Absence of a Jurist)* by Sheikh-e Sadouq. The six Sunni source books on Hadith are *Sonan-e Nessa'i (Traditions of Nessa'i)* by Nessa'i, *Sahih-e Moslem (The Book of Moslem)* by Moslem-e Hajjaj, *Jame'-e Tarmazi (Complete Works of Tarmazi)* by Tarmazi, *Sahih-e Bukhari (The Book of Bukhari)* by Bukhari, *Sonan-e ibn Majeh (Traditions of Ibn Majeh)* by Ibn Majeh, and *Sonan-e Abi Davood (Traditions of Abi Davood)* by Abi Davood. These were also written in the ninth and tenth centuries.

10. Associated Press, dispatch from Washington, 25 February 1992, quoting an official of the People's Mojahedin Organization of Iran.

11. *The New York Times*, 29 April 1982.

12. *British Petroleum Statistical Review of World Energy* (1991).

13. This issue was frequently raised during discussions on the future of the Central Asian republics. But many analysts believe the difference carries particularly less weight in the former Soviet republics. For example, Paul Goble, a former U.S. State Department expert on the Soviet nationalities, noted that the distinction is a lot less relevant among Soviet Muslims. (*The Washington Post*, 2 February 1992). The view is commonly shared by the general public in these republics: A militant in the Uzbek city of Namangan told *Time* magazine: "It doesn't matter that they are Shi'ite over there and we are Sunni. The Ayatollah made Iran strong and glorious, while in Sunni Turkey they have weakened Islam." (*Time*, 20 April 1992)

14. Hamid Enayat, *Tafakkor-e Novin-e Siassi Dar Islam (Modern Islamic Political Thought)* (Tehran: Amirkabir Publishing House, 1983), p. 20.

15. Khomeini's message on the founding of the Islamic Republic Party of Iran, *Kayhan*, Tehran, 3 April 1979.

16. Tehran mullahs have followed the same course after Khomeini's death. Anis Mansour, a famous Egyptian journalist, wrote in *Al Ahram* in January 1992: "He lies to himself and to all the people who says that [Khomeini] was an Iranian. He is ignorant who says: 'How does this concern us? Those are problems that relate to the Shi'ah sect and we are Sunnis.'"

17. *The Glorious Qur'an*, translation and commentary by A. Yusuf Ali (USA: American Trust Publications, 1987), *Sura IV: Nisaa*, Verse 59, p. 198.

CHAPTER VI

1. Jack Anderson and Dale Van Atta, "Iran's Spurious Holy War," *The Washington Post*, 5 October 1986.

2. Confidential policy paper on the Iran-Iraq War, prepared by the ruling Islamic Republic Party. A copy was obtained by the People's Mojahedin Organization of

Iran. In January 1983, the movement published excerpts of this document in its Farsi-language organ, *Mojahed*.

3. *Kayhan*, Tehran, 27 September 1980.

4. *Bamdad*, Tehran, 14 April 1980.

5. *Jomhouri Islami*, Tehran, 9 August 1980.

6. This map, produced by the Guards Corps during the Iran-Iraq War, was extensively distributed among the G.C. Staff at the war fronts. It encompasses Tehran's plans to establish an Islamic empire by using Iraq as a springboard for this strategy. A copy of the map was obtained by the People's Mojahedin Organization of Iran. (See Appendix.)

7. In 1983, the Mojahedin initiated an extensive domestic and international campaign to discredit Khomeini's war effort. This was subsequent to a peace meeting between Massoud Rajavi and Tariq Aziz, then deputy prime minister of Iraq, at Rajavi's Paris headquarters on January 9, 1983. Rajavi proposed a peace plan in March of that year, which Iraq accepted as a suitable basis for a negotiated settlement of the conflict. The peace plan was endorsed by more than 10,000 parties, dignitaries, and political personalities from 70 countries around the world.

8. The National Council of Resistance of Iran (NCR) was founded by Massoud Rajavi in July 1981 in Tehran. It is a coalition of democratic Iranian opposition organizations and personalities, representing a broad spectrum of different political views within Iran. In its nine-day session in December 1992, the NCR expanded to 150 members and it was agreed that it will act as the National Legislative Assembly for the transition period after the mullahs' overthrow.

9. Hashemi-Rafsanjani Friday prayer sermon, Tehran radio, 9 August 1991.

10. For instance, invalids took part in a major antigovernment demonstration on April 16, 1992, in the southern city of Shiraz, the capital of Fars Province. (Reuters, dispatch from Tehran, 16 April 1992.)

11. Khomeini had warned repeatedly against peace and its consequences for the regime, a view also shared by senior Iranian officials. On August 7, 1986, in a message addressed to Iranians who had gathered in Mecca for the hajj pilgrimage, Khomeini said: "Those who talk of peace are traitors to Islam and the interest of Muslims. Peace with these criminals has at all times resulted in the dishonor of Islam and the Muslim countries. For us, compromise and an imposed peace have a meaning worse than war." In light of such background, he described his forced acceptance of the cease-fire in July 1988 as "drinking a chalice of poison."

12. *Al-Jumhuriya*, Baghdad, 20 January 1992. Muhammad Hamzah Az-Zubaidi, the Iraqi prime minister, reiterated the same point during an interview with the Iraqi national television in January 1992. As the minister of transportation and communications, he was a member of an Iraqi delegation which visited Iran on several occasions during the Persian Gulf crisis.

13. The formation of the National Liberation Army of Iran, the military arm of the Iranian Resistance, was announced on June 20, 1987, by Massoud Rajavi, its commander in chief. This all-volunteer army, which is based along the Iran-Iraq frontier, has evolved from an infantry force to a full-fledged armored army with tank, mechanized infantry, artillery, air defense and air assault units, communications and combat engineering units. The NLA's largest offensive was the Eternal Light Operation. In summer 1988, 35 NLA brigades thrust 170 kilome-

ters inside Iran to the gates of the western provincial capital of Kermanshah. The NLA inflicted 55,000 casualties on the enemy's forces.

14. In the wake of the Persian Gulf War, the Tehran regime took advantage of the circumstances and launched major offensives in March and April 1991 to destroy the NLA. Although the National Liberation Army deployed only one-fifth of its forces in these defensive battles, it crushed the mullahs' 25,000-strong force. Thousands were killed, a number captured, and the rest routed. Forty-three NLA combatants were killed during the battles, code-named Operation Pearl.

CHAPTER VII

1. Ali Khamenei, Tehran radio, 4 April 1992.
2. Bruce Clark and Anatol Lieven, "US, Turkey and Iran Chase Power in Central Asia," *Times*, London, 17 February 1992.
3. Editorial, *Ressalat*, Tehran, 29 December 1991.
4. Richard Curtis, "Iranian Opposition Leader Charges Rafsanjani Regime Backing Algeria," *The Washington Report on Middle East Affairs*, April 1992.
5. Claude Van England, "Iran Concerned with Independence Movement," *Christian Science Monitor*, 23 September 1991.
6. Martin Sieff, "Iran Seeks Global Power for Islamic Nations," *The Washington Times*, 17 February 1992.
7. Ahmad Khomeini speech to bassij forces, *Kayhan*, Tehran, 11 January 1992.
8. Graham Fuller interview, Voice of America, 27 January 1992.
9. *Jomhouri Islami*, Tehran, 29 December 1991.
10. Roger Boyes, "Islam Stokes the Regional Ember," *Times*, London, 11 January 1992.
11. Internal document of the Iranian government, a copy of which was obtained by the People's Mojahedin Organization of Iran.
12. *The Economist* wrote on February 29, 1992, "The newly founded Caspian Council (which links Iran, Turkmenistan, Kazakhstan, Azerbaijan, and Russia) is an open attempt to cut Turkey out and bolster the region against the plotting of America through the Turks."
13. Tehran radio, 9 February 1992.
14. *Jomhouri Islami*, Tehran, 17 December 1991.
15. *Jomhouri Islami*, Tehran, 22 October 1991.
16. Jane Kokan, "Mullahs Tussle for Soviet Hearts," *Sunday Times*, 1 March 1992. To that effect, *Foreign Report*, on February 20, 1992, reported that construction of a 185-mile railway between the holy city of Mashad in Iran and the northern half of Sarakhs in Turkmenistan has begun. President Niyazov said he is giving priority to establishing regular flights and direct telephone links between Ashkhabad and Tehran.
17. *Jomhouri Islami*, Tehran, 24 November 1991.
18. Iranian Foreign Ministry confidential policy paper (Tehran: April 1992). A copy of the paper was obtained by the People's Mojahedin Organization of Iran.
19. British Broadcasting Corporation, Persian Service, 26 January 1992.
20. The People's Mojahedin Organization obtained a copy of the communication intercepts.

21. Tehran radio, 24 April 1992.

22. *Bei'at* is the oath of allegiance that all believers should lend to the vali-e-faqih.

23. Jannati Friday prayer sermon, Tehran radio, 8 May 1992.

24. News of this type was repeatedly reported by the Iranian media: "Hojjatolislam Mazari, the President of Leadership Council of the Islamic Coalition Council of Afghanistan, entered Kabul amid cheers of *Allah-o-Akbar* [God is Great]" (Tehran radio, 11 May 1992); or "Hojjatolislam Mansouri, Leader of the Islamic Coalition Council of Afghanistan, was welcomed by thousands of residents and dignitaries of the city of Mazar Sharif" (Tehran radio, 7 May 1992).

25. Hashemi-Rafsanjani speech in Ferdows city (Khorassan Province), Tehran radio, 16 May 1992.

26. *Shah-nameh*, or the *Book of Kings*, written by one of Iran's most famous poets, Abolqassem Ferdowsi, at the beginning of the eleventh century, is one of the most widely read masterpieces of Persian literature. *Shah-nameh* contains between 35,000 and 60,000 verses in short rhyming couplets. It deals with the history of Iran from its beginnings.

27. Dostum interview, Tehran radio, 13 May 1992.

28. Ibid.

29. *Ettela'at*, Tehran, 7 August 1991.

30. Mazari interview, Tehran radio, 13 May 1992.

31. Reuters, 9 May 1992.

32. Tehran radio, 7 May 1992.

33. *Foreign Report*, 30 April 1992.

34. Tom Post and Melinda Liu, "The Great Game, Chapter Two," *Newsweek*, 3 February 1992.

35. According to *The Guardian* of 18 March 1992, the president of the Democratic Party of Tadzhikistan stressed that "we want close relations [with Iran]. Our historical destiny was linked to Persia and will be."

36. Voice of America, Farsi Service, 9 May 1992.

37. Voice of America, Farsi Service, 13 February 1992.

38. Voice of America, Farsi Service, 9 May 1992.

39. "Mosque as Carapace," *The Economist*, London, 29 February 1992.

40. Ibid.

41. According to the Sunday *Telegraph* of 1 March 1992, as the euphoria of the Turkish family reunion starts to die down, the ability of Turkey to compete with Iran has become an increasingly pressing question. A Western diplomat wondered, "How in the absence of the vast amounts of cash that Ankara's Iranian and Arab competitors have at their disposal, will Turkey be able to promote Western ideals effectively in these states?"

42. Rowland Evans and Robert Novak, "Ignoring Tehran's Threat," *The Washington Post*, 2 March 1992.

43. *Kayhan*, Tehran, 17 March 1992.

44. Reuters, dispatch from Ankara, 13 March 1992.

45. Henry Kissinger, CSPAN TV, USA, 28 February 1992.

46. *Time* magazine of April 20, 1992, reported a growing fear in the West that if

democratic values fail to take root in Central Asia and the Caucasus, the whole southern rim of the old Soviet empire will inexorably slide into the embrace of Islamic fundamentalism.

47. In a commentary in *The Washington Times* on January 25, 1992, a Western observer noted that "an Iranian success in this endeavor is an alarming prospect. It inevitably would result in adverse repercussions for the West. The stability of Saudi Arabia and others in the Middle East would be threatened. Oil once more could become a weapon wielded against the West."

CHAPTER VIII

1. Tehran radio, 3 March 1991.
2. *Kayhan Airmail*, Tehran, 11 March 1992.
3. Ibid.
4. *Al Watan Al Arabi*, Paris, 25 October 1991.
5. *Jomhouri Islami*, Tehran, 19 August 1991.
6. Tehran radio, 1 February 1992.
7. Michael Evans, "Jibril's Camps Moved to Iran," *Times*, London, 14 March 1992.
8. *Al Watan Al Arabi*, Paris, 25 August 1991.
9. *Asharq Al Owsat*, London, 13 October 1991.
10. Abd al-Salam Sid Ahmed, "Iran, Sudan and Algeria—A Setback in the Grand Plan?" *Middle East International*, London, 20 March 1992.
11. *Jomhouri Islami*, Tehran, 20 June 1991.
12. Tehran radio, 15 January 1992.
13. *Abrar*, Tehran, 29 June 1991.
14. Tehran radio, 4 January 1992.
15. *Independent*, London, 1 January 1992.
16. Ian Black, Deborah Pugh, and Simon Tisdall, "Militant Islam's Saudi Paymasters," *The Guardian*, London, 29 February 1992.
17. *Asharq Al Owsat*, London, 23 March 1992.
18. Tom Post, Jeffrey Bartholet, and Carol Berger, "A New Alliance for Terror," *Newsweek*, 24 February 1992. *The New York Times* on January 20, 1992, reported that, according to Tunisian officials, Rachid Al-Ghannouchi also travels with an Iranian diplomatic passport under the alias Muhammad Jamal Aouidh.
19. *Jomhouri Islami*, Tehran, 31 March 1992.
20. *Realities*, Tunis, September 1991.
21. Christopher Walker, "Arab Leaders Fight to Defuse Islamic Militant 'Time Bomb,'" *Times*, London, 15 January 1992.
22. *Asharq Al Owsat*, London, 23 January 1992. Meanwhile, *The New York Times* reported from Tunis on January 20, 1992, that Tunisian officials contended that Tunisian fundamentalists, with active support from the Iranians, tried to organize two armed uprisings and assassinate the president and five cabinet ministers. The plan, these officials assert, was thwarted by security officials last fall.
23. *El-Moudjahid*, Algiers, January 1992.
24. Tehran radio, 10 January 1992.

25. Abd al-Salam Sid Ahmed, "Tehran-Khartoum: A New Axis or a Warning Shot?" *Middle East International*, London, 7 February 1992.

26. Abd al-Salam Sid Ahmed, "Iran, Sudan, and Algeria—A Setback in the Grand Plan?" *Middle East International*, London, 20 March 1992.

27. *Der Spiegel*, Hamburg, 23 December 1991.

28. *Ash-Shira*, Beirut, January 1992.

29. Ibid.

30. Scott Peterson, "Sudan's Islamic Regime Cultivates Ties with Iran," *Christian Science Monitor*, 31 March 1992.

31. Agence France-Presse, 27 December 1991.

32. *Al Ahram*, Cairo, 10 February 1992.

33. David Ignatius, "U.S. Fears Sudan Becoming Terrorists' 'New Lebanon,'" *The Washington Post*, 31 January 1992.

34. Jennifer Parmelee, "Sudan Denies 'Khartoum-Tehran Axis' to Promote Islamic Regimes in Africa," *The Washington Post*, 12 March 1992. It has also been reported that Majid Kamal has been stationed in Khartoum since 1989, and in 1991 he was promoted from charge d'affaires to ambassador.

35. *Al Osbou Al Arabi*, Beirut, 18 May 1992.

36. *Al-Ahram*, Cairo, 10 February 1992.

37. Reuters, dispatch from Cairo, 10 February 1992.

38. Reuters, dispatch from Cairo, 16 January 1992.

39. Ignatius, op. cit.

40. *Al Watan Al Arabi*, Paris, 17 January 1992.

41. Christopher Walker, "Sudan's Link with Iran Alarms West," *Times*, London, 18 December 1991.

42. British Broadcasting Corporation, World Service, 2 February 1992.

43. Parmelee, op.cit.

44. Rafsanjani's office confidential document, Tehran, July 1991. A copy was obtained by the People's Mojahedin Organization of Iran.

45. Moussa interview, in *Al-Musawar*, Cairo, 24 May 1992.

46. *Jomhouri Islami*, Tehran, 26 August 1991.

47. *Ressalat*, Tehran, 23 May 1991.

48. *Kayhan*, Tehran, 3 October 1991.

49. British Broadcasting Corporation, World Service, 25 January 1992. *The Times* of London reported from Cairo on the same day that, according to Muhammad Abdel-Halim Moussa, the Egyptian interior minister, those arrested had infiltrated Egypt to agitate on streets and carry out terrorist attacks.

50. *Al Akhbar*, Cairo, 19 February 1992.

51. Reuters, dispatch from Cairo, 9 March 1992.

52. *Al Ahram*, Cairo, 9 March 1992.

53. *Al Watan Al Arabi*, London, 6 December 1991.

54. Ibid., 20 September 1991.

55. *Kayhan*, Tehran, 2 August 1987.

56. Reuters, dispatch from Washington, D.C., 25 February 1992.

57. Reuters, dispatch from Riyadh, 27 February 1992.
58. *Jomhouri Islami*, Tehran, 21 January 1992.
59. Tehran radio, 12 July 1991.
60. Agence France-Presse, 15 July 1991.
61. Tehran radio, 18 June 1991.

CHAPTER IX

1. *Ettela'at*, Tehran, 7 August 1991.
2. Hashemi-Rafsanjani, Tehran radio, 3 November 1992.
3. Moussavi interview, in *Kayhan*, Tehran, 21 February 1985.
4. Manoucher Muhammadi, *Principles of the Foreign Policy of the Islamic Republic of Iran* (Tehran: Amirkabir Publishing House, 1987), p.70.
5. Ibid.
6. Internal memorandum, Iranian government's Supreme National Security Council, March 1991. A copy of the memorandum was obtained by the People's Mojahedin Organization of Iran.
7. *Kayhan*, Tehran, 21 December 1991.
8. Iranian television, 30 August 1992.
9. Internal document of the Qods Force, a copy of which was obtained by the People's Mojahedin Organization of Iran.
10. Ibid.
11. Ibid.
12. *Abrar*, Tehran, 17 December 1991.
13. United Press International, dispatch from Ankara, 29 January 1993.
14. Internal document of the Qods Force, op. cit.
15. Internal report of the Qods Force, August 1991. A copy was obtained by the People's Mojahedin Organization of Iran.
16. United Press International, dispatch from Ankara, 4 February 1993.

CHAPTER X

1. Hashemi-Rafsanjani Friday prayer sermon, *Ettela'at*, Tehran, 6 May 1989. (See Appendix.)
2. Letter from Mir-Hussein Moussavi to Khamenei, 6 September 1988. A copy of the letter was obtained by the People's Mojahedin Organization of Iran. (See Appendix.)
3. In an interview with the French TF1 television, Lutfi stated: "They had more serious targets and planned to kill prominent personalities, including Jacques Chirac, Regis Debres, Laurent Fabius, and Jack Lang. They also had plans to blow up a nuclear center and had predicted that 10,000 would be killed."
4. *The Washington Times* quoted Western intelligence sources as saying that "Tehran convened an international conference in February 1992 involving 80 senior participants from 20 organizations involved in terrorism. Participating groups included Hizbullah from Lebanon, the Popular Front for the Liberation of

Palestine General Command, the Tunisian Islamic Movement, Hizbullah of Kuwait, the Egyptian Islamic Jihad, the Liberation Front of Bahrain, the Islamic Revolutionary Organization of the Arabian Peninsula, the Organization for the Advancement of Shi'ite Ideology in Pakistan, the Patani Front of Thailand, the Radical Muslim Organization of the Philippines and the Revolutionary Muslim Movement of South Africa."

5. Hashemi-Rafsanjani, Friday prayer sermon, Tehran radio, 19 December 1986.

6. *Ettela'at*, Tehran, 7 November 1986.

7. *Times*, London, 9 August 1991.

8. During the 1986 hajj pilgrimage, a group of about 170 terrorists from the Guards Corps and other terrorist organs of the Khomeini regime were dispatched to Saudi Arabia in the guise of pilgrims. The group carried large quantities of arms as well as various explosive materials, such as TNT and plastic bombs. But soon after the group's arrival in the country, Saudi police discovered they were carrying weapons and ammunition and arrested more than 100 of them. After extensive efforts by Rafsanjani (then the majlis speaker), Mohsen Rezaii, the G.C. Commander in Chief, and Ali Nikan-Qomi (Tehran's former ambassador to Saudi Arabia), the arrested terrorists were released the next day.

9. On April 1, 1992, Reuters reported the German newspaper *Die Rheinpfalz* had learned through well-informed Lebanese sources that the attack was carried out "with the full approval and support of Iran." *Die Rheinpfalz* said that the bombing was planned at a secret conference in a Beirut Hotel December 24–26, 1991. The conference was led by Iranian representatives and attended by members of the radical Shi'ite Muslim groups. The paper added that the information was obtained from a "volunteer helper of the attack planners."

10. Reuters, dispatch from Washington, D.C., 7 May 1992.

11. Hashemi-Rafsanjani, Tehran radio, 4 November 1986. Rafsanjani made these remarks while addressing a rally on the seventh anniversary of the U.S. embassy takeover in Tehran in 1979.

12. *Ressalat*, Tehran, 20 July 1987. (See Appendix.)

13. *Jomhouri Islami*, Tehran, 14 February 1992.

14. *The New York Times*, 2 November 1992.

15. Caryle Murphy, "Iranian Sees No Breakthrough in U.S. Ties," *The Washington Post*, 1 February 1993.

16. Tehran radio, 14 February 1993.

17. *Hurriyet*, Istanbul, 7 March 1990.

18. Reuters, dispatch from Beirut, 15 January 1992.

19. United Press International, dispatch from Ankara, 29 January 1993.

20. United Press International, dispatch from Geneva, 22 June 1990.

21. According to the press statement of the People's Mojahedin on July 16, 1989, Muhammad-Ja'far Sahrarudi was at the time commander of the Directorate of Operations of the Guards Corps 15th Corps, based at Ramadhan Headquarters near the western Iranian city of Kermanshah. According to the same statement he used a diplomatic passport and the pseudonym "Rahimi."

22. Stephen Kinzer, "Iran Kurdish Leader Among 4 Killed in Berlin," *The New York Times*, 19 September 1992.

23. Reuters, dispatch from Bonn, 10 August 1992.

24. In 1986 when Hussein Mala'ek was appointed as the regime's ambassador to Berne, the U.S. Department of State protested the acceptance of his credentials by the Swiss government because of his involvement in hostage taking.

25. VEVAK (*Vezarat-e Ettela'at Va Amniyat-e Keshvar*), Ministry of Intelligence and Security, previously known as SAVAMA, is in charge of state security and intelligence matters. The minister is Ali Fallahian. This organ was called SAVAK under the shah.

26. *Die Welt* reported in May 1992 that for the year 1991, Germany's exports to Iran were DM 6 billion ($3.6 billion.)

27. *Khaneh Behdashte-Iran* is located near Cologne. It is closely linked to the Union of Islamic Associations in Europe, and many of the latter's meetings are held there. Under the direct supervision of the Iranian Embassy in Bonn, it acts as a logistical support base for the regime's terrorist activities.

28. Located at 27 Rue Maurice Berteux, Paris, this center is a gathering place for joint activities of pro-Khomeini Shi'ite Arabs and Iranian agents. The center has direct contacts with the Iranian Embassy in Paris and the Muslim Students Association, a proregime student outfit.

29. Reuters, dispatch from Paris, 11 March 1992.

30. Reuters, dispatch from Ankara, 13 March 1992. The Turkish interior minister, Ismet Sezgin, in March 1992 stated that the Hizbullah, which "is an Iranian group, was aiming to destroy the Turkish state and break it up."

31. Jeff Kamen, "Terror Threat Carries Nuclear Cloud," *Defense News*, 24 February 1992.

32. As Dove Zakheim, an expert on the subject commented on the Voice of America radio on March 2, 1992, "They [Iranians] have supported terrorism, sponsored it when they thought it was worthwhile. There is no great evidence, regardless of what any individual Iranian leader, and that includes the president, might say, these people are not functioning on the same wavelength as the West is."

33. Caryle Murphy, "Questions Remain About New Image Touted by Iran," *The Washington Post*, 21 April 1992.

CHAPTER XI

1. *Kayhan*, Tehran, 21 October 1991. (See Appendix.)

2. *Abrar*, Tehran, 20 October 1991.

3. *Jomhouri Islami*, Tehran, 26 August 1991.

4. *Kayhan*, Tehran, 20 October 1991.

5. *Kayhan Airmail*, Tehran, 23 October 1991.

6. Hashemi-Rafsanjani, speech to the Conference to Support Palestine's Islamic Revolution in Tehran, *Jomhouri Islami*, Tehran, 20 October 1991.

7. *Kayhan*, Tehran, 19 October 1991.

8. *Jomhouri Islami*, Tehran, 3 December 1991.

9. *Jomhouri Islami*, Tehran, 22 October 1991.

10. Hashemi-Rafsanjani, *Jomhouri Islami*, Tehran, 20 October 1991.

11. *Kayhan*, Tehran, 21 October 1991.

12. Reuters, dispatch from Nicosia, 27 March 1992.

13. *Kayhan*, Tehran, 20 October 1991.
14. Iranian television, main evening news broadcast, 26 January 1993.
15. Caryle Murphy, "Iranian Sees No Breakthrough in U.S. Ties," *The Washington Post*, 1 February 1993.

CHAPTER XII

1. Reuters, dispatch from Nicosia, 23 October 1991.
2. *Suddeutsche Zeitung*, Munich, 5 October 1991.
3. Tony Banks and James Bruce, "Iran Builds Its Strength," *Jane's Defense Weekly*, 1 February 1992.
4. Ibid.
5. *Corriere della Serra*, Milan, 13 January 1992.
6. Banks and Bruce, op. cit.
7. Ibid.
8. Associated Press, dispatch from Washington, D.C., 12 February 1992.
9. *Sunday Telegraph*, London, 1 June 1992.
10. Banks and Bruce, op. cit.
11. Eric Rosenberg, *Defense Week*, Washington, D.C., 13 January 1992.
12. *Die Tageszeitung*, Berlin, 5 January 1992.
13. Patrick Cockburn, "Russia Helps Iran Equip Its Warplanes from Iraq," *Independent*, London, 13 January 1992.
14. Associated Press, dispatch from Washington, D.C., 7 January 1992.
15. Cockburn, op. cit.
16. Arnold Beichman, "Arms and the Goals of Iran," *The Washington Times*, 1 March 1992.
17. Ibid.
18. Owen Ullmann, Knight-Ridder Newspapers, Washington, D.C., 11 February 1992.
19. Rowan Scarborough, "China to Boost Iran's Navy," *The Washington Times*, 22 April 1992.
20. *Defense News*, 17 February 1992.
21. *Aviation Week*, Washington, D.C., 9 November 1992.
22. Richard Sia and Mark Mathews, "Iran Buying Submarines to Control Gulf Entrance," (Baltimore) *Sun*, 5 February 1992.
23. Rosenberg, op. cit.
24. *Middle East Economic Digest*, London, 17 April 1992.
25. Rowland Evans and Robert Novak, "Baker's Chinese Friends," *The Washington Post*, 18 November 1991.
26. *Der Spiegel*, Hamburg, December 1991.
27. Rosenberg, op. cit.
28. Press conference by Alireza Jafarzadeh, U.S. spokesman for the People's Mojahedin Organization of Iran, in Washington, D.C., 5 February 1992.
29. "Nuclear Journey," *Issues*, Paris, March 1992.

30. Rowland Evans and Robert Novak, "Beijing's Tehran Connection," *The Washington Post*, 26 June 1991.

31. Jim Mann, "Iran Determined to Get A-Bomb, U.S. Believes," *Los Angeles Times*, 17 March 1992.

32. Jafarzadeh, op. cit.

33. Reuters, dispatch from Brussels, 26 February 1992.

34. Reuters, dispatch from Nicosia, 28 November 1992.

35. Tehran radio, 14 February 1993.

36. The Hamburg-based Messerschmitt, Boelkow, Blohm Co. signed a "memorandum of understanding" with the Khomeini regime to issue licenses for the manufacture of TRANSALL cargo planes and to build a center in Iran for their maintenance in December 1985 at the height of the Iran-Iraq War. The bid was for the Khomeini regime to buy 12 military TRANSALL C-160 aircraft valued at $424 million.

37. Agence France-Presse, dispatch from Cyprus, 16 November 1991.

38. Rowland Evans and Robert Novak, "Baker's Chinese Friends," *The Washington Post*, 18 November 1991.

39. *Le Monde*, 2 January 1992.

40. David Hoffman, "Iran's Rebuilding Seen as Challenge to West," *The Washington Post*, 2 February 1992.

41. "Fear of Flying," *Newsweek*, 17 February 1992.

CHAPTER XIII

1. Hashemi-Rafsanjani, Tehran radio, 28 May 1992. He made these remarks in the opening session of the Fourth Majlis.

2. Andrew Borowiec, "Iran's Nuclear Effort, Arms Buys Trigger Concerns," *The Washington Times*, 8 February 1992.

3. Report on the Human Rights Situation in the Islamic Republic of Iran by the Special Representative of the United Nations Commission on Human Rights, Reynaldo Galindo Pohl, pursuant to the Commission resolution 1991/82, E/CN.4/1992/34, 2 January 1992, pp. 77–89.

4. Ibid., p. 90, par. 474.

5. Press communique by Judge Roland Chatelain, 20 June 1990.

6. United Nations General Assembly Resolution, A/C.3/47/L.76, 2 December 1992.

7. *Salam*, Tehran, 18 October 1991.

8. Ali Avazzadeh, majlis deputy from Shirvan, *Ettela'at*, Tehran, 6 January 1992.

9. *Ettela'at Political-Economic Survey*, Tehran, October 1989.

10. *Salam*, Tehran, 1 May 1991.

11. *Salam*, Tehran, 18 October 1991.

12. *Le Monde*, 21 June 1991.

13. *Kayhan*, Tehran, 27 July 1991.

14. *Le Monde*, 21 June 1991.

15. Seyyed Reza Nourizadeh, majlis deputy from Asfarayen, *Ressalat*, Tehran, 12 June 1991.

16. Mostafa Mo'azenzadeh, majlis deputy from Kerman, *Ressalat*, Tehran, 15 January 1992.

17. Tehran radio, 4 and 29 April 1992.

18. *Kayhan*, Tehran, 8 October 1989.

19. Associated Press, dispatch from the United Nations, New York, 31 December 1991.

20. Jassem Jaderi, majlis deputy from Dasht-e-Azadegan, *Jomhouri Islami*, Tehran, 14 November 1991.

21. Associated Press, dispatch from the United Nations, New York, 31 December 1991.

22. Reuters, dispatch from Nicosia, 16 April 1992.

23. Associated Press, dispatch from Nicosia, 25 May 1992.

24. Reuters, dispatch from Tehran, 2 June 1992.

25. Several factors explain the mullahs' failure to quell the mounting public protests. While the deteriorating economic situation, pervasive poverty, and the denial of the most basic social and individual rights of citizens are the underlying causes of continuing unrest, another essential factor in fomenting these protests is the crucial role of the Mojahedin's network across the country. Through this nationwide underground network, the Mojahedin's Command Headquarters inside Iran has distributed hundreds of thousands of antigovernment fliers, statements, and pamphlets. In addition, it has recruited many volunteers, some of whom eventually cross the border to join the National Liberation Army, the Resistance's military arm. Others are given the task of organizing acts of protest in different sectors of society. Videotapes about the NLA and cassette recordings of statements, messages, and interviews by the Resistance's leaders Massoud and Maryam Rajavi are also distributed by the network's members. In addition, the Mojahedin have made effective use of their daily nationwide radio broadcasts to offer direction and guidance to the citizenry, urging them to defy government clampdown. The success of the campaign has aroused grave concern among the ruling clerics, who have been compelled to publicly acknowledge the effectiveness of the Mojahedin in organizing the protests and their emboldening of the public. Nowhere was this more evident than during the majlis elections, when the clerical authorities, including Khamenei, lashed out at the Mojahedin's call for the election boycott during a speech in Mashad on April 4, 1992: "Through their radio broadcasts and publications, the Mojahedin are attempting to make these elections worthless. They do this to weaken the system politically, economically, and militarily."

26. *The Economist*, London, 13 June 1992.

27. Associated Press, dispatch from Tehran, 8 May 1992.

28. *Jomhouri Islami*, Tehran, 26 April 1992.

29. Associated Press, dispatch from Nicosia, 26 July 1992.

30. Associated Press, dispatch from Nicosia, 6 July 1992.

31. Hashemi-Rafsanjani, Friday prayer sermon, Tehran Radio, 17 July 1992.

32. Tehran Radio, 29 July 1992.

33. *The New York Times*, 12 October 1992.

34. Associated Press, dispatch from Nicosia, 15 October 1992.

35. Ahwaz radio, local news broadcast, 20 February 1993.

36. Hashemi Rafsanjani, Tehran Radio, 12 June 1992.

CHAPTER XV

1. Maryam Rajavi interview, Voice of Mojahed national radio, quoted in *NLA Journal*, November 1991, p. 9.

2. Hashemi Rafsanjani Friday prayer sermon, *Ettela'at*, Tehran, 7 June 1986.

3. Mullah Sadoughi, quoted in *Mojahed*, Tehran, 19 November 1979.

4. Tehran radio, 25 June 1980.

5. The Organization of the Iranian People's Fedayeen Guerrillas(OIPFG) was an indigenous, independent Iranian Marxist group which took up armed struggle against the shah's regime in 1970. But it underwent numerous splits after the 1979 revolution. A 'Majority' faction was assimilated into the pro-Moscow Tudeh Party, and smaller splinter groups gradually withered away as a result of their political inclination toward the clerical regime. The only surviving, independent offshoot of the OIPFG is a member organization of the National Council of Resistance of Iran.

6. *Nahj ol-Balagha (The Road to Eloquence)* is a compilation of sermons, letters, and sayings of Imam Ali ibn Abi Talib.

7. A 12-point statement, *Ettelaye Taeen-e Mavaze-e Sazeman-e Mojahedin-e Khalq-e Iran (Statement on the Positions of the People's Mojahedin Organization of Iran)*, was drawn up in autumn 1975 to define the Mojahedin's stance vis-a-vis the Marxist coup that led to the organization's temporary disintegration in the mid-1970s, paving the way for Khomeini's rise to power.

8. Ibid.

9. Massoud Rajavi interview, in *Nashriye Ettehadiye Anjomanhaye Daneshjuyane Mosalman Khareje Keshvar (Journal of the Union of Muslim Iranian Students Societies Outside Iran)*, (Paris, 9 January 1982), p. 1.

10. Letter of the Tudeh Party to the French Government, 30 July 1981.

11. Rajavi interview, op. cit., p. 2.

12. Massoud Rajavi's message on the anniversary of the Iranian Revolution, Voice of Mojahed national radio, 11 February 1987.

13. Constitution of the National Council of Resistance of Iran, Paris, ratified in March 1982.

14. "The Principal Tasks of the Transitional Period," ratified by the National Council of Resistance of Iran, Paris, March 1982.

15. Rajavi interview, op. cit. Here Rajavi is alluding to Imam Ali's reluctance to accept the leadership of the Muslim community until he was assured of the people's *bei'at* (oath of allegiance).

16. Ayatollah Mirza Hussein Na'ini, *Tanbihol Umma va Tanzihol Millah (Raising the People's Awareness and Purifying the Ideology)*.

17. *The Glorious Koran*, a bilingual edition with English translation, introduction and notes by Marmaduke Pickthall (London: George Allen & Unwin, 1976), *Sura LX: Mumtahana*, Verse 8, p. 735.

18. Program of the National Council of Resistance and Provisional Government of

the Democratic Islamic Republic of Iran (Paris: 1981), Chapter 3, Article 4.

19. Ali ibn Abi Taleb, *Nahj ol-Balagha*, translation and commentary by Haj Alinaqi Faiz ol-Islam (Tehran: Faiz ol-Islam Publications, 1972), sermon 27, pp. 95–97.

20. *The Glorious Qur'an*, translation and commentary by A. Yusuf Ali (USA: American Trust Publications, 1987), *Sura V: Ma'ida*, Verse 35, p. 252.

21. Ibid., *Sura XXVIII: Qasas*, Verse 77, p. 1024.

22. Ibid., *Sura II: Baqara*, Verse 83, p. 39.

23. Ibid., *Sura XVI: Nahl*, Verse 90, p. 680.

24. Maryam Rajavi's Iranian New Year message, Voice of Mojahed national radio, 21 March 1990.

25. Tehran radio, 1 January 1990.

26. *Kayhan*, Tehran, 1 October 1989.

27. *Kayhan*, Tehran, 16 November 1991.

28. Fahimeh Arvani is from Tabriz, capital of East Azerbaijan Province in northwest Iran. During the two years preceding her election as the deputy secretary general of the Mojahedin Organization, she had worked closely with Maryam Rajavi as her senior aide and was directly associated with the Mojahedin's achievements during that period.

29. Massoud Rajavi's Iranian New Year message, Voice of Mojahed national radio, 21 March 1982.

Appendix

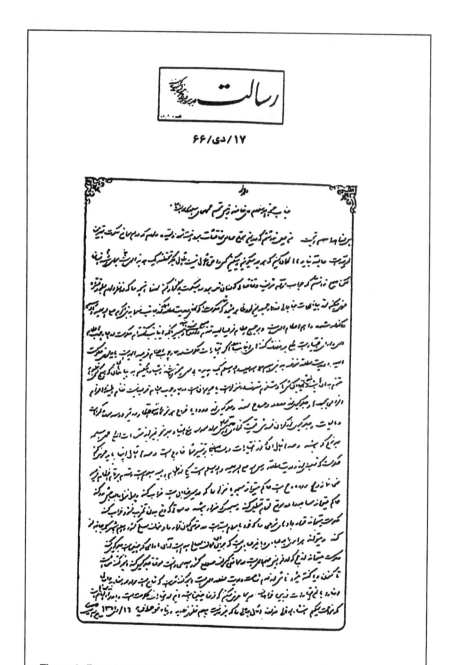

Figure 1. *Ressalat*, 7 January 1988. Text of Khomeini's open letter to then President Ali Khamenei lambasting his "understatement" of vali-e-faqih's powers.

Figure 2. *Ettela'at,* 24 June 1981, No. 16460. Photographs of executed detainees whose identities were not established when they were shot by firing squad. The parents were ordered to go to Evin Prison to identify their children.

Figure 3. The text of Montazeri's letter to judicial officials on 15 August 1988 in which he warned about the repercussions of summary executions of the Mojahedin.

Figure 4. Text of Montazeri's letter to Khomeini on 31 July 1988, complaining that mass execution of Mojahedin prisoners will only enhance their legitimacy and popular appeal.

*Cover of the booklet containing
some of Khomeini's decrees on war.*

Figure 5. Khomeini's religious decrees, sanctioning the execution of Iraqi prisoners of war.

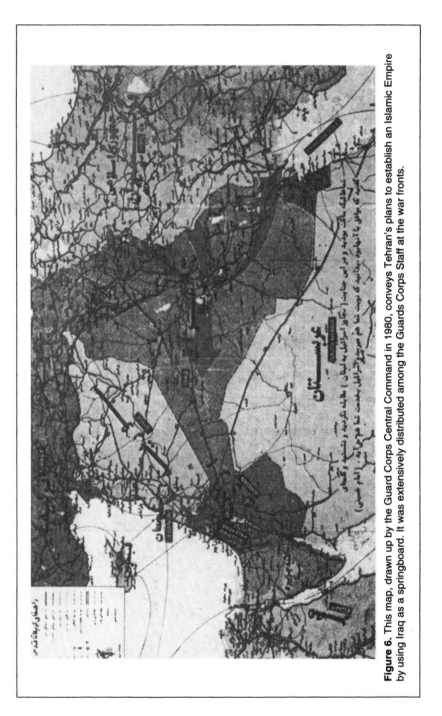

Figure 6. This map, drawn up by the Guard Corps Central Command in 1980, conveys Tehran's plans to establish an Islamic Empire by using Iraq as a springboard. It was extensively distributed among the Guards Corps Staff at the war fronts.

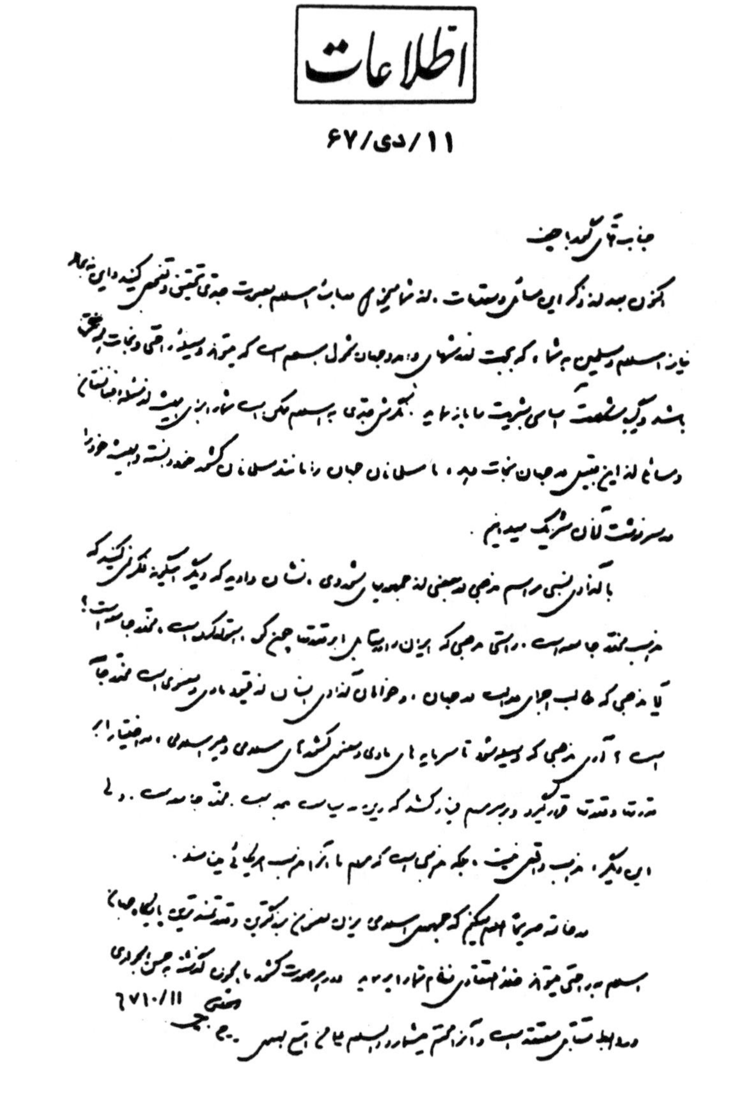

اطلاعات

۱۱/دی/۶۷

Figure 7. *Ettela'at*, 9 January 1989. The concluding paragraph of Khomeini's letter to Mikhail Gorbachev, in which he wrote: "I declare . . . that the Islamic Republic of Iran . . . can easily fill the ideological void of your system."

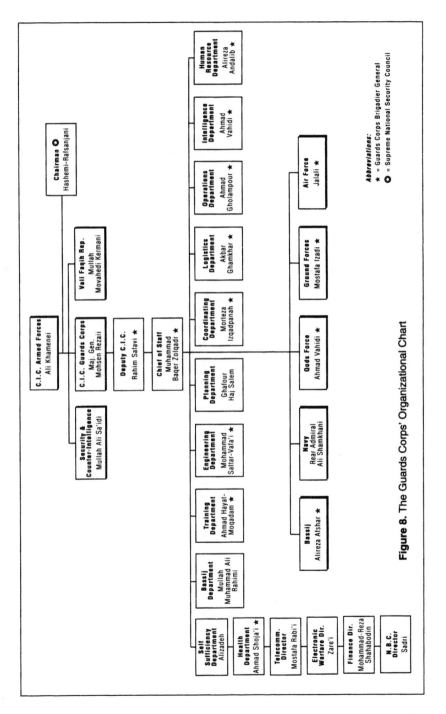

Figure 8. The Guards Corps' Organizational Chart

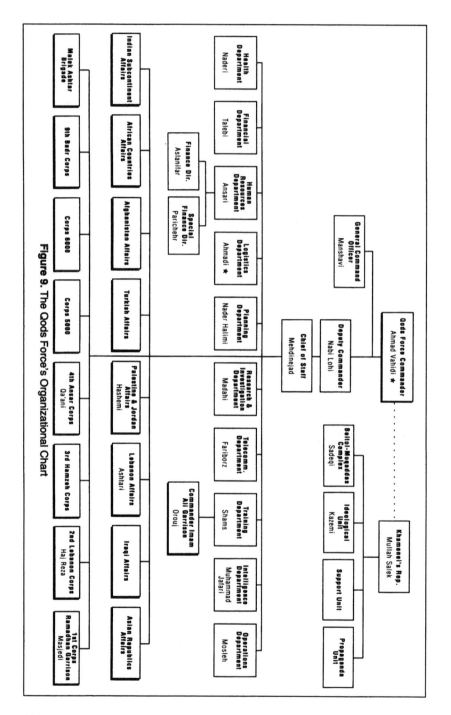

Figure 9. The Qods Force's Organizational Chart

Figure 9a. The Qods Force's Organizational Chart

The Qods (Jerusalem) Force is one of the five major branches of the Islamic Revolutionary Guards Corps. All the extraterritorial activities of the Guards Corps fall under the responsibility of the Qods Force. Commanded by GC Brigadier General Ahmad Vahidi, the Qods Force now has the most experienced Guards Corps officers on its staff. Although organizationally under the command of GC Commander in Chief Mohsen Rezaii, Vahidi takes his orders directly from Khamenei and Rafsanjani.

The Qods Force has its own autonomous staff groups and directorates for logistics, planning, operations, intelligence, telecommunications (signals and intelligence), etc. But a specific feature of the Force's organization is a separate staff group dealing with the political aspects of the Qods Force's activities. The body, called the General Staff of the Export of Revolution, handles issues related to the export of fundamentalism to different countries. Specific assignments are surveyed and organized to take place in different countries by the different directorates of the Qods Force, including the directorates for:

1. Iraq
2. Palestine, Lebanon, and Jordan
3. Turkey
4. Afghanistan, Pakistan, and the Indian subcontinent
5. Western countries (Europe, United States)
6. North Africa (Egypt, Tunisia, Algeria, Sudan, and Morocco)
7. Arabian Peninsula
8. Republics of the former Soviet Union

The main branches of the Qods Force, each of which is responsible for the Force's activities in a particular country or region, are as follows:

1. The 1st Corps, based in Ramadhan Headquarters, is responsible for all Guards Corps activities in Iraq, including the northern and southern parts of the country.
2. The 2nd (Lebanon) Corps is stationed in the Bekaa Valley and southern Lebanon.
3. The 3rd (Hamzeh) Corps provides logistical support for operations in northern Iraq and Turkey.
4. The 4th (Ansar) Corps is responsible for Guards Corps' activities in Afghanistan, Pakistan, and Asian republics.
5. Corps 5,000 is responsible for terrorist activities in the West, especially bombings and assassinations.
6. Corps 6,000 is responsible for military activities in Africa.
7. The 9th (Badar) Corps, made up chiefly of Iraqi POWs, operates under the command of Ramadhan Headquarters.

اطلاعات

/۲۶/اردیبهشت/۶۸

تهران ـ خبرگزاری جمهوری اسلامی:
نماز پرشکوه جمعه در تهران دیروز با حضور انبوه اقشار مختلف مردم که
پس از انجام راهپیمائی عظیم روز قدس در میعادگاه دانشگاه تهران اجتماع
کرده بودند برگزار شد.
حجت‌الاسلام والمسلمین هاشمی رفسنجانی امام جمعه موقت تهران در
خطبه‌های نماز جمعه دیروز تهران تاکید کرد که تنها راه نجات قدس شریف
مبارزه مسلحانه مجاهدین فلسطینی در خارج و قیام مردمی در داخل
فلسطین است.
امام جمعه موقت تهران خاطرنشان ساخت: اگر در برابر هر فلسطینی که
توسط مزدوران اسرائیل به شهادت می‌رسد پنج نفر آمریکائی یا فرانسوی
به قتل برسند آنها دیگر چنین جنایاتی را مرتکب نمی‌شوند وی خطاب به
مبارزین فلسطینی افزود: شما باید انتقام خون ملت مظلوم فلسطین را از
ستمگران بگیرید و دشمنانتان نباید احساس آرامش کنند.
آقای هاشمی رفسنجانی اظهار داشت: مجاهدین فلسطینی ممکن است
بگویند در این صورت دنیا ما را تروریست خطاب می‌کند اما من می‌گویم
مگر حالا هم همین را به شما نمی‌گویند؟!

Figure 10. *Ettela'at,* 6 May 1989. Hashemi-Rafsanjani: "If for every Palestinian martyred by Israeli mercenaries, five American or French citizens are murdered, they would no longer commit such crimes. . . . The Palestinians might say, In that case the world will call us terrorist. I say, however, do they not label you already?"

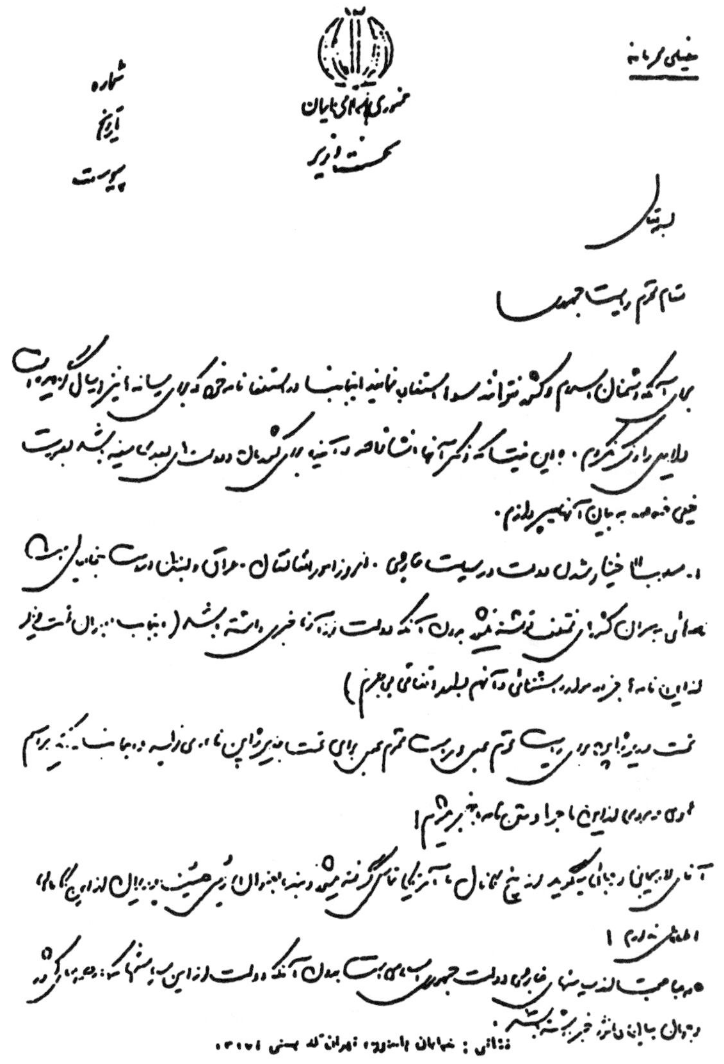

خیلی محرمانه

جمهوری اسلامی ایران

نخست وزیر

شماره

تاریخ

پیوست

بسمه تعالی

مقام محترم ریاست جمهوری

Figure 11. Mir-Hussein Moussavi, the clerical regime's longest-serving prime minister, wrote a "strictly confidential" letter to Khamenei in 1988, outlining the reasons for his resignation. He complained of the higher authorities' constant interference with the government's work and cited as an example the regime's terrorist activities in Lebanon and Saudi Arabia.

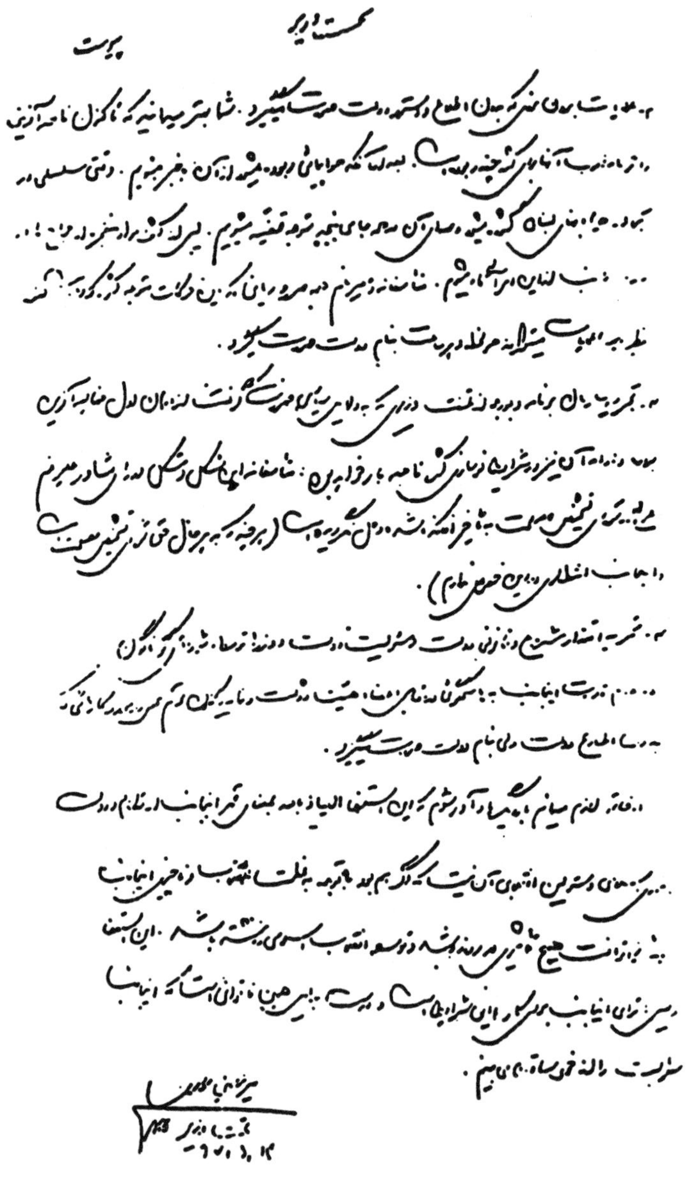

پیوست

[handwritten Persian letter text]

Figure 11. (continued)

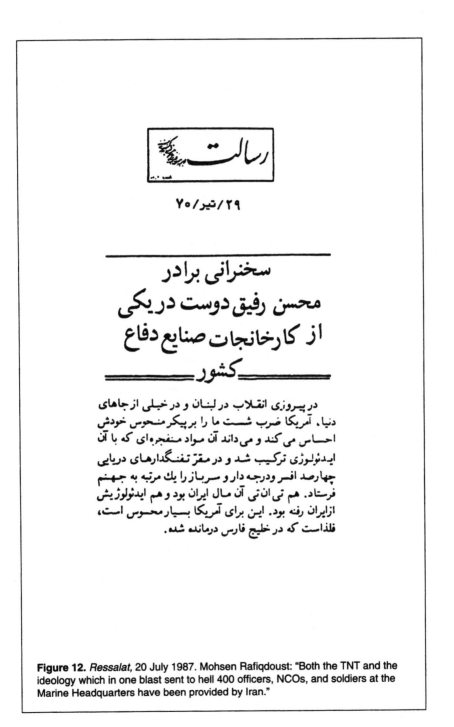

Figure 12. *Ressalat*, 20 July 1987. Mohsen Rafiqdoust: "Both the TNT and the ideology which in one blast sent to hell 400 officers, NCOs, and soldiers at the Marine Headquarters have been provided by Iran."

کیهان

۲۹/مهر/۷۰

‏❋ سرلشگر محسن رضایی فرمانده کل سپاه پاسداران : روزی جرقه‌های خشم‌و کینه مسلمانان در دل واشنگتن زبانه خواهد کشید.

آمریکا هرچه اسرائیل را بیشتر تقویت کند و در حفظ آن بیشتر بکوشد، کینه‌بیشتری از مسلمانان خریده است و روزی جرقه‌های این خشم و نفرت در دل واشنگتن زبانه می‌کند و مسئولیت عواقب آن نیز بر عهده آمریکاست. آمریکا حتی مسئول بی‌خانمانی ملت یهود نیز خواهد بود . چرا که روزی خواهد رسید که در هیچ‌جای این دنیا آنها نیز مانند سلمان رشدی نتوانند خانه‌ای برای سکونت پیدا کنند . وقتی از صهیونیسم دفاع می‌کنید چه انتظاری دارید که جان و مال و سرمایه‌گذاری‌هایی که در ممالک اسلامی کرده‌اید و می‌کنید در امان باشد؟

Figure 13. *Kayhan,* 21 October 1991. Mohsen Rezaii: "The Muslims' fury and hatred will burn the heart of Washington some day and America will be responsible for its repercussions . . . The day will come when, like Salman Rushdie, the Jews will not find a place to live anywhere in the world."

List of Victims of the Mullah Regime's Terrorist Activities Abroad

Date / Location	Target	Description
6/12/99 Baghdad, Iraq	6 Mojahedin members (Fariba Mouzarmi, Massoumeh Goudarzi, Bijan Aghazadeh, Abbass Rafii, Akbar Qanbarnezhad, and Javad Fotouhi)	A huge car bomb explosion on a highway north of Baghdad at 8 A.M. (local time) wrecked two passenger buses, leaving dead (including 6 members of the Mojahedin) and scores injured.
2/10/99 Panjgour, Pakistan	Reza Pirzadi	Ex-political prisoner. Kidnapped and injured.
8/1/98 Karbala-Najaf, Iraqi Kurdistan	Ayatollah Agha Mirza Ali Ghoravi	Iranian cleric. Assassinated by the mullahs in Iraq.
6/18/98 Najaf, Iraq	Sheikh Morteza Broujerdi	An Iranian cleric. Assassinated by the Intelligence Ministry of the Iranian regime.
4/25/98 Sulaymaniyah, Iraqi Kurdistan	5 KDPI members	5 members of the Kurdistan Democratic Party of Iran (KDPI) were assassinated.
12/15/97 Sulaymaniyah, Iraqi Kurdistan	Salah Bigzadi	Khebat supporter. Assassinated.
12/8/97 Koysanjaq, Iraq	Seyed Jamal Nikjouyan	A member of the KDPI. Killed.
12/3/97 Sulaymaniyah-Karkuk Highway, Iraq	Taher Feizi	4 terrorists of the regime opened fire on a vehicle belonging to the Khebat organization and killed one of its Peshmargas in this attack.
11/15/97 Sulaymaniyah, Iraqi Kurdistan	Hassan Zinati	Assassinated.
10/25/97 Ba'aqoubeh, Iraq	Changiz Hadikhanlou	Mojahedin member. Slain in an ambush.
10/19/97 Sulaymaniyah, Iraqi Kurdistan	Taher Feyzi	Car belonging to the Khebat came under fire, one person killed.

Date / Location	Target	Description
10/18/97 Sulaymaniyah, Iraqi Kurdistan	Saeid Moradi, Ali Zokaleh, and Ismael Namaki	3 members of the KDPI were killed and 9 others wounded after their minibus, which was going to Sulaymaniyah, came under heavy machine gun attack by the regime's terrorists.
8/19/97 Sulaymaniyah, Iraqi Kurdistan	Anjad Mowlaei	The mullah regime's terrorists killed him and another KDPI member.
8/14/97 Sulaymaniyah, Iraqi Kurdistan	Ghalib Alizadeh	The mullah regime's terrorists killed him and another KDPI member.
8/14/97 Panjvein, Iraqi Kurdistan	Ebrahim Gagoli	Abducted and assassinated.
8/14/97 Sulaymaniyah, Iraqi Kurdistan	2 Peshmargas of the Khebat	2 Peshmargas of the Khebat organization were injured after a bomb detonated in their vehicle.
6/26/97 Sulaymaniyah, Iraqi Kurdistan	Farhad Babaii	Attack against a car belonging to the KDPI killed 1 person and injured 2 others.
6/8/97 Sulaymaniyah, Iraqi Kurdistan	Khaled Abbassi	Assassinated.
6/4/97 Khalkan, Iraq	Abdollah Khani	Active member of Kurdistan Democratic Party. Killed.
6/3/97 Iraq	3 KDPI members	3 members of the KDPI were murdered.
5/5/97 Erbil, Iraqi Kurdistan	Latif Naghshbandi	Assassinated.
5/1/97 Sulaymaniyah, Iraqi Kurdistan	6 members of a Kurdish group	6 members of Iranian Kurdish group were killed by the regime.
3/11/97 Kanigherjaleh, Iraqi Kurdistan	Salim Karimzadeh	Assassinated.

Date / Location	Target	Description
3/2/97 Rwandooz, Iraqi Kurdistan	Abdollah Pirootzadeh	Assassinated.
12/9/96 Sulaymaniyah, Iraqi Kurdistan	Abbas Rahmani	A Khebat member. Assassinated.
12/1/96 Koysanjaq, Iraq	5 people belonging to KDPI families	The mullah regime's terrorists attacked a number of members of the KDPI and their families and wounded a number of people. Among the dead was a 4-year-old child.
11/19/96 Zahedan, Iran	Abdolaziz Kazemi Vajd	Professor at Zahedan University and a leader of Sunnis. Kidnapped and killed by the regime's terrorists.
11/12/96 Islamabad, Pakistan	Ali Mowlaei	An Iranian dissident. Assassinated.
11/11/96 Sulaymaniyah, Iraqi Kurdistan	Hamed Salimi	Attack against a KDPI camp led to the death of one person.
11/4/96 Halabche, Iraq	Ali Garmaei	An Iranian Kurd and member of the Khebat organization. Killed by the regime's terrorists.
11/3/96 Sulaymaniyah, Iraqi Kurdistan	Mohammad Nanwa	An Iranian Kurd and member of the Khebat organization. Killed by the regime's terrorists.
9/29/96 Paris, France	Reza Mazlouman	Former minister under the shah. Assassinated.
5/28/96 Iraqi Kurdistan	Osman Rahimi	Assassinated.
3/18/96 Iraqi Kurdistan	Taher Azizi	Assassinated.
3/18/96 Sulaymaniyah, Iraqi Kurdistan	Taher Rouhani	Assassinated.

Date / Location	Target	Description
3/18/96 Iraqi Kurdistan 3/11/96 Baghdad, Iraq	Faramarz Keshavarz Hamed Reza Rahmani	2 Iranian Sunni clerics assassinated by the regime in Pakistan.
3/7/96 Karachi, Pakistan 3/4/96 Pakistan	Mowlavi Mollahzadeh Abdul-Nasser Jamshid-Zehi	2 Iranian Sunni clerics assassinated by the regime.
3/4/96 Istanbul, Turkey	Abdul-Ali Muradi	Supporter of the People's Mojahedin Organization (PMOI) of Iran. Assassinated.
2/20/96 Baghdad, Iraq	Three Mojahedin members	Three members of the PMOI were shot dead in Baghdad.
2/3/96 Sulaymaniyah, Iraqi Kurdistan	Hassan Bazargan	Assassinated.
2/2/96 Istanbul, Turkey	Zahra Rajabi	Senior member of the National Council of Resistance of Iran. Assassinated in Turkey by the Iranian regime's terrorists while on a mission to aid Iranian refugees.
1/2/96 Sulaymaniyah, Iraqi Kurdistan	Rahman Sha'abannejad	Assassinated.
1/2/96 Sulaymaniyah, Iraqi Kurdistan	Haji Abdollah Salehzadeh	Assassinated.
12/31/95 Koysanjagh, Iraqi Kurdistan	Sedigh Abdollahi	Assassinated.
12/31/95 Erbil, Iraqi Kurdistan	Osman Rooyan	Assassinated.
12/31/95 Raniya, Iraqi Kurdistan	Hassan Jit	Assassinated.

Date / Location	Target	Description
12/31/95 Koysanjagh, Iraqi Kurdistan	Ghafour Mehdizadeh	Assassinated.
12/31/95 Koysanjagh, Iraqi Kurdistan	Ali Amini	Assassinated.
12/31/95 Erbil, Iraqi Kurdistan	Aboubakr Chegel Mostapha	Assassinated.
12/10/95 Iraqi Kurdistan	Omar Dehestani	Assassinated.
9/12/95 Raniya, Iraqi Kurdistan	Rahim Kolseii	Assassinated.
9/12/95 Erbil, Iraqi Kurdistan	Najmodin Shaiatpanah	Assassinated.
8/23/95 Erbil, Iraqi Kurdistan	Seyedali Partovi	Assassinated.
7/10/95 Baghdad, Iraq	Yarali Gartabar	Assassinated along with 2 other Mojahedin members when their car came under fire by the regime's terrorists.
7/1/95 Baghdad, Iraq	Effat Haddad and Fereshteh Esfandiari	Effat Haddad (mother of 4) and Fereshteh Esfandiari (anchorwoman), officials of the PMOI. Assassinated by the mullah regime's terrorists.
5/19/95 Paris, France	Shahpour Bakhtiar	The shah's last prime minister and Soroush Katibeh, his personal secretary. Bakhtiar's throat was slit and his aide stabbed to death at Bakhtiar's home near Paris.
5/1/95 Basormeh, Iraqi Kurdistan	Soleiman Chekloudeh	Assassinated.
4/25/95 Erbil, Iraqi Kurdistan	Najmeddin Sharifzadeh	Assassinated.

Date / Location	Target	Description
3/21/95 Ghaladiza, Iraqi Kurdistan	Saleh Aminpour	Assassinated.
3/21/95 Sulaymaniyah, Iraqi Kurdistan	Roonak Hosseini	Assassinated.
3/21/95 Sulaymaniyah, Iraqi Kurdistan	Moslem Hosseini	Assassinated.
3/21/95 Seyedsadegh, Iraqi Kurdistan	Mohammad Soureii	Assassinated.
3/21/95 Sulaymaniyah, Iraqi Kurdistan	Mansour Fedayi	Assassinated.
3/21/95 Diana, Iraqi Kurdistan	Majid Saldouzi	Assassinated.
3/21/95 Dookan, Iraqi Kurdistan	Karim Shoghi	Assassinated.
3/21/95 Ghandil, Iraqi Kurdistan	Hossein Ramheh	Assassinated.
2/8/95 Raniya, Iraqi Kurdistan	Saadoun Barezan	Assassinated.
2/8/95 Raniya, Iraqi Kurdistan	Hassan Azarbarzin	Assassinated.
12/23/94 Gol-Ali beik, Iraqi Kurdistan	Mohammad Amin Bayazidi	Assassinated.
12/23/94 Gol-Ali beik, Iraqi Kurdistan	Mohammad Darakhshani	Assassinated.
11/26/94 Chowarghorneh, Iraqi Kurdistan	Westa Hassan Ojaghi	Assassinated.
11/6/94 Iraqi Kurdistan	Omar Kurd	Assassinated.

Date / Location	Target	Description
10/14/94 Halabja, Iraqi Kurdistan	Mohammad Rashid	Assassinated.
10/10/94 Hajiabad, Iraqi Kurdistan	Moloud Salim Savol	Assassinated.
10/5/94 Diana, Iraqi Kurdistan	Aboubakr Saboktakin	Assassinated in his friend's residence.
9/8/94 Sulaymaniyah, Iraqi Kurdistan	Aliakbar Teymouri	Assassinated.
8/4/94 Baghdad, Iraq	Ghafour Hamzeii	Assassinated in his residence.
6/25/94 Mavet, Iraqi Kurdistan	Khaleh Momgooleh	Assassinated.
4/7/94 Iraqi Kurdistan	Saleh Jahangiri	Assassinated.
3/21/94 Halabja, Iraqi Kurdistan	Wase Jahangiri	Assassinated.
3/21/94 Momghelich, Iraqi Kurdistan	Mohammad Saeed Ghaderi	Assassinated.
3/21/94 Rwandooz, Iraqi Kurdistan	Mohammad Bookani	Assassinated.
3/21/94 Barian, Iraqi Kurdistan	Mohammad Mohammadpour	Assassinated.
3/21/94 Sulaymaniyah, Iraqi Kurdistan	Mam Sharif	Assassinated.
3/21/94 Bahrkeh, Iraqi Kurdistan	Hassan Ebrahimzadeh	Assassinated.
3/21/94 Erbil, Iraqi Kurdistan	Awla Soovar	Assassinated.
3/21/94 Sulaymaniyah, Iraqi Kurdistan	Abdollah Izadi	Assassinated.

Date / Location	Target	Description
3/21/94 Iraqi Kurdistan	Abdollah Ryani	Assassinated.
3/16/94 Sulaymaniyah, Iraqi Kurdistan	Reshad Karimi	Attacked by several terrorists and killed.
2/12/94 Sweden	Abubakr Hedayati	Blinded when he tried to open an envelope sent to his wife. According to the police, the package had been sent by the Iranian embassy.
2/2/94 Nawtagh, Iraqi Kurdistan	Shahrokh Moradi	Assassinated.
1/22/94 Raniya, Iraqi Kurdistan	Osman Osmani	Assassinated.
1/17/94 Chroom, Turkey	Taha Kermany	Assassinated by a shot fired at his head by the regime's terrorists.
12/24/93 Sulaymaniyah, Iraqi Kurdistan	Sedigh Rashidi	Assassinated.
12/15/93 Ranieh, Iraq	Mahmoud Mojahedi	Assassinated by the regime's terrorists in his house in Haji-abad camp.
12/11/93 Baghdad, Iraq	Majid-Reza Ibrahimi	Ibrahimi was killed and his companion wounded when the Khomeini regime's terrorists opened fire on them while they were shopping at a store in Baghdad's As-Sha'ab district.
10/17/93 Raniya, Iraqi Kurdistan	Dr. Bahram	Assassinated.
10/16/93 Sulaymaniyah, Iraqi Kurdistan	Jamal Nami	Assassinated.
10/6/93 Diana, Iraqi Kurdistan	Mola Ahmad Darwishi	Friday prayer leader of Delzian village. Assassinated by gunfire in his residence.

Date / Location	Target	Description
9/10/93 Ankara, Turkey	Behran Azadfer	Fatally shot by two Farsi-speaking gunmen at his house. A third person stood guard in the garden.
8/26/93 Diana, Iraqi Kurdistan	Mola Mohammad Bigzad	Assassinated by the regime's agents.
8/26/93 Turkey	Mohammad Ghaderi	Abducted then killed by the regime's agents.
8/2/93 Raniya, Iraqi Kurdistan	Saadoun Abbassi	Assassinated.
8/2/93 Raniya, Iraqi Kurdistan	Ahmad Fatemi	Assassinated.
6/6/93 Karachi, Pakistan	Mohammad Hassan Arbab	Member of the Mojahedin. Assassinated around noon in front of his residence by 4 terrorists dispatched by the Khomeini regime.
6/6/93 Rome, Italy	Mohammad Hossein Naghdi	Representative of the National Council of Resistance of Iran in Italy. Shot dead by two terrorists astride a motorcycle in broad daylight as he went by car from his home to his office.
5/31/93 Raniya, Iraqi Kurdistan	Kamran Shafei	Assassinated.
3/16/93 Pakistan	Mohammad Amin Mirlashari	Chief of the Mirlashar tribe in Iranian Baluchistan. Shot and wounded in the street.
3/9/93 Baghdad, Iraq	PMOI and National Liberation Army (NLA)	Terrorists planted a bomb in a city bus in Baghdad, knowing it was used by the Mojahedin and NLA. No one was injured in the blast.
3/9/93 Pakistan	Delaviz Narou'i and Heybatollah Narou'i	Chiefs of the Narou'i tribe in Iranian Baluchistan. Shot to death in the street.

215

Date / Location	Target	Description
2/22/93 Germany	Mehdi Ha'eri	Cleric opposed to the regime. Terrorists posing as acquaintances made an appointment to see him by phone. Aware his life was in danger, he notified the police, who arrested 1 man and discovered a knife and a silencer-equipped gun in his car.
1/24/93 Oslo, Norway	Mehdi Baba'l	Mojahedin supporter. Two terrorists from the regime's embassy in Oslo brutally assaulted him. They fled when police arrived. Baba'i required hospitalization.
1/18/93 Iraq	Gholam-Hossein Kazemi	Member of the Mojahedin and combatant in the National Liberation Army of Iran. Assassinated while driving between NLA bases. The other occupants of the car were wounded.
1/12/93 Istanbul, Turkey	Abbas Golizadeh	Former bodyguard to the shah. Kidnapped from his home in a suburb of Istanbul and later killed.
12/26/92 Germany	Mohammad Sadeq Sharafkandi	Leader of the KDPI, 3 other Kurds (Homayoun Ardalan, Fattah Abdolahi, and Nuri Dehkordi), and an unidentified individual. Sharafkandi and the 3 Kurds were shot dead when terrorists sprayed them with machine gun fire.
9/29/92 Nawtagh, Iraqi Kurdistan	Taher Manouchehri	Assassinated.
9/29/92 Nawtagh, Iraqi Kurdistan	Salah Moradi	Assassinated.
9/29/92 Nawtagh, Iraqi Kurdistan	Rashid Rostami	Assassinated.

Date / Location	Target	Description
9/29/92 Nawtagh, Iraqi Kurdistan	Mohammad Mehrban	Assassinated.
9/25/92 Nawtagh, Iraqi Kurdistan	Mahmoud Khezri	Assassinated.
9/17/92 Berlin, Germany	Sadegh Sharafkandi	Gunned down along with 3 other people in the restaurant Mikonos. The Berlin Court later condemned two agents of the mullahs' regime and blamed Khamenei, Rafsanjani, and Velayati for the crime.
9/15/92 Germany	Fereidoun Farokhzad	Entertainer. Stabbed to death.
8/9/92 Germany	Homayoun Maraghe'I	Head of the overseas office of the People's Party. Wounded with a knife.
8/6/92 Dubai	Gholam Ghahremani	Supporter of Mojahedin seeking political asylum. Kidnapped from his residence and transferred to Evin Prison in Tehran.
8/5/92 Iraqi Kurdistan	Kashtmir Abbassi	Assassinated.
8/3/92 Iraq	Members of the KDPI	Terrorist infiltrators poisoned food at the KDPI's headquarters. 7 persons were hospitalized in critical condition, 3 of whom subsequently died Hadi Mahmoudi, Ali Nanoureh, and Fakhroddin Moradi.
7/29/92 Basormeh, Iraqi Kurdistan	\Mam Morad Mohammadzadeh	Assassinated.
7/24/92 Raniya, Iraqi Kurdistan	Ebrahim Rahmani	Assassinated.
7/24/92 Raniya, Iraqi Kurdistan	Ali-asghar Almaspour	Assassinated.

Date / Location	Target	Description
7/8/92 Panjvein, Iraqi Kurdistan	Karim Balafkan	Assassinated.
7/1/92 Sulaymaniyah, Iraqi Kurdistan	Kamran Mansour	Assassinated.
6/23/92 Turkey	Mojahedin supporters	Car bomb planted in a car used by Mojahedin supporters was defused before it went off. Car bomb planted in a car used by Mojahedin supporters in Istanbul destroys the vehicle.
6/10/92 Halabja, Iraqi Kurdistan	Salar Saedpanah	Assassinated.
6/10/92 Halabja, Iraqi Kurdistan	Hadi Mahmoudi	Assassinated.
6/10/92 Halabja, Iraqi Kurdistan	Fakhredin Moradi	Assassinated.
6/10/92 Halabja, Iraqi Kurdistan	Ali Tatooreh	Assassinated.
6/5/92 Istanbul, Turkey	Ali-Akbar Ghorbani	Mojahedin member. Kidnapped by Tehran's terrorists in front of his home. Terrorists arrested admitted having been trained in Iran and having turned Ghorbani over to Iranian agents, who tortured and then murdered him. They led police to a shallow grave in the outskirts of Istanbul, where they found the tortured body.
6/4/92 Iraq	Kamran Mansour Moqadam	Member of the Communist Union. Murdered by machine gun fire.
6/3/92 Iraq	Shahpour Firouzi	Member of the KDPI Revolutionary Leadership. Assassinated by machine gun.

Date / Location	Target	Description
5/31/92 Iraq	Seifollah Seimanpour	Refugee. Killed by machine gun fire.
5/8/92 Karachi, Pakistan	Abdollah Delavar	Assassinated.
5/1/92 Netherlands	Kamal Reza'l	Member of the Mojahedin. Terrorists set an ambush for him near his residence, but he escaped the trap.
4/11/92 New Jersey, United States	Nareh Rafi'zadeh	Wife and sister-in-law of former intelligence agents under the shah. Assassinated as she left her car at her New Jersey residence.
3/26/92 Versailles, France	Abolhassan Banisadr	Khomeini's first president. The would-be assassins, who had entered his home in Versailles, fled when French security agents opened fire.
3/25/92 New Jersey, United States	Nareh Rafizadeh	Assassinated.
3/21/92 Sulaymaniyah, Iraqi Kurdistan	Seyfollah Soleimanpour	Assassinated by the mullahs' regime.
3/21/92 Iraqi Kurdistan	Mohammad Sheikhpour	Assassinated.
3/21/92 Panjvein, Iraqi Kurdistan	Karim Gagol	Assassinated by the mullahs' regime.
3/21/92 Panjvein, Iraqi Kurdistan	Ahmad Gagol	Assassinated by the mullahs' regime.
2/17/92 Baghdad, Iraq	Mojahedin office in Baghdad	Around midnight, 4 terrorists dispatched by the regime attempted to enter one of the Mojahedin's offices. Confronted by a security guard, one escaped, two were arrested, and the fourth, who attempted to open fire, was shot and killed.

Date / Location	Target	Description
12/23/91 Iraqi Kurdistan	Khaleh Hemeh	Assassinated by the mullahs' regime.
12/6/91 Iraq	Members of the KDPI	A bomb-laden minibus was detonated in the path of a bus carrying KDPI members and their families. 3 persons were killed and a number, including small children, wounded.
10/29/91 Iraq	Saeed Yazdanpanah	Member of the Revolutionary Union of the Kurdish People, and Sirous Katibeh, his secretary. Terrorist infiltrators stabbed both to death at Yazdanpanah's residence.
10/5/91 Bouli, Iraqi Kurdistan	Mollah Rasoul Kurdi	Assassinated by the mullahs' regime.
10/5/91 Bouli, Iraqi Kurdistan	Jalil Jalili	Assassinated by the mullahs' regime.
9/23/91 Bouli, Iraqi Kurdistan	Hassove Alipour	Assassinated by the mullahs' regime.
9/17/91 Bouli, Iraqi Kurdistan	Kuri Zuri	Assassinated by the mullahs' regime.
9/7/91 Paris, France	Jahangir Mehrani	Assassinated 10 hours after the assassination of Shapour Bakhtiar.
9/5/91 Pishdar, Iraqi Kurdistan	Saber Farhadi	Assassinated.
6/8/91 Paris, France	Abdolrahman Boroumand	Aide to Bakhtiar. Stabbed to death in the street.
4/18/91 Iraq	Ahad Aqa	Member of Kurdistan Democratic Party. Assassinated in the street.
1/1/91 Iraqi Kurdistan	Saeed Yazdanpanah	Assassinated by the mullahs' regime.
1/1/91 Iraq	Khaled Hosseinpour	Member of the Khebat. Assassinated.

Date / Location	Target	Description
10/31/90 Paris, France	Sirous Elahi	Shot and killed at his residence in Paris.
10/31/90 Iraq	Komeleh Headquarters	A Peshmarga was killed when a bomb planted by terrorists went off at the headquarters.
10/23/90 Turkey	Gholam Reza Nakha'i	Iranian political refugee. Killed in his hotel room by a severe blow to the head.
10/1/90 Sweden	Amir Qazi	Member of KDPI. His wife, Effat Qazi, was killed when she opened a letter bomb addressed to her husband.
9/6/90 Turkey	Ali Kashefpour	Member of the KDPI Revolutionary Leadership. Terrorists kidnapped him from his home in a refugee quarter. His tortured body was later found in a roadside ditch.
9/1/90 Sulaymaniyah, Iraqi Kurdistan	Mohammad Fathi	Assassinated.
6/10/90 Koysanjaq, Iraq	Mohammad Mostafaei	Member of KDPI. Kidnapped and killed 2 days later.
5/28/90 Coppet, Switzerland	Professor Kazem Rajavi	Representative of the National Council of Resistance of Iran, elder brother of Massoud Rajavi, leader of the Iranian Resistance. Shot to death in his car in Coppet, near Geneva. Swiss police confirmed at least 13 terrorists with Iranian service passports.
4/24/90 Istanbul, Turkey	Hossein Mir-Abedini	Mojahedin member. Shot and critically wounded en route by car to Istanbul Airport.

Date / Location	Target	Description
3/14/90 Taftan, Pakistan	Hadj Balouch Khan	Royalist. Assassinated by a Guards Corps commando squad.
3/5/90 Gouhaln, Iraqi Kurdistan	Kamal Ghaderzadeh	Assassinated.
2/16/90 Karachi, Pakistan	Hossein Keshavarz,	Mojahedin sympathizer. A hail of machine gun fire gravely wounded him in Karachi, leaving him paralyzed in both legs.
11/26/89 Iraq	Seyed Mohammad Heidari	A member of the KDPI. Shot and killed a day later in the hospital.
9/14/89 Iraq	Sadiq Kamangar	Member of Komeleh. Infiltrators assassinated him at his headquarters.
8/26/89 Cyprus	Bahman Javadi and Youssef Rashidzadeh	Members of Komeleh. Javadi was shot and killed in the street. Rashidzadeh was wounded.
7/13/89 Dubai	Ata'ollah Bayahmadi	Former military intelligence colonel under the shah. Assassinated in his hotel room.
6/26/89 Vienna, Austria	Abdol Rahman Qassemlou	Leader of the KDPI. Abdullah Qaderi-Azar, Fadel Mala, and Mahmoud Rassoul (his aides) were also shot dead while meeting secretly with representatives of Rafsanjani. A senior Guards Corps commander oversaw the murders.
6/4/89 Germany	Gathering of Mojahedin sympathizers	A bomb exploded in front of the door to the meeting hall, wounding 3 persons.

Date / Location	Target	Description
2/1/89 Karachi, Pakistan	Iranian refugees	Iranian refugees waiting outside the UNHCR office in Karachi attacked. One person killed, 5 wounded.
12/3/88 Istanbul, Turkey	Javad Ha'eri	Dissident. Stabbed to death by 2 men at this home.
12/1/87 Paris, France	Behrouz Bagheri	Former Air Force commander. Bomb planted in his store.
11/28/87 Quetta, Pakistan	Iranian refugees	A bomb was planted in a hotel. Police arrested Guards Corps members. One Iranian was killed, another wounded.
10/31/87 Istanbul, Turkey	Abolhassan Mojtahedzadeh and Mostafa Abrari of the Mojahedin	Kidnapped by Iranian embassy personnel. Abrari escaped his captors. The police discovered Mojtahedzadeh in the trunk of an Iranian embassy car with diplomatic plates near the Iran-Turkey border.
10/26/87 Pakistan	Anti-Khomeini students	One student was murdered in an attack by the regime's agents.
10/11/87 London, United Kingdom	Ali and Noureddin Nabavi Tavakoli	Father and son royalists. Shot in the back of the head in the living room of their London home.
10/4/87 London, United Kingdom	Ali Nabavi	Killed along with his son.
10/3/87 Geneva, Switzerland	Ahmad Talebi	Fighter pilot and refugee. Assassinated on the street by two armed men.
9/10/87 Istanbul, Turkey	Mohammad Hassan Mansouri	Anti-Khomeini dissident, and another person. Assassinated by two men at Mansouri's home.

Date / Location	Target	Description
8/25/87 Karachi, Pakistan	Alireza Hassanpour, Emambakhsh Mirbaluch and Faramarz Aqa'i	13 homes in Karachi and Quetta were attacked with RPG rockets and submachine guns. Hassanpour, Mirabaluch, and Aqa'i were killed and 33 persons wounded. 9 men identified by police as Guards Corps members were arrested at the Iran-Pakistan border.
7/8/87 Kuwaiteh and Karachi, Pakistan	Mojahedin supporters	3 persons injured in terrorist attack on their center.
7/8/87 United Kingdom	Amir-Hossein Amir-Parviz	Affiliate of the shah's last prime minister, Bakhtiar. Severely injured in a car bomb.
5/31/87 Vienna, Austria	Hamidreza Chitgar (Hamid Bahmani)	First secretary of the Workers Party. Assassinated in a house. His body was discovered by police on July 12, 1987.
3/21/87 Germany	Ali Akbar Mohammadi	Former pilot for Rafsanjani. Assassinated in the street by two men.
12/29/86 Pakistan	Vali Mohammad Van	Shot five times and killed.
12/29/86 Turkey	Ahmadhamed Monfared (Hamid Farzaneh)	Former Army colonel. Assassinated by 2 men armed with silencer-equipped pistols.
10/24/86 United Kingdom	Reza Fazeli	Assassination attempt by a bombing that killed his son.
1/1/86 Istanbul, Turkey	Aziz Moradi	Former colonel in the shah's army. Assassinated.
12/23/85 Karachi, Pakistan	Mir Monavat	Majlis deputy from Baluchistan under the shah. Murdered at his home by 3 armed men.

Date / Location	Target	Description
9/28/85 Istanbul, Turkey	Behrouz Shahvardilou	Police colonel under the shah. Assassinated in the Koucheh Kyabi district of Istanbul.
8/21/85 Paris, France	Gholam-Ali Oveissi	Former commander of the shah's army and his brother, a former general. Assassinated.
2/7/84 Paris, France	Iranian refugee	Attacked by armed terrorists in the UNESCO Building.
2/1/84 Turkey	Hamid Farzaneh	Gunned down by the regime's terrorists.
12/6/82 India	Abdol-Amir Rahdar	Terrorists armed with knives and machetes attacked a demonstration protesting human rights abuses in Iran. Amir Rahdar was murdered and 20 others seriously wounded.
9/10/82 Karachi, Pakistan	Ahmad Zolanvar	Two terrorists astride motor-cycles attacked him and his companions, causing wounds resulting in brain hemorrhaging. He was subsequently transferred to Denmark for emergency surgery, where he died.
6/20/82 India	Shahram Mirami and other anti-Khomeini students	100 terrorists armed with clubs, knives, and machetes attacked the Aligarh dormitory, where a group of Iranian students wase holding a hunger strike to protest executions in Iran. Shahram Mirami was murdered and 9 other students seriously wounded.

Date / Location	Target	Description
6/6/82 Mainz, Germany	University students supporting the Mojahedin	150 terrorists armed with clubs, knives, chains, brass knuckles, and tear gas attacked a student dormitory. A young German woman was killed and 28 Iranian students severely wounded.
4/24/82 Sweden	Anti-Khomeini Iranian student	Attacked by Khomeini's terrorists at a bus stop. The following day, he was again attacked in retaliation for speaking to the press about the incident.
3/27/82 Turkey	Saeed Aghapour	Mojahedin supporter. Killed in an armed attack.
3/27/82 Manila, Philippines	Esfandiar Rahimi	Supporter of the PMOI. Stabbed to death by regime's agents.
3/9/82 Manila, Philippines	Iranians attending funeral service	Terrorist lobbed a grenade into the gathering; 3 persons were hospitalized with critical wounds.
1/15/82 Manila, Philippines	Shahrokh Missaqi	Supporter of the People's Feda'ii. Stabbed and killed.
8/31/81 Washington, D.C., United States	Ali-Akbar Tabataba'i	Diplomat under the shah. Shot and killed at his home.
7/23/80 Paris, France	Shahpour Bakhtiar	The shah's last prime minister. A five-man hit squad tried to shoot its way into his Paris home. A policeman and a neighbor were killed and 3 policemen wounded.

Index

A

Abaii, Mullah, 79

Abdoh, Muhammad, 14, 151

Abdulhamid, 15

Abru, Hafiz, 8

Abtahi, Muhammad-Ali, 101

Abu Bakr, 55

Adam, Muhammad Kamal, 96

Adeli, Muhammad-Hussein, 71

Afghanistan, 40, 51
  relations with Iran, 72–76
  Shi'ism in, 73–74
  Soviet invasion of, 52

Africa, North. See also individual nations.
  fundamentalism exported to, 86–94, 110
  Guards Corps in, 110
  recruitment of terrorists in, 121

Ahari-Mostafavi, Mehdi, 99, 120

Ahl al-Beit, 121

Akhtari, Muhammad-Hassan, 126

Akhundzadeh-Basti, Muhammad-Mehdi, 100

Al-Azhar University of Cairo, 55

Al-Baghlani, Abu Bakr, 6

Al-Bazzaz, Saad, 64

Al-Ghannouchi, Rachid, 89, 92

al-Ghazzali, Abu Hamid Muhammad, 5

Al-Kawakibi, Abdur-Rahman, 13–14

al-Ketab, 46

Al-Moussavi, Abdul-Hussein Sharafoddin, 55

Al-Nawawi, Hafiz Yahya, 6

Al-Tamheed, 6

Albania, 40

Alborzi, Muhammad-Reza, 119

Algeria, 40, 43, 48, 51, 53–54, 94
  and Islamic movement, 3, 38
  relations with Iran, 87–88, 100

Ali ibn Abi Taleb, or Imam Ali, 4–5, 57, 61, 103, 167, 170, 173 (n. 6), 189 (n. 6), 190 (n. 19)

Amrollahi, Reza, 138

An-Nahdha movement, 89

Anwar ot-Tanzil va Asrar ot-T'avil (The Rays of the Quran and Secrets of Interpretation), 45

Aqazadeh, Gholamreza, 71

Aqiqi, 117

ar-Rashid, Harun, 46

Arab-Israeli War, 49
  and Soviet Union, 51

Arefina, 93

Argentina
  offering military aid, 129
  terrorism in, 116

Arvani, Fahimeh, 171, 190 (n. 28)

Asia, Central
  fundamentalism exported to, 48, 67, 69–70, 77, 80–81
  as "major crisis point," 81

Assad Abadi, Seyyed Jamal od-Din, 14–15

Assass ol-Balaghah (The Fundamentals of Eloquence), 46

Austria
  terrorism in, 118

Avecinna (Ibn Sina), 45, 68

Ayat, Hassan, 11, 175 (n. 10)

Azadi, Muhammad, 119–120

Azari-Qomi, Ahmad, 24–25, 28

Azerbaijan, 67, 76
  leaders' meeting with Rafsanjani, 69
  relations with Iran, 70–71

Aziz, Tariq, 178 (n. 7)
Azizi, Ahmad, 89

B

Baghdad Pact (CENTO), 51
Bahrain, 98
Baker, James, 77
Bakhtiar, Shapour, 109, 118, 119, 120
Bangladesh, 40
Bangladesh War, 152
Baqeri, Muhammad-Reza, 100
Bassij. *See* Guards Corps Mobilization
Bayhaqi, Bu'l Fazl-i, 46
Bazargan, Mehdi, 32, 162, 175 (n. 11)
Behbahani, Seyyed Abdullah, 11
Beheshti, Muhammad-Hussein, 32, 174 (n. 10)
Beit ol-Moqaddas, 111
Belgium
    offering military aid, 129
Besharati, Ali-Muhammad, 83
Birouni, Abu-Rayhan, 68
Bongo, Omar, 48
Bonyad-e-Mostaz'afin (Foundation for the Deprived), 133
Bourguiba, Habib, 89
Brazil
    offering military aid, 129, 131
Brezhnev, Leonid, 51
Bulgaria
    offering military aid, 129
Bush, George, 77

C

Cambodia, 41
Casablanca Summit, 94
CENTO, 51
Chad, 40
Chamberlain, 53
Chatelain, Roland, 118
China, 41
    offering military aid, 90, 129, 130, 131, 132, 134–137, 138

Conference to Support Palestine's Islamic Revolution, 84, 126
Congo, 96
Cyprus
    terrorism in, 122

D

Daqiqi, 68
Dar Al-Hadith, 6
Daryaei, Nasser, 121
Dastjerdi, Vahid, 139
Decrees on Defense and the Front, 62
Demirel, Suleyman
    trip to Central Asia, 76, 77
Democracy. *See also* Liberalism.
    in Mojahedin, 165–167
Djibouti, 92
Dostum, Rasheed, 74
Dumas, Roland, 53

E

Economic Cooperation Organization (ECO), 70, 71, 77, 81
Ecuador, 48
Egypt, 40, 43, 49, 51, 53, 182 (n. 49)
    accusations toward Sudan, 91–92
    liberalism in, 153
    relations with Iran, 55, 92–94
Ethiopia, 40, 92

F

Fadhlullah, Sheikh Muhammad-Hussein, 28, 86, 115
Fallahian, Ali, 90, 102, 148
Farahani, Faramarz, 122
Farrokhzad, Fereidoon, 119
Farsi, Hamid, 122
Farzaneh, Hamid, 122
Fatemi, Hussein, 12
Feda'ian-e-Islam, 12, 160
Ferdowsi, Abolqassem, 180 (n. 26)

France
offering military aid, 134
terrorism in, 118, 120–121
Freedom Movement, 162, 175 (n. 11)
Fundamentalism, Islamic
costs, xxiii
defined, xxiii
and despotism, 5
exportation of, 21–22, 39–40, 47, 53,
95–96
to Central Asia, 48, 67, 69–70,
77, 80–81
to Eastern Mediterranean, 83–85
Farsi's role, 71, 72, 75, 79
to Iraq, 61, 65
to North Africa, 86–94, 110
oil's role, 47–50
religion's role, 70, 77–78
to Saudi Arabia and Persian Gulf
states, 94–95
trade's role, 70
growth as nationalism declined, 47
training, xiii, 37
Western misinterpretations of, 155–
156
women's status under, 170

G

Gabon, 48
Galindo Pohl, Reynaldo, 142
Ganjavi, Nezami, 68
Ganji, Sadeq, 101
Geha, Mustapha, 117
Gellner, Ernest, 41
Germany
offering military aid, 129, 131, 132,
134, 137, 187 (n. 36)
terrorism in, 109, 118–119, 120
Ghailuli, Abu-Bakr, 96
Ghorbani, Ali-Akbar, 108
Goble, Paul, 177 (n. 13)
Golestan, Treaty of, 68, 79
Gorbachev, Mikhail, 52, 68
Great Britain, 51
terrorism in, 109
Greece, 41
Guards Corps Mobilization, 20

H

Hadith
source books on, 45
Haj Azim, Mansour, 136, 137
Hanifnejad, Muhammad, 42, 159, 160,
174 (n. 8)
arrest and death, 160
background, 176 (ch. 5, n. 5)
Hashemi, Mahmoud, 101
Hedayat, Kamal, 107
Hezb-i-Vahdat-e-Islami (Islamic
Unionist Party), 73
Hindizadeh, Massoud, 121
Hitler, Adolf, 53
Hizbullah, 28, 91
leaders' meeting with Rafsanjani, 86
Hojjatieh, 57
Hulagu Khan, 15
Hungary
offering military aid, 135
Hussein bin Ali, or Imam Hussein, 6,
42
Hussein, King, 46, 85
Husseinzadeh, 91

I

Ibn Taymiyah, 5
Ibrahim, Haj, 121
Ikhwan as-Safa (Brethren of Purity), 7
Imam Ali University, 110
India, 40, 96
Muslim population, 74
offering military aid, 129
Indonesia, 40, 43, 96
Muslim population, 48
International Committee of the Red
Cross, 175–176 (n. 14)
Iran. *See also* Iran-Iraq War; Khamenei,
Ali; Khomeini, Ruhollah; Media,
Iranian; Hashemi-Rafsanjani, Ali-
Akbar.
and Persian Gulf War, 64–65
as "Mother of All Islamic Lands,"
37–38, 47

Atomic Energy Organization, 134, 137
beneficial geopolitical location of, 78–79
economy, 79–80, 143–144
employment, 143
executions in, 31, 33, 97
foreign relations
  with Afghanistan, 72–76
  with Algeria, 87–88, 100
  with Azerbaijan, 70–71
  with Egypt, 55, 92–94
  with Jordan, 84–85, 100
  with Lebanon, 85–86, 100
  with Saudi Arabia, 94–95
  with Sudan, 90–92
  with Tadzhikistan, 71–72, 75
  with Tunisia, 88–90
  with Turkey, 76–77, 100, 180 (n. 41)
  with Turkmenistan, 71
government
  Abbasid dynasty, 6, 15, 46
  anti-shah groups, 159-161, 172–173 (n. 18)
  Assembly of Experts, 23, 27
  communists in, 154, 159, 161, 189 (n. 5)
  constitution, 23–25, 28, 29–31
  Council for Constitutional Revision, 24
  Council for the Determination of Exigencies of the State, 24, 30, 146
  Council of Guardians, 10, 24, 30, 73, 142
  foreign policy, 39–40. *See also* Fundamentalism, Islamic, exportation of.
  Ghaznavid dynasty, 46
  Khwarezm-Shah dynasty, 46
  Ministry of Foreign Affairs, 72, 99–101
  Ministry of Intelligence, 102
  Ministry of Islamic Culture and Guidance, 36, 101–102
  Office of Political and International Studies, 72
  Oil Ministry, 133
  Qajar monarchy, 9

  Safavid dynasty, 5, 8, 9
  Sasanid dynasty, 45
  Supreme Judicial Council, 31
  Twelfth Bureau, 72
  Umayyad dynasty, 6, 15, 46
  under Khomeini. *See* Khomeini, Ruhollah.
  under Rafsanjani, 31, 32–33, 35–38, 48, 68–69, 129, 142, 143, 146
  velayat-e-faqih, 17–19, 21–25, 28–31, 33, 36, 56
history
  anti-monarchic revolution, 2, 41–42
  Constitutional Revolution, 10–13, 152, 153, 166
  cultural, 45–47
  democratic Islamic movements, 7–8
  military, 45, 59
military aid, 129. *See also individual nations.*
military spending, 129
Muslim population, 40
oil nationalization movement, 152
oil revenues, 49
political repression in, 142–143
protests in, 21, 144–148, 164, 174 (n. 9), 188 (n. 25)
secret police, 20, 42, 160, 185 (n. 25)
strikes, 148
view toward Middle East, 125–127
vision of as democracy, 171
voters, 145–146
weaponry
  chemical and biological, 131–132
  conventional, 130–131
  nuclear, 133–139
West's appeasement toward, 53
women's status in, 31, 142, 170–171
Iran-Iraq War, xxi, 59–65, 121
  aftermath, xiii, 57, 129, 144
  and Mojahedin, 63
  as "divine blessing," 22, 59
  capture of Faw, 62
  cease-fire, 64
  fortifying velayat-e-faqih, 61–62
  Guards Corps' role in, 97–98, 103
  human toll, 63-64

Iraqi withdrawal, 63
Islamic Republic Party's analysis of, 59
Khomeini's religious decrees during, 62
Khomeini's unfulfilled dream, 64
killing of civilians and POWs, 62
monetary costs, 63, 64
nuclear site destroyed during, 136
objectives, 60–62
Iraq, 51
    and Shi'ism, 61
    fundamentalism exported to, 61, 65
    Guards Corps in, 110
    Muslim population, 40
    nationalism in, 152
    occupation of Kuwait, 64
    oil reserves, 61
Islam
    and Ottomans, 18
    cultural significance, 44–47
    described by Rajavi, 161
    embedded in velayat, 17
    encyclopedia, 7
    history, 2–15
    location of followers, 40–41
    marriage under, 25
    modern objectives, 41
    modern, democratic vs. fundamentalism, 157–158, 165–171
    Mojahedin's vision of, 165, 169, 170
    revived as colonialism declined, 43–44
    teachings, 1. *See also* Muhammad, Prophet; Quran.
Islamic Conference Organization, 80
Islamic Free University, 170
Islamic Government, 56
Islamic Propaganda Organization, 99
Islamic Republic Party
    analysis of Iran-Iraq War, 59–60
    founding, 175 (n. 10)
Islamic Revival Party (IRP)
    in Tadzhikistan, 75
    in Uzbekistan, 72
Islamic Revolutionary Committees, 20
Islamic Revolutionary Courts, 20
Islamic Revolutionary Guards Corps, 20

2nd (Lebanon) Corps, 98–99, 107
3rd (Hamzeh) Corps, 107
4th (Ansar) Corps, 107–108
9th Badr Corps, 110
in Algeria, 88
Ansar Garrison, 69
Ansar Headquarters, 99
and chemical weapons, 132–133
collaborating with communists, 162
Corps 5,000, 108–109
Corps 6,000, 110
formation of new units, 98–99
founding, 97
in Lebanon, 85, 122–123
Liberation Movements Unit, 98, 119
and nuclear weapons, 133–134, 136, 138
organization, 103–110
Ramadhan Headquarters, 99
role in Iran-Iraq War, 97–98, 103
Special Qods (Jerusalem) Force, 69, 72–73, 102–103, 119
    in Afghanistan, 73
as targets of protest, 147, 148
training, 110–111
Islamic Unionist Party, 73
Israel, 83–84, 124
Italy
    offering military aid, 129
    terrorism in, 109, 115, 117

J

Jahad-e-Sazandegi (the Construction Crusade), 132
Jame' ol-Bayan (A Comprehensive Statement), 46
Jame' ot-Tawarikh (A Comprehensive History), 46
Jannati, Ahmad, 73
Japan
    terrorism in, 109, 117
Jibril, Ahmed, 28, 86
Jihad
    members arrested in Egypt, 93
Jordan, 40, 53, 83, 100–101
    relations with Iran, 84–85, 100
Jowri, Hassan, 7–8

K

Kamal, Majid, 91, 182 (n. 34)
Kan'ani, Ahmad, 89
Kani, Haji Molla Ali, 9
Kashani, Ayatollah Abolqassem, 11
Kashef Al-Qeta', Muhammad-Hussein, 55
Kasravi, Ahmad, 12
Katibeh, Soroush, 118
Kazakhstan, 67, 70, 71, 81, 138, 139
Kemal, Mustafa, 152
Kenya, 92
Khalkhali, Sadeq, 12
Khamenei, Ali, 175 (n. 10)
  and Shi'ite traditionalists, 57
  calling for security, 148
  commenting on Algeria, 88
  commenting on Middle East peace talks, 125
  commenting on Palestine, 126
  commenting on Salman Rushdie, 117
  lambasted by Khomeini, 19
  named vali-e-faqih, 27–28
  securing loyalties, 28
  terrorism and, 114
Khansari, Muhammad-Kazem, 101
Kharajites, 4–5
Kharazmi, 68
Kharrazi, Kamal, 100
Khatami, Muhammad, 36, 101
Khaz'ali, Abolqassem, 28
Khomeini, Ahmad, 70, 127, 146
  defining Islamic Republic's objective, 39
Khomeini, Ruhollah. *See also* Iran, government.
  book by, 18, 56
  death, xxii, 27
  decrees against Mojahedin, 3
  describing his role in post-shah government, 19
  describing vali-e-faqih, 17
  dismissing successor, 27
  endorsing killing of civilians and POWs, 62
  government under, 18, 23
  in Iraq, 61, 160, 161
  lambasting Khamenei, 19
  letter to Gorbachev, 52
  model for, 10, 13
  opposed by Shi'ites, 18
  ordering death of Salman Rushdie, 117
  and Palestine, 126
  popularity, 22
  religious decrees during Iran-Iraq War, 62
  rise to power, 15, 50, 155
  and Shi'ih-Sunni conflict, 55
  supported by Marxists, 22
  tomb damaged, 148
  treatment of Sunnis, 56
  two-pronged policy, 20–22
  using religious justification, 12–13
  views toward war, 22–23
  views toward Mojahedin, 158, 161
  warning against peace, 178 (n. 11)
Khomeiniism. *See also* Fundamentalism, Islamic.
  in former Soviet Union, 76
Khosrojerdi, Hassan, 120
Khosrow-Shahi, Seyyed Hadi, 89
Kissinger, Henry, 81
Komitehs. *See* Islamic Revolutionary Committees.
Korea, North
  offering military aid, 129, 130, 132
Kowsari, Moussa, 119
Kuwait, 48, 98
  Iraqi occupation in, 64
  Shi'ism in, 123
  terrorism in, 116, 123
Kyrgyzstan, xiv, 67, 71, 80

L

Larijani, Muhammad-Javad, 35–36
Lebanon, 83, 84. *See also* Hizbullah.
  Guards Corps in, 85, 86, 107, 122–123
  Islamic movement in, 80
  relations with Iran, 85–86, 100
  terrorism in, 86, 115, 117, 122–123

Liberalism, 44, 152–153. *See also* Democracy.
Libya, 48, 51, 94, 131
Lutfi, 114, 183 (ch. 10, n. 3)

M

Mahgoub, Rifaat, 92
Majlisi, Mullah Muhammad Baqir, 8
Mala'ek, Muhammad-Hussein, 99, 119
Malaysia, 96
Malik ol-Motekallemin, Haj Mirza Nasrollah, 9
Manshavi, 104
Mansour, Anis, 177 (n. 16)
Martyrs Foundation, 99
Marxism, 44, 153–154, 159
  in Iran, 189 (n. 5)
  supporting Khomeini, 22
Mauritania, 94, 96
Mazandarani, Sheikh Khalifa, 7
Media
  Iranian
    commentaries on Soviet Union, 70, 71
    describing political parties, 21–22
    producing Tadzhik programs, 72
    reporting on Afghanistan, 73, 74–75
    reporting executions, 174 (n. 9)
    reporting on Middle East peace talks, 125–126
    reporting on Persian Gulf War, 64
    reporting protests, 148
    reporting on Turkey, 76
    warning Turkey, 107
  Western
    describing Iranian military, 129, 131, 139
    describing Popular Defense Forces of Sudan, 91
Melal (Nations) Training Center, 111
Middle East
  liberalism in, 152–153
  Marxism in, 153–154
  nationalism in, 151–152

peace talks, 125
Mir Damad, 9
Modaressi, 98
Mohajerani, Ata'ollah, 129, 133
Mohtaj, Abbas, 138
Molla Sadra, 9
Montazeri, Hussein-Ali
  named Khomeini's successor, 175 (n. 1)
  dismissed by Khomeini, 27
  writing on Iraq, 61
Moqtada'i, Morteza, 170
Morocco, 51, 94
Moslehi, Hussein, 103
Mossadeq, Muhammad, 11, 152, 159, 174 (n. 18)
Motalebov, Ayaz, 78
Mottaki, Manouchehr, 99
Moussa, Muhammad Abdel-Halim, 93, 182 (n. 49)
Moussavi, Abbas, 86
Moussavi, Mir-Hussein, 32, 98, 114
Moussavi-Ardebili, Abdulkarim, 32
Mubarak, Hosni, 92
Mugniyeh, Imad, 86
Muhammad, Prophet, 6. *See also* Islam; Quran.
  calling for compassion, 169
  teachings, 1
  traits, 3
Muhammad-Doust, Bake, 139
Muhammad-Rayshahri, Muhammad, 114
Muhammadi, Ali-Asghar, 93
Mumcu, Ugur, 109, 111, 117
Muslim Brotherhood, 84–85
Muzaffar od-Din Shah, 10
Myanmar (Burma), 41

N

Nabiyev, Rahman, 75
Nadim, 151
Nahj-ol Balaghah, 45, 160, 189 (n. 16), 190 (n. 19)

Na'ini, Ayatollah Mirza Hussein, 11
  warning against religious tyranny,
  166–167
Najafabadi, Hadi, 99
Najafi, Aqa, 9
Najibullah, 72
Naqashan, Hamid, 119
Naser od-Din Shah, 9, 14
Nasrullah, Seyyed Hassan, 86
Nasser, Gamal Abdel, xxii, 51, 55, 152
Nasseri, Sirous, 99, 118, 119
National Council of Resistance
  (NCR), 63, 165, 169, 174
  founding, 178 (n. 8)
National Front, 159
National Liberation Army (NLA), 65
  founding, 178 (n. 13)
Nationalism, 44, 151–152
  in Arab world, 43, 47
Navvab Safavi, Mojtaba, 12
Nigeria, 40, 49, 96
  Muslim population, 48
Nouri, Reza, 122
Nuri, Sheikh Fadhlullah, 10–11

O

October War, 51
Oil
  Azerbaijani contracts with Iran, 71
  prices, 48–49
  production, 47–48
  role in exportation of fundamental-
  ism, 47–50
Organization for Islamic Propaganda
  dispatches to Central Asia, 70
Organization of Petroleum Exporting
  Countries (OPEC), 48
Organization of the Caspian Sea
  Countries, 70, 80
Organization of the Iranian People's
  Fedayeen Guerrillas (OIPFG), 189
  (n. 5)
Orouj, 104, 110
Ottoman Caliphate, 18
Ozal, Turgut, xiii

P

Pahlavi, Shah Muhammad-Reza, 11
Pakistan, 40, 49, 101, 108
  liberalism in, 153
  offering military aid, 129, 134, 137,
  138
  terrorism in, 123
Palestine, 83, 126
Panzdah Khordad Foundation, 117
Pasdaran (Guardians) of Islamic
  Revolution. *See* Islamic Revolutionary
  Guards Corps.
People's Mojahedin Organization of
  Iran, xviii, xxiii. *See also* Hanifnejad,
  Muhammad; Rajavi, Massoud.
  attacked by Guard Corps, 65
  and compassion, 169–170
  coup within, 161
  founding, 159, 160–161, 176 (ch. 5,
  n. 5)
  and human rights, 169
  ideology, 44, 160
  Khomeini's decrees against, 3
  members murdered, 21, 27
  opposing velayat-e-faqih, 162–163
  prominent members, 42
  proposed peace plan of, 63, 178
  (n. 7)
  and religious tolerance, 168–169
  role in protests, 145, 148, 164
  and tolerance of opponents, 167–
  168
  victimized by Khomeini's agents,
  164
  view of democracy and government,
  165–167
  women's role in, 157, 170–171
Persian Gulf
  oil production, 47
Persian Gulf War, xxi, 144
Philippines, 41, 96
Pipes, Daniel, 44
Poland
  offering military aid, 129
Popular Defense Forces of Sudan, 91
Popular Front for the Liberation of
  Palestine, 28

Pour-Muhammadi, Muhammad-
Mehdi, 101

Q

Qa'ani, Isma'il, 107
Qaderi, Abdullah, 118
Qassemlou, Abdul-Rahman, 104, 118
Qatar, 48
Qazi, Bayzawi, 45
Quran
    Al-Kawakibi's interpretation of, 14
    teachings, 1, 169–170

R

Rafiqdoust, Mohsen, 114, 116
Rafsanjani, Ali-Akbar Hashemi-, 76,
114, 141, 148, 162, 175 (n. 10)
    calling for security, 147
    commenting on Guards Corps
    commenting on hajj riots in Mecca,
    94–95
    commenting on Iran-Iraq War, 63
    commenting on Middle East peace
    talks, 125
    commenting on Palestine, 126, 127
    commenting on Salman Rushdie,
    117
    commenting on Sudan, 90
    commenting on terrorism, 113
    considering rebuilding Silk Road to
    China, 79
    delaying hostages' release, 115
    describing women, 158
    developing Iran's nuclear capacities,
    134–135
    meeting with Hizbullah leaders, 86
    as "moderate," 3 –33, 146
    role in Khomeini rule, 32, 35
    support for, xxiii
    visit to China, 13
    visit to Moscow, 68
    visit to nuclear site, 1
    visit to Sudan, 39
    visit to Syria, 85
Raja'i-Khorassani, Muhamm '-Sa'id,
29, 37

Rajavi, Kazem, 99, 109, 118, 119, 120,
142, 169, 174
Rajavi, Maryam, 157, 170, 171, 190
(n. 28)
Rajavi, Massoud, 42, 118, 122, 165,
178 (nn. 8, 13)
    arrest, 160
    assassination attempts, 106, 120–121
    background, 174 (n. 8)
    commenting on Iran-Iraq War, 63
    commenting on popular vote, 166
    describing a democratic Iran, 171–
    172
    describing democratic Islam, 161
    lectures, 163
    popularity, 22
Rasa'il (Letters), 7
Razi, Fakhr-e, 45
Razi, Zakariya-ye, 45
Rezaii, Kamal, 119
Rezaii, Mohsen, 74, 90, 96, 97, 107,
125, 127, 134
Romania
    offering military aid, 129
Royaye Sadeqeh (Truthful Dreams), 9
Rudaki, 68
Rushdie, Salman, 117
Russia, 70. *See also* Soviet Union.
    annexing Central Asian republics,
    68

S

Saber, Ali, 122
Sadat, Anwar, 53
Sadeqi-Meibodi, Mustafa, 120
Sahraroudi, Muhammad-Ja'far, 104,
118, 184 (n. 21)
Salari, Alireza, 71
Saleh, Al-Zubair Muhammad, 92
Salek, Ahmad, 104
Sane'i, Hassan, 117
Sarbedaran movement, 7–8
Sarhaddi, Zein ol-Abedin, 120
Sarhadizadeh, Abolqassem, 93
Satanic Verses, 109

Saudi Arabia, 40, 48
  oil production, 49
  relations with Iran, 94–95
SAVAK, 20, 42, 160, 185 (n. 25)
SAVAMA, 185 (n. 25)
Senegal, 40, 96
Seqat ol-Islam-e Tabrizi, Aqa Mirza Ali
Seqat, 11
Sevan, Benon, 72
Seyyed-e-Razi, 119
Shabestari, Mullah Mohsen, 29
Shah Abbas, 8
Shah-Ibrahim, Nariman, 122
Shah of Iran. *See* Iran, government.
Shah-nameh (*Book of Kings*), 180
(n. 26)
Shahrbanoo, 46
Shaltout, Sheikh Mahmoud, 55
Shamkhani, Ali, 138
Shams, 104, 110
Sharafkandi, Sadeq, 118
Sharif University of Technology, 163
Sharif, Muhammad, 72
Sheikh-Attar, Alireza, 80
Sheikh-Attar, Hussein, 121
Sheikh ol-Islam, Hussein, 99
Sheyzari, Mahmoud, 121
Shi'ah-Sunni conflict, 1
  attempt to resolve, 55–56
Shi'ism
  ban on teaching lifted, 55
  established as official religion, 5, 8
  followers massacred, 46
  in Afghanistan, 73–74
  in Azerbaijan, 70
  in Iraq, 61
  in Kuwait, 123
  opposing Khomeini, 18, 56
  schools, 18
  and velayat-i-faqih, 56
Shirvani, Khaqani, 68
Sibevayh, 45
Six Day War, xxii, 51
Somalia, 92

Soviet Union, 47. *See also individual
republics*; Central Asia; Russia.
  disintegration's impact on Guards
  Corps, 108
  effects of disintegration, xxi, 38, 50,
  69–70, 78–79, 154
  foreign aid, 51
  invasion of Afghanistan, 52
  Middle East policy, 52–53
  offering military aid, 129, 130–131,
  135, 136
  religious state of, 70, 77
Spain, 122
Students Following the Imam's Line, 99
Sudan, 53, 100
  fundamentalist training in, xiii
  and Islamic movement, 38, 39, 40
  relations with Iran, 90–92
  terrorist base in, 123
Suez Canal crisis, 152
Sunnism, 13–15
  raising jihad against shah, 55
Supreme Islamic Cultural Revolutionary Council, 163
Sweden
  offering military aid, 129
  terrorism in, 119
Switzerland
  terrorism in, 99, 109, 115, 118, 119–
  120
Syria, 51, 83, 84
  nationalism in, 152

T

Tabari, Muhammad Jarir-e, 46
Tabatab'i, Seyyed Muhammad, 11
Tabaye' ol-Istibdad (*Nature of Despo-
tism*), 13
Tadzhikistan, 67, 69, 75, 138
  relations with Iran, 71–72, 75
Taherian, Muhammad-Ibrahim, 72
Tahtawi, Rafi'at, 151
Taiwan
  offering military aid, 129
Talebi, 104
Tale'i, Javad, 107

Taleqani, Ayatollah Seyyed Mahmoud, 12, 163, 166, 172 (n. 18)
    Tanbihol Umma va Tanzihol Millah (*Raising the People's Awareness and Purifying the Ideology*), 11
Tanzania, 96
Tarikh ol-Omam-e val Molouk (*The History of Nations and Kings*), 46
Tasfir-e Kashaf (*A Comprehensive Interpretation*), 46
Taskhiri, Muhammad-Ali, 101
Terrorism, 89, 98, 106, 108, 109
    in Argentina, 116
    by assassination, 89, 98, 99, 109, 111, 116–119, 142–143
    in Austria, 118
    by bombing, 109, 114, 116, 122
    by bombing Pan Am flight, 109
    by hijacking, 115–116
    by taking hostages, 114–115
    in Cyprus, 122
    in France, 118, 120–121
    in Germany, 109, 118–119, 120
    hajj riots, 94–95, 116, 184 (n. 8)
    in Italy, 109, 115, 117
    in Japan, 109, 117
    in Kuwait, 116, 123
    in Lebanon, 86, 115, 117, 122–123
    in Pakistan, 123
    in Sweden, 119
    in Switzerland, 99, 109, 115, 118, 119–120
    in Thailand, 116
    in Tunisia, 81
    in Turkey, 108–109, 116, 117, 121–122
    prospects, 123–124
    religion used to legitimize, 114
    state-sponsored, 113–114
Thailand, 41
    terrorism in, 116
Tijansila, Sheikh Ahmad, 96
Torkan, Ali Akbar, 90, 91, 129, 131
The True Visage of Mossadeq ol-Saltaneh, 11
Tudeh Party, 22, 154, 159, 162, 189 (n. 5)

Tunisia, 40, 53, 92, 94, 181 (n. 22)
    relations with Iran, 88–90, 100
    terrorism in, 81
Turkey, 43, 49
    geopolitical location of, 78
    Islamic movement in, 47
    liberalism in, 153
    Muslim population, 40
    promoting Pan-Turkism, 76
    relations with Iran, 76–77, 100, 180 (n. 41)
    supported by the West, 77
    terrorism in, 108–109, 116, 117, 121–122
Turkmanchay, Treaty of, 68, 79
Turkmenistan, 67, 70, 78
    president's meeting with Rafsanjani, 69
    relations with Iran, 71

U

Ukraine, 138
Umar, 45, 55
Umm ol-Qura (*The Mother of All Lands*), 13
United Arab Emirates, 48, 92, 139
United Nations Human Rights Sub-Commission, 31
United States, 52
    embassy takeover, xviii, 22, 99, 114–115, 119
    oil production, 48
    support of Turkey, 77
    view toward Sudan
    view toward Sudan-Iran relations, 99
Uthman, 55
Uzbekistan, 67, 72

V

Vahidi, Ahmad, 102, 103, 119
Va'iz, Seyyed Jamal od-Din, 11
Vakili-Rad, 119
Velayat-e-faqih. *See* Iran, government.
Velayati, Ali-Akbar, 53, 93, 96, 130
    touring Central Asia, 69
Venezuela, 48

VEVAK, 185 (n. 25). *See also* Iran, government.
Von Kremer, A., 5

W

War. *See individual entries*.
Women
  in Mojahedin, 157, 170–171
  suppression of, 142, 170

Y

Yang, Shang Kun, 137
Yazdegerd III, 46
Yazdi, Ibrahim, 60
Yazdi, Muhammad, 126, 176 (n. 14)
Yeltsin, Boris, 68
Yemen, South, 51, 52, 95, 154
Yugoslavia, 41
  offering military aid, 129

Z

Zakheim, Dove, 185
Zakzaki, Ibrahim, 96
Zamakhshari, 46